SMITHSONIAN INSTITUTION
BUREAU OF AMERICAN ETHNOLOGY
BULLETIN 193

ARCHEOLOGICAL INVESTIGATIONS IN THE PARITA AND SANTA MARIA ZONES OF PANAMA

By JOHN LADD

U.S. GOVERNMENT PRINTING OFFICE
WASHINGTON : 1964

For sale by the Superintendent of Documents, U.S. Government Printing Office
Washington, D.C., 20402 - Price $2.50 (Cloth)

LETTER OF TRANSMITTAL

SMITHSONIAN INSTITUTION,
BUREAU OF AMERICAN ETHNOLOGY,
Washington, D.C., June 28, 1963.

SIR: I have the honor to submit the accompanying manuscript, entitled "Archeological Investigations in the Parita and Santa Maria Zones of Panama," by John Ladd, and to recommend that it be published as a bulletin of the Bureau of American Ethnology.

Very respectfully yours,

FRANK H. H. ROBERTS, Jr.,
Director

DR. LEONARD CARMICHAEL,
Secretary, Smithsonian Institution.

CONTENTS

Contents

ILLUSTRATIONS

PLATES

(All plates follow page 276)

TEXT FIGURES

PREFACE

This report is based on an analysis of the ceramic remains from five prehistoric sites located near the Santa Maria and Parita Rivers of western Panama. These sites, along with others, were excavated by two expeditions in 1948 and 1952: The first, sponsored jointly by the Smithsonian Institution and the National Geographic Society, was led by Matthew W. Stirling, then director of the Bureau of American Ethnology, Smithsonian Institution. Dr. Stirling was assisted by Gordon R. Willey. Mrs. Stirling and Richard H. Stewart, photographer for the National Geographic Society, completed the party. Among the sites excavated during this season were He-4 (El Hatillo), the largest site treated in the report, He-1 (Sixto Pinilla), and He-2 (Leopoldo Arosemena). The second expedition, in 1952, sponsored by the Peabody Museum of Harvard University and directed by Gordon R. Willey, excavated, among others, the Co-2 (Girón) and He-8 (Delgado) sites. Dr. Willey was assisted by Charles R. McGimsey and James N. East. Although these and other excavations conducted by the two expeditions have been discussed in earlier publications,[1] some, like the Monagrillo site (He-5) in detail, none of these five has been reported thoroughly in print.[2]

In acknowledging the contributions of others, my primary thanks go to Dr. Willey. This report was prepared under his patient guidance, and his advice and support were always available and often utilized. Dr. Samuel K. Lothrop not only offered full use of his excellent library, but provided warm hospitality and much helpful advice as well as fruitful contacts with members of the Archaeological Society of Panama. The support and cooperation of Dr. Clifford Evans, of the Smithsonian Institution, are gratefully acknowledged, as is the cooperation of Dr. J. O. Brew, director of the Peabody Museum at Harvard. I also wish to thank Dr. H. E. D. Pollock and Dr. Stephen Williams, who, in addition to Dr. Willey, kindly read the report and contributed helpful suggestions.

Preparation of the report would have been impossible without the aid of funds provided by grants from Harvard University and the American Philosophical Society. In some cases, photographs were

---

[1] See Stirling, 1949, 1950; Willey, 1951; Willey, and McGimsey, 1952, 1954; and Willey and Stoddard, 1954.

[2] Since this report was written, the results of subsequent El Hatillo site excavations by Dade, Mitchell, Acker, and other members of the Archaeological Society of Panama, have been published in the Panama Archaeologist, vol. 4, No. 1, 1961.

supplied through the courtesy of Mr. Richard H. Stewart, of the National Geographic Society, and others were obtained from the University Museum, University of Pennsylvania. Dr. Frederick J. Dockstader, director of the Museum of the American Indian, Heye Foundation, New York City, kindly made available for study the extensive Panamanian collection at his disposal, although only a small portion of it was examined in detail. Dr. Russell H. Mitchell, president of the Archaeological Society of Panama, was especially helpful in making available photographs and manuscripts dealing with comparable material, and Dr. Leo P. Biese, also of the Canal Zone, made available his manuscript of the Panamá Viejo report before publication.

Full credit for the excellent drawings of the He-4 material goes to Mrs. Svetlana Rockwell and to Miss Symme Burstein for the careful preparation of the tables and maps. Others who helped with considerable skill in the restoration of vessels are Trois Johnson and Jane Fishburne, while sherd washing and restoration work were performed cheerfully by David Piper and Walter Spaulding. Fellow graduate students who contributed ideas and encouragement include, among others, Donald Lathrap, James Deetz, Elizabeth Baldwin, James Gunnerson, James C. Gifford, and Olga Linares.

Upon completion of the report, the bulk of the material from He-1, He-2, and He-4 was returned to the Smithsonian Institution.

1962   PEABODY MUSEUM
                                         HARVARD UNIVERSITY

ARCHEOLOGICAL INVESTIGATIONS IN THE PARITA AND SANTA MARIA ZONES OF PANAMA

By JOHN LADD

INTRODUCTION

GEOGRAPHY

The geography of Panama is best visualized in terms of the volcanic cordillera which, running in a generally east-west direction, separates the wet and dense tropical forests of the Caribbean coast from the drier and somewhat more seasonal savannas and hilly areas of the southern watershed. This distinction is somewhat blurred in the corridor of the Canal Zone, but even in Darien to the east, where the cordillera is lower and more scattered and where dense tropical growth extends to the Pacific shore, the southern coast remains the drier.

The area between the Santa Maria and Parita Rivers at the base of the Azuero Peninsula lies in the southern hilly and savanna zone which extends westward through southern Veraguas to the low mountainous area bordering the Tabasará River. It then continues on as a narrower coastal strip in Chiriquí and southeastern Costa Rica. To the east, from the base of the Peninsula, the zone continues through Coclé Province until pinched off between Chamé Bay and the eastern terminus of the cordillera at La Campana. Southward, the zone extends with increasing hilliness almost to the end of the Peninsula, where it terminates in mountainous terrain rising to 7,000 feet.

Disregarding local variation, the rainy season for this zone extends from May through November; the remaining months are hot, dry, and windy. The hillier portions support livestock. Crops, often concentrated in the broader river valleys, include corn, beans, and sugarcane in contrast to the tropical forest of Darien and the Caribbean coast where manioc and other tubers dominate the agriculture, which, however, includes corn in some quantity. The fauna includes deer and jaguar and smaller mammals such as peccary, coati, arma-

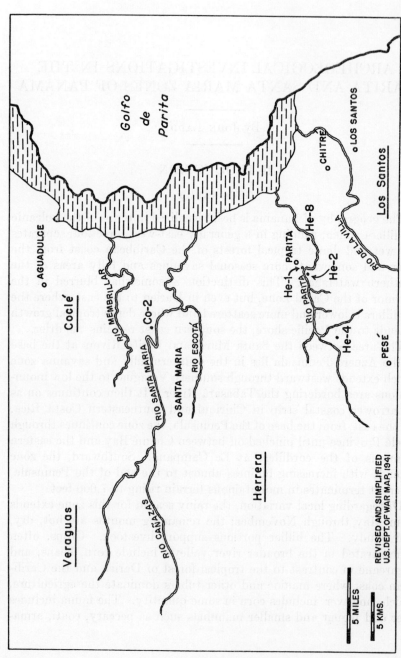

MAP 1.—Map of the Parita–Santa Maria zones of Panama. (From Willey and McGimsey, 1954.)

dillo, raccoon, and bats. Reptiles, including snakes and turtles, are present, and alligators are especially common along the coastal areas. Fish and shellfish abound along the coast.

ETHNOGRAPHY

Panama today is inhabited by three main native groups: the Guaymí west of the Chagres River, and the Cuna and Chocó to the east. All three are linguistically affiliated with South rather than Middle America. The Guaymí and Cuna speak languages classified as Macro-Chibchan and the Chocó speak a language assigned to the Paezan subfamily, formerly held to be a member of the Chibchan family but now seen as possibly having affinities with the Andean-Equatorial phylum (Greenberg, 1956; Tax, 1960). The Guaymí, although divided at the time of the Conquest into fairly clear-cut and compact political groupings, today live either in loose communities or as extended family households fairly well separated from each other. Subsistence is based on hunting and fishing and a combination of slash and burn farming. Their horticulture includes such crops as maize, beans, and sweet manioc (Johnson, 1948). The Cuna, located on the San Blas Islands east of the Chagres River and on the adjacent mainland, combine island trading with cultivating bananas, plantain, corn, and sweet manioc. Hunting is definitely a secondary activity, and their settlement pattern is one of compact villages (Stout, 1948 a). The Chocó, living in dwellings scattered along the rivers to the east and south, are seminomadic hunters, fishers, and farmers. The relative importance of agriculture as opposed to hunting and fishing varies with the environment (Stout, 1948 b).

Linares (MS., 1962) has made a persuasive argument for a roughly similar distribution of the aboriginal tribes at the time of the Conquest, i.e., that the Indians encountered by the Spaniards west of Chamé were Guaymí, and that those to the east of Chamé who spoke the Coiba and Cueva languages may correspond to the present-day Cuna. In support of the first portion of this thesis, Linares cites two main points: (a) that the names of the chiefs listed by the Spaniards for western Panama are now recognized as Guaymí names and (b) that the only native vocabulary from Coclé Province (Pinart, 1882) is also Guaymí. Steward and Faron (1959), however, believe that the archeology of Coclé (with the possible and significant exception of Sitio Conte) is definitely representative of native Cuna.

The inhabitants of western Panama described in the 16th-century chronicles (see Lothrop, 1937, for a detailed description based on these sources) may be classified with the Circum-Caribbean culture as presented by Steward in 1948. They were grouped together in

4 BUREAU OF AMERICAN ETHNOLOGY [Bull. 193

alliances of subchiefs under the control of more powerful "great chiefs" such as Parita, Natá, Urracá, and Escoria. Social classes are indicated by the presence of chiefs and slaves. Villages were fortified with stockades and were relatively small compared to the great urban concentrations in Mexico and Peru. Thus, Natá's "capital," one of the largest settlements in the area, was estimated by Espinosa to have a population of only 1,500 persons (Lothrop, 1937, p. 14). The houses of Natá were circular with cane walls and thatched conical roofs. Subsistence, based on a combination of hunting, fishing, and the cultivation of maize, peppers, sweet manioc, sweetpotatoes, yucca, calabashes and gourds (Lothrop, 1937, p. 16), was apparently much like that of today with the exception of post-Conquest introduced crops. Although it is not clear whether cotton was grown or imported, it was utilized for ceremonial robes and armor. Dress was minimal for other than religious or warlike activities; body tattooing fulfilled the decorative function of clothing, and gold, stone, and shell jewelry was worn by the wealthier classes. In hunting, considerable use was made of nets, snares, traps, and pits, and game drives were organized with dogs and grass fires. Presumably the large animals such as deer were dispatched with spears. Lothrop does not mention the use of the bow and arrow specifically except for the killing of birds, which were also taken by noose and net. Fish were caught by net and hook and line, and this reliance on nets for both game and fish may help explain the paucity of stone or bone points, at least in the Parita sites. Weapons utilized for fighting included wooden clubs, darts, and long spears or pikes although, again, these were not fitted with stone blades or points but were made of chontal, a hardwood which can be sharpened to a tough edge or point. Cotton armor was reported for the warriors of Coiba Island off the coast of southern Veraguas. One gains the impression that warfare, carried out for the purposes of acquiring prestige, territory, and, probably, slaves, was a frequent and important activity. Funerary practices reported by the Spaniards included the desiccation of the bodies of nobles over fire, and the burial of nobles together with their wives and servants. It is not clear from Oviedo's narrative (as given by Lothrop, 1937, pp. 46–47) whether fire was involved in the latter ceremony. The account does state, however, that the pit with the dead and the stupefied retainers was filled with earth, faggots, and timbers so that the women quickly smothered to death. Evidence of burning connected with burials containing Azuero and Coclé design style polychrome vessels is fairly common in the Parita sites herein discussed. The bodies of the common people and slaves, according to the Spaniards, were taken to deserted areas and abandoned.

CERAMIC TYPOLOGY

The aim of this typological classification is to achieve descriptive ceramic units which will have chronological or areal validity. The type-variety system (Wheat, Gifford, and Wasley, 1958; Smith, Willey, and Gifford, 1960) was used in classifying the polychrome pottery, since this scheme offers considerable flexibility and is coming into increasing use in nearby areas such as Middle America. In its simplest form, the system consists of establishing small ceramic units (varieties) on the basis of shared modes or attributes and then progressively linking these into larger and more inclusive units (types) which are bound together by fewer shared attributes. Types, in turn, are combined if necessary into ceramic groups (Gifford, MS.). Again following Gifford, the term "design style" is used herein to express a general similarity of decorative style which may, and usually does, crosscut the typological groupings.

Essentially, the groupings evolved out of an examination of the sample. The whole vessels decorated in Azuero design style polychrome were described vessel by vessel, primarily in an attempt to become familiar with the various elements comprising the designs, but also to bring to the fore whatever other attributes of surface treatment or construction might be significant. Then a card containing the descriptive data was prepared for each vessel. By the time this process was completed, certain groupings had become apparent on the basis of shared design elements, styles of depicting these elements, and/or modes of shape or construction details. These groups were then further refined by study of the sherds and of complete vessels from other collections. Some varieties were given new substance by the discovery of additional vessels which clearly belonged in what had previously been very weakly represented groups. Additional element combinations found on a characteristic shape enlarged the definition of some varieties as did the admission of previously unrecognized shapes to a characteristic combination of designs and vessel form. No single category of attribute was considered dominant or decisive in all cases as a criterion for distinguishing varieties. The main unifying attribute in one variety might be shape; in another, design. For example, the El Hatillo variety includes a great many shapes, none of which is especially frequent, but all of which are decorated in a distinctive style with characteristic elements present. The Níspero variety, however, is based on one distinctive shape combined with a characteristic decorative arrangement and style which occur regularly enough to be classified as a variety. As a result of this lack of consistency, some varieties stand out as easily recognizable entities, whereas with others the line of demarcation is not as clear. There are a few varieties which have conflicting or vague affiliations with the types as established. Thus, the Ortiga variety, although placed with the Parita type, shares various elements with the Macaracas type, and the Calabaza and Ceritó varieties, which were grouped as a separate Calabaza type, may prove to be sufficiently related to one of the three major types at the site to be combined with it. Others, for example the Higo and the Pica-pica, possibly should be combined since their shapes coincide and their design elements are so frequently shared. However, such difficulties are inherent in any system of classification which deals with as many possible variables and subtleties of impression as are included in the Azuero or Coclé styles. It is worth noting, as well, that the typology used in this report was necessarily established without benefit of adequate stratigraphic checks. These varieties, then, are my impressions of ceramic units, or clusters of attributes, which may have chronological and areal significance. The classifications should be used with the obvious caveat that since they are based on a fairly limited sample of total aboriginal manufacture at a particular time and place, they are subject to revision in the light of subsequent knowledge.

In the same way that no one category of attributes was chosen as decisive in distinguishing varieties from each other, I followed no explicit rule in grouping varieties into types. In a sense, the types obtruded themselves from the material at hand; in many cases the larger grouping was apparent first, and varieties within it were distinguished later. The El Hatillo type is based primarily on a similarity of design style and, to some extent, shapes which appeared to me to be readily distinguishable from other vessels; the varieties within it were separated out only after further examination. Although some attributes are obviously shared between types, the final decision as to whether a variety belonged in type A or type B was made on the basis of the subjective impression that it was more similar to the varieties of one type than to those of another. In some cases (e.g., the Calabaza variety) this was difficult to determine and the variety, although in this case placed within a type, is left with a vague status.

The ceramic group as used here is simply a more inclusive grouping at a higher level of generalization; a device which is handy, for example, in discussing the differences or similarities between the pottery complexes of the Late Period Coclé graves at Sitio Conte and the "classic" Chiriquí grave complex, or that found at He-4 and other sites on the base of the Azuero Peninsula. It includes both characteristic polychrome and other ceramics, bichromes, plain and plastic decorated wares. As distinct from the pottery or ceramic "complex," it presumably includes only pottery of local manufacture that is characteristic of the area and time and excludes trade sherds or vessels.

The term is used here as a general referent rather than as a rigidly defined concept.

Procedure.—The ceramics from He-1 were analyzed first since they seemed, on preliminary examination, to be representative of all major ceramic classifications in the collection and were more manageable than those from the He-4 site. Not only was the amount smaller, but the major portion appeared to fit readily into the ceramic schemes already established by Lothrop for Sitio Conte and by Willey and McGimsey for the Co-2 (Girón) site. Descriptive cards were made out for each of the whole vessels from graves and caches. The sherds were sorted according to the schemes mentioned above although, at this preliminary stage, all "El Hatillo" or Azuero Group polychrome sherds were lumped together for subsequent reexamination after study of the He-4 material. On completion of the sherd counts, percentages of the different categories in each excavation level were computed. Detailed comparisons of the cache and grave pottery were postponed until the He-4 study had been completed. Photographs and descriptive notes were used in the analysis of the whole vessels retained by the Museo Nacional de Panamá, roughly one-half of the total from He-1, He-2, and He-4.

In dealing with the material from the He-4 (El Hatillo) site, a different problem was faced; that of establishing a typology for polychromes which had not previously been analyzed in detail. As mentioned above, descriptive cards were prepared for each whole vessel covering such characteristics as dimension, temper, shape, paste coloring, construction details or anomalies and, primarily, design elements. As new elements were discovered they were added to the element list. Finally, a photograph was taken of each vessel and a print attached to the back of the card. After card entries had been made for all of the whole vessels present at the Peabody Museum or left in Panama but available through notes and photographs, a provisional grouping into varieties was made. This primary grouping was then further refined as the varieties were grouped into types, although this was, in some cases, a two-way process involving both the consolidation of smaller groups into larger and the subdivision of some larger groups into varieties as consistent differences were noted. Next, the sherds were sorted according to types and varieties within the polychrome wares and according to rim, handle, and base characteristics in the Red-buff wares. Previously existing categories were naturally included here as at He-1. During the sorting procedure, the occurrence of new design element combinations, or of known combinations on new or different shapes, was noted and further modified the typology. Additional modification resulted from subsequent study of Azuero design style pottery at the Heye Museum of the American

Indian and study of photographs and descriptive notes of vessels at the University Museum of the University of Pennsylvania. Returning to the sherd count, percentages were computed and a stratigraphic analysis of the material by trenches was made. Finally, with the varieties and types well solidified, all grave lots and caches with more than one vessel were typed in an effort to test certain conclusions suggested by the stratigraphic analysis. Stone, bone, shell, and metal content of the graves and caches was noted, but a full analysis of the nonceramic material was not attempted at that time.

As a last step in the ceramic analysis, the cache and grave material at He-1 was reexamined and the Azuero design style sherds there were sorted, and the cache and grave ceramics at He-2 were typed and the sherds sorted. Willey and Stoddard's detailed type descriptions then were consolidated into the sections of the report dealing with the Girón(Co-2) and Delgado (He-8) sites.

Technique.—In describing shapes, eight basic categories were adhered to, e.g., plates, shallow open bowls, deep bowls, collared and collarless jars, bird effigy jars, bottles, and miscellaneous items such as pot covers and incensarios. In some cases (e.g., plates and shallow bowls, bowls versus jars) the categories overlap in the sense that an individual vessel might be placed in one as well as another, but since the classification was made for descriptive purposes only and not for statistical comparison, this overlapping is inconsequential. Measurements of maximum diameter, maximum height and in some cases of minimum orifice were taken in the metric system to the nearest 0.5 centimeter. Pedestal heights were noted. Handles are categorized as either loop (circular cross section) or strap (flattened cross section), and their location (shoulder, rim, etc.) and position (vertically placed or horizontally placed) were noted. Bases are described as either plain or unmodified: i.e., as having varying degrees of roundness; a ring, that is with a low annular base generally not more than 1–1.5 cm. in height; and pedestal, a category which ranged from a short collarlike base to the tall flaring pedestals which sometimes account for as much as ⅔ to ¾ of total vessel height. Such distinctions as were made within the latter category, i.e., "collarlike," "low," "tall," should be clear from the illustrations of the material.

Sherds of those complete vessels which arrived for study in a fragmentary condition were examined under magnification for temper characteristics, but only gross distinctions between crushed rock, sherd, and sand were attempted. Paste firing color was noted and the range of hues follows the Munsell Soil Color Charts (Munsell Color Co., Baltimore, 1954). Paste and surface finish colors for the Girón and Delgado sites were described by Willey and Stoddard according to the Maerz and Paul system (Maerz and Paul, 1930) and their classifications have been retained. In dealing with the designs of the Azuero group, colors are described in terms of everyday usage, i.e., red, black, purple, etc., and, I believe, carry sufficient preciseness for the purposes of this typology. Red may vary from bright, or almost crimson, to dark or a burnt carmine, and purple ranges from burnt carmine to lilac, but these variations did not appear to have any consistent correlation with other attributes. It is possible, although unlikely, that finer color distinctions may become valuable in later analyses, but their usefulness is not apparent at this stage.

REVIEW OF PANAMANIAN ARCHEOLOGY

HISTORICAL

As is frequently pointed out in the literature, despite the long history of archeological interest in Panama, dating from the discovery of the Chiriquí cemeteries of Bugabita, Bugaba, and Boquete in 1858–59 (McGimsey, 1959), the area still lacks a long and sound chronological sequence and continues to present a fluid archeological picture. In the Coclé region a sequence with gaps exists and to the west, in the Chiriquí-Costa Rica region, chronological order is beginning to appear, but elsewhere, in Veraguas and Darien, there is still very little to go on.

This situation may be attributed to archeology as practiced in the country and to the nature of the sites themselves. With regard to the latter, most of the sites so far excavated have been either funerary or ceremonial in nature with little or no opportunity present for the use of stratigraphic analysis. When middens have been excavated, they have normally been shallow and lacking in a long record of cultural change. Probably as a reflection of this situation, most of the archeological activity in Panama until recently has been concerned with the excavation of the more spectacular ceremonial sites or the typological analysis of funerary ware unearthed by huaqueros and assembled in private collections. The various ceramic classifications which have resulted from the analyses of these collections (Holmes, 1888; MacCurdy, 1911; Osgood, 1935, and, more recently, Haberland, 1959), regardless of their typological merit, have yet to be arranged in chronological order on the basis of stratigraphic excavation. Holmes' and MacCurdy's work was based largely on the excavations, notes, and collections of J. A. McNeil, as well as the small collection of de Zeltner (de Zeltner, 1865, 1866) and made use of earlier works by J. King Merritt (1860) and Bollaert (1860).

In general, there was little or no professional archeological excavation in Panama until the 1920's. In 1925 A. Hyatt Verrill excavated a ceremonial site in Coclé Province near Penonomé (Verrill, 1927 a, 1927 b), but published the material in only a preliminary fashion. Not until the arrival of the Swedish expedition under Baron Erland Nördenskiöld was there a major and controlled program of archeological excavation in Panama which resulted in full publication (Linné, 1929). In this case, the interest was centered primarily in the eastern and Atlantic coastal areas of Panama. Although Hartman had engaged, around the turn of the century, in systematic excavation of graves in Costa Rica, excavation in Panama west of the Canal Zone was limited, with the exception of Verrill's scantily published work, until the 1930's to huaqueros' activities and unpublished investigations by interested amateurs. In that decade, however, the Peabody Museum of Harvard University sponsored extensive excavations in Coclé Province under the direction of Henry B. Roberts and Samuel K. Lothrop. These resulted in Lothrop's two volumes (1937, 1942) which presented not only a sensitive and extremely thorough description of the rich ceremonial remains uncovered at the Sitio Conte, but also the first chronological scheme for any area of Panama based on field excavation and the first systematic survey of the archeology of Coclé and Herrera provinces. In the same decade, Linné reported the results of a small but careful tomb excavation in Chiriquí (Linné, 1936) and J. Alden Mason (1942) undertook further excavations at Sitio Conte in 1940.

Lothrop's interest continued, resulting in his 1950 publication of a description of the archeology of southern Veraguas based on a study of museum collections and a few small-scale excavations. However, no additions to the chronology so far established were made until the 1950's. This decade saw more serious archeological investigation and publication for the Panama area than at any time since the period of Holmes and MacCurdy. Lothrop undertook excavations at Venado Beach, the findings of which are soon to be published. The Smithsonian Institution expeditions in 1948 and 1949, under the direction of Matthew W. Stirling, excavated in the Parita Bay area, at Utivé near the Pacora River east of the Canal Zone, at La Pita in Veraguas, and at Barriles in Chiriquí. These were followed by a Harvard expedition to the Parita area in 1952. Much of the Parita material has been published (Willey, 1951; Willey and McGimsey, 1952, 1954; and Willey and Stoddard, 1954) while other portions of it are in preparation or have been published in a preliminary fashion (Stirling, 1949, 1950). In addition, McGimsey (1956) excavated the preceramic site of Cerro Mangote in the same area, thereby extending the range of Panama archeology back to about 5000 B.C. The above-listed publications of Willey, Stoddard, and McGimsey, along with Ladd, 1957, provided a relative chronology for early ceramics at Monagrillo and intermediate phases (with some gaps) up to the Coclé sequence at Sitio Conte.

In recent years Marshall has published the analysis of a museum collection from Far Fan Beach in the Canal Zone (Marshall, 1949), Wassén (1960) and Mahler (1961) have both published the results of grave collections or excavations in Veraguas, and Haberland (1956, 1960) has given preliminary publication to his excavations in the Chiriquí area of Panama. Feriz (1959) has also published the results of two small-scale excavations in which he took part in the Parita area and in Chiriquí. In addition, the amateur archeologists who have long played an important role in the archeology of Panama organized, with the encouragement of Dr. Lothrop and others, the Archaeological Society of Panama which publishes a yearly bulletin, the "Panama Archaeologist." The Society has encouraged its members to utilize formal archeological techniques and to follow these up with systematic reports. As a result, in the last few years, a number of new sites such as Rancho Sancho de la Isla in Coclé Province (Dade, 1960), Chamé area sites (Bull, 1959), Las Filipinas in Veraguas (Dade, 1959), and Panamá Viejo in the Canal Zone (Biese, 1964), have been reported. There have also been a number of articles of a comparative nature dealing with projectile points, burial practices, spindle whorls, etc.

The next few years, besides seeing increasingly valuable work done by the members of the Archaeological Society of Panama, should also witness publication of Lothrop's excavations at Venado Beach, of Stirling's excavations at Barriles, and the results of McGimsey's and Linares' excavations, especially those along the Pacific coast of Panama in the summer of 1961.

GEOGRAPHICAL

Although the archeological regions into which Panama has been traditionally divided, Chiriquí, Veraguas, Coclé, and Darien, are losing their cultural distinctness as our knowledge increases (see pp. 221–225; and Lothrop, 1959), with the addition of the Canal Zone they nevertheless provide a suitable framework for a brief recapitulation of the archeological situation to date (chart 1).

CHIRIQUÍ

Despite the fact that a beginning is being made in the establishment of a sequence in Chiriquí through the dating of scarified and alligator wares, the filling out of the chronological framework with additional cultural content awaits the publication of Haberland's work in the Concepción area and the results of McGimsey's and Linares' 1961 excavations. At the present time we are limited almost entirely to descriptive analyses of funerary complexes.

The beginning of the sequence in Chiriquí rests, at the present time, on the Concepción Phase (Haberland, 1959; Sander, 1960), so far not fully described in print, but apparently based on graves found with scarified ware. Examples of the latter ware have been found in a grave at Pueblo Nuevo below a layer of charcoal which has been dated at 2045±45 B.P. (Feriz, 1959, p. 186). Corrected for the industrial effect (Suess effect), this date reads 2290±45 B.P., or 340±45 B.C. (personal communication from Dr. J. C. Vogel, Groningen Laboratory). The characteristic heavy, reddish slipped ware of the phase is found in shallow graves lined with river boulders

	CHIRIQUI	VERAGUAS	COCLÉ	CANAL ZONE	DARIEN
1952 Conquest	(Iron tools) Alligator ware	Herrera	La Arena / El Tigre — Herrera		La Villa (1775) Escarromalo Rectangular dwellings (Pearl Is.)
		Late Coclé	Late Coclé	[R.C. A.D. 960]?	Girón bowl at gulf of San Miguel
			Early Coclé	Early Coclé [R.C. A.D. 210]?	
A.D. / B.C.	Scarified ware (R.C. 340 B.C.)	Santa Maria	Santa Maria		Circular dwellings (Pearl Is.)
			GAP	Fluted points	
2000 B.C.			Sarigua Monagrillo (R.C. 2130 B.C.) Cerro Mangote (R.C. 4853 B.C.)		
5000 B.C.					

CHART 1.—Sequences of Panamanian archeological regions.

but lacking the stone slab covers so often accompanying graves or tombs containing the "classic" Chiriquí wares. Pottery stamps of the same scarified ware, some carved in the form of human figurines, have also been reported from the Concepción graves (Sander, 1960). Since scarified ware has not been found in association with "classic" Chiriquí wares, and one of the latter, alligator ware, has been found associated with iron tools (Stone, 1958, p. 48), it is evident that scarified ware and the Concepción Phase are the earlier development.

The main "classic" Chiriquí wares consist of plain wares with modeled adornos (armadillo-terra cotta ware; Osgood, 1935), a modeled ware with red geometric and daub designs (fish-tripod-handled ware), and two polychrome wares with shared designs but different techniques, i.e., negative and positive painting (lost color ware and alligator ware). Vessels of these wares are generally found together in many of the deeper oval or rectangular graves of the Chiriquí area. Associated with this complex are gourd-shaped rattles (identical in shape to Calabaza variety vessels at Parita), spindle whorls decorated with nodes and incisions, "needle cases," polychrome figurines, "stools" of clay, modified hourglass-shaped vessels which may have been drums, and double-tubed whistles. Also found in the cemeteries are metates of both the simple type and the ornately carved type, triangular cross section arrowheads, bronze bells (Holmes, 1888, p. 49) and gold or tumbaga ornaments. Although all this material has been recovered from "cemeteries" or "graves," very little human bone is reported. The finding of iron tools associated with alligator ware fixes the terminal date for this complex, but the duration of its prior existence is unknown. Ceramic affinities of the complex extend up into Costa Rica but not to any great extent to the east, other than in terms of broad traditions such as use of modeling and tripod supports on plain or red-slipped wares, both of which are found in quantity in Veraguas. The dragon motif is also found in Herrera and Coclé, and one very specific similarity, the gourd bottle shape, does exist between the lost color ware and the Calabaza variety of Parita, suggestive of a late date for the latter variety. Probable trade vessels of the Late Coclé and Azuero design styles illustrated in Holmes and MacCurdy include representatives of Macaracas, Parita (Yampí and Ortiga varieties), and Calabaza types, all of which are of generally late position, and suggest that the "classic" Chiriquí complex was coeval with the Late Coclé and Herrera Phases of the Coclé region.[3]

---

[3] The term "phase" is used here to conform to current practice, but both the Early and Late Coclé Phases correspond to Lothrop's Early and Late Coclé Periods at Sitio Conte (Lothrop, 1942, pp. 183-199), while the Herrera Phase was set up on the basis of the He-4 material. See charts 1 and 2 and pp. 13, 19.

VERAGUAS

The archeology of Veraguas has been fully treated in Lothrop's 1950 volume, and little has been accomplished since then to alter the picture.

No sequence has yet been determined for the area, although much of what is known from the numerous grave collections appears, on the basis of its association with either Late Coclé or Azuero design style vessels, to be late. Lothrop (1950, p. 79) and Mahler (1961), however, report the presence of Early Coclé Phase vessels in Veraguas tombs, at least one of which also contained a typical Veraguas plain ware jar with looped ribbon legs. Sites excavated up to 1946 are divided by Lothrop into two types: (a) refuse beds containing burials and (b) deep shaft tomb burials. The former are known only from the Montijo Gulf area including the western shore of the Azuero Peninsula (Lothrop, 1950, p. 16; Dade, 1959) and contain urn burials with pottery vessel covers and associated funerary offerings, some of which were Coclé style ceramics. The graves of these refuse beds are pits, 2–3 meters deep with earthen floors. The deep shaft graves have been found in practically all other areas of southern or lowland Veraguas. These shaft graves have been likened to those of Colombia, but not other areas of Panama, although conical pits similar in shape to those of Lothrop's type "d" graves, but without the deep upper shaft or stone slab, were found at He-1.

The ceramics of Veraguas as characterized by Lothrop are of a single dull red to dark brown ware which is often covered with a partly transparent orange wash. Shapes include collarless globular jars with either strap or loop handles placed vertically or horizontally on the shoulder, jars with angled shoulders, tripod bowls with conical legs and tripod jars, vessels with looped ribbons of clay for legs (a characteristic only of Veraguas), three-lobed vessels, tetrapod vessels, half jars, double rim bowls, and others. Other pottery forms include hollow pottery rings, effigy whistles, and "drums."

Although in 1946, when Lothrop completed his volume on southern Veraguas, it appeared that most if not all of the 200 or more polychrome vessels found in Veraguas graves (Lothrop, 1950, p. 76) were traded from the province of Coclé or the Azuero Peninsula, it becomes increasingly probable, as suggested by Dade and others (Dade, personal communication to Lothrop) that many of the vessels, in the Azuero design style at least, were actually manufactured in Veraguas. Additional finds published by Mahler (1961) and Wassén (1960) as well as discoveries by Dade and Mitchell of Panama (Mitchell, personal communication) further reinforce the conclusion that the manufacture of Azuero design style vessels had a distribution which included at least the eastern portions of southern Veraguas.

The stone industry encountered in the cemeteries shows affinities primarily toward Chiriquí in its triangular cross section points, celts with diamond-shape cross section and completely polished surface, and ornately carved three- and four-legged metates.

Although a sequence based on stratigraphy is at present still lacking for the Veraguas area, grave associations, as pointed out by Lothrop (1950, p. 76) would include a span covering at least the Early and Late Coclé Phases. The date of A.D. 782 for a stela at Copán, under which was found a gold figurine of probable Veraguas origin, would be well within the Coclé time span as revised by Venado Beach dates. As for the Azuero styles, Wassén in 1960 illustrates four Macaracas type vessels (Higo and Pica-pica varieties) which were associated in a grave at La Peña with typical Veraguas half jars and ribbon-legged vessels, and Mahler (1961) also illustrates Macaracas type vessels from a grave at the same site associated with Veraguas plain ware. The outside limits of the sequence as far as I know are also suggested in the Mahler article, the earliest being Santa Maria Phase ceramics noted in private collections in the area and the terminal date of Conquest or later suggested by the discovery in two instances of iron tools in typical deep shaft graves. The finding of El Hatillo type vessels (Espalá variety) (Lothrop, 1942, fig. 229; 1950, fig. 134) and the affinities in shape between the double-rimmed bird effigy jars and Níspero variety vessels from Parita would also indicate a post Late Coclé time period.

DARIEN

Linné's report on the Nördenskiöld expedition survey and excavations along both the Atlantic and Pacific coasts of Panama is still the primary work on the area. In fact, the only accounts of excavations in Panama east of the Canal Zone published since 1929, of which I am aware, are the preliminary description of the site of Utivé on the upper Pacora River (Stirling, 1950) and Cruxent's (1958) report of excavations undertaken in 1954 in an attempt to trace Balboa's route across the Isthmus. Neither of these later works suggests a sequence for the region. On the Pearl Islands, however, Linné found two types of sites; one with round dwelling sites in middens which contained shells of locally extinct species of mollusk [4] and unpainted pottery, and another with rectangular dwelling areas characterized by both plain and polychrome pottery. Linné postulates an early chronological position for the round dwelling sites, on the basis of the absence of painted pottery and the presence of the cold water mollusks. Linné notes both the lack of ceramic affinities of the

[4] *Strombus peruvianus* with a distribution from Peru to western Colombia, *Ostrea chilensis* normally found from Chiloe Island to Ecuador, and *Solen* (*Tagelus*) *dombey* occurring from Valdivia to Tumbez in Peru. These distributiofis are from W. H. Dall in 1909 as cited in Linné, 1929, p. 129.

round dwelling sites with Central America including western Panama and, on the other hand, the "very great resemblances" of the painted ceramics to Azuero and Coclé design styles (Linné, 1929, pp. 134–136). I concur in the latter part of this statement,[5] but feel that some of the incising (Linné, 1929, fig. 26-*F*, -*G*) is reminiscent of the same technique since found on Venado Beach Incised variety ceramics.

The pottery at Utivé is primarily modeled and unpainted ware with a great variety of forms, but a few sherds of black on red painted ware with geometric designs were found. These may have affinities to Venado Beach and the Aristide group (Stirling, 1950).

As a result of his Darien excavations in 1954, Cruxent set up two pottery styles: (*a*) the Escorromulo style encountered in sites along the eastern shores of Darien (i.e., the west shore of the Gulf of Urabá), and (*b*) the La Villa style which is characteristic of the pottery he recovered along the Rio Chucunaque and about the headwaters of the Gulf of San Miguel. The former style, consisting of unpainted vessels with finger impression, incision and punctation, was found associated with 16th-century European pottery and iron tools, and Cruxent notes the similarities between it and the ceramics of Trigana and La Gloria farther down the coast. The La Villa style dated at A.D. 1775 (Cruxent, 1958, p. 183) also consists of unpainted ware decorated with notching along the lips, and notched V-shaped applique ribbons which Cruxent believes has its closest similarities to the El Tigre Phase ceramics of the Parita Delta to the west. Comparison of the illustrations for the two groups reveals similarities in shape and decoration,[6] as well as differences, and supports Cruxent's suggestion that La Villa is probably somewhat later than El Tigre.

Also in the vicinity of the Gulf of San Miguel on the western side of the San Lorenzo Peninsula near the village of Gonzalo Vasquez, Cruxent found additional evidence of western influence, in this case a Girón type Interior Banded variety open bowl (Cruxent, 1958, pl. 13). He notes that the Pearl Islands are visible from the beach, and it is possible that the vessel was obtained by trade from the islanders. Certainly, however, with the exception of these San Miguel examples, the general ceramic affinities of Darien as known

---

[5] Linné, 1929, figure 24, is identical in shape and horizontal banding of the rim to Girón sherds at He-1 and He-2. Figure 25-*B* illustrates a rectangular scroll design similar to Achote variety motifs, and the ray motif of figure 23 is similar in general feeling, though not in details of execution, to those of the Macaracas and Parita types.

[6] Attributes shared by the El Tigre Phase pottery and the La Villa style include olla and deep open bowl shapes, rounded bases, and identical lip notching on a few sherds. Differences include: the casuela shape (common in La Villa, absent in El Tigre); the bottlelike jar (present in La Villa, absent in El Tigre); ring bases (occasional in La Villa, absent in El Tigre); applique ribbons festooned in V patterns (*escotadura*) which are present in La Villa and absent in El Tigre; horizontal lugs just below the rim (absent in La Villa, present in El Tigre); and the squaring off of bowl rims, a common feature in El Tigre, but apparently rare in La Villa which more often has thickened and rounded or slightly pointed rims.

to date are more to the northwestern portion of Colombia with its incised and modeled wares than to western Panama.

CANAL ZONE

The Canal Zone may be viewed as a transitional area between Darien with its emphasis on unpainted, modeled, and incised pottery, and the Coclé-Parita-Azuero area to the west with the highly developed polychrome tradition. Thus polychromes of the Coclé style and other vessels with affinities to the Santa Maria Phase have been found at Venado Beach, while at a cemetery site near the Chame River to the west, modeled and incised urns have been recovered (Bull, 1959) which appear to be more in the Darien tradition. Similar modeled and incised ware has been described from Far Fan Beach (Marshall, 1949).

With regard to chronology, this area may have provided some of the earliest material in Panama in view of the few projectile point fragments demonstrating fluting which have been found on islands in Madden Lake, as well as fragments of other points from the region which show an exceedingly fine chipping technique not characteristic of other regions of Panama (Mitchell, 1959, 1960; Sander, 1959). Beyond these faint indications of a possible Paleo-Indian occupation there is a long gap to the early polychrome pottery recovered at Venado Beach and Panamá Viejo (Biese, 1964). At both these sites open bowls with white ovate spaces in black rectangles, which are duplicated on sherds from Santa Maria Phase levels at the Girón site, were recovered. At Venado Beach, Early Coclé style vessels were also recovered as well as examples of what I have called Smoked ware type, Venado Beach Incised variety, a variety also found at He-1 and He-2 and apparently contemporary with Early Coclé. Carbon-14 dates from "typical urns" containing infant burials are reported by Lothrop as 1,750 years ago (ca. A.D. 210) and 1,000 years ago (ca. A.D. 960) (Lothrop, 1960). The answer as to which of these dates is correct, or whether both are, indicating a long timespan for the Girón type Banded Lip variety, awaits further investigation.

COCLÉ, PARITA, AZUERO

It is in this region of Panama that the greatest degree of time control over the archeology has become apparent. First, Lothrop's grave sequence at Sitio Conte suggested a two period breakdown for the polychrome styles there. Then Willey and Stoddard's work on the material from the Girón site suggested an earlier Santa Maria Phase characterized by pottery with black on red or buff geometric designs. The Monagrillo site next provided the earliest pottery for

DATE	PHASE	CERAMIC GROUPS	TYPES
Modern	La Arena		La Arena Plain La Arena Red
Conquest	El Tigre		El Tigre Plain
	Herrera	Azuero	El Hatillo Polychrome ? Parita Polychrome Red and Cream Delgado Red Calabaza Polychrome
	Late Coclé	Azuero-Coclé	Macaracas Polychrome Late Coclé styles at Sitio Conte ? Smoked Ware Red Line (Red Daubed) Delgado Red (?)
	Early Coclé	Coclé	Early Coclé styles at Sitio Conte Girón Polychrome Smoked Ware Red Line (Red Daubed)
	Santa Maria	Aristide	Escotá Polychrome Escotá Red Escotá Plain Girón Polychrome Girón Red Girón Plain Plastic decoration Red Line (Red Daubed)
		GAP	
	Sarigua		Sarigua Plain Sarigua Applique Sarigua Shell Stamped Sarigua Punctated Sarigua Striated
2000 B.C.	Monagrillo		Monagrillo Plain Monagrillo Red Monagrillo Incised Monagrillo Thin Yellow
5000 B.C.	Cerro Mangote	Lithic, Pre-Ceramic	Pebble tools

CHART 2.—Coclé region

Panama with a carbon-14 date of roughly 2,000 B.C. and the Cerro Mangote site pushed the archeological horizon back to a pre-ceramic stone complex with a date of 4853 ± 100 B.C. (McGimsey, 1956; Willey, 1958).

Recapitulating the culture history for this area of Panama we begin with the Cerro Mangote material characterized by a crude chopper and pebble grinder complex, recovered from a shell midden located near the old shoreline.   With these were found pebble manos, shallow basin boulder metates, flakes and cores, and two shell ornaments, but no pottery to speak of (five sherds only, all but one from the surface) and very little worked bone.   Both flexed and secondary burials were found, with the latter the more frequent.   Shell and bone remains indicated a dependence on oysters, crabs, and small bivalves in the lower layer changing to oysters alone in the upper layers.   The mammal ratio remained fairly constant, with deer the most popular followed by small mammals, turtles, birds, and fish in that order.

The next phase, Monagrillo, also is found in shell heaps along the old shoreline (at least four sites bearing Monagrillo pottery have been excavated) and suggests very much the same kind of life as that for Cerro Mangote but with the addition of pottery.   At the Monagrillo site, a pebble grinder and chopper stone complex identical to that at Cerro Mangote was recovered with the addition of a stone bowl fragment.   The pottery complex is composed primarily of plain thick ware bowls and beakers (88–96 percent of all pottery per stratum) and secondarily of a buff ware painted with red geometric designs.   In addition, there were 200 to 300 sherds of thin yellow ware and 70 sherds of incised ware with both broad and fine lines and predominantly curvilinear motifs.   Oyster and *Tivela* shells comprised the bulk of the midden, and the diet suggested by the bone remains included deer, turtle, fish, and fresh water crab.

The Sarigua Phase, which apparently follows close on the heels of the Monagrillo Phase (scanty evidence at the Monagrillo site suggested it was either contemporaneous with or immediately postdated the Monagrillo occupation), also is represented by shell midden sites on the flats of an old lagoon.   This phase is based entirely on the presence of a very thin monochrome pottery with plastic decoration, i.e., applique, punctation, and striation, and appeared to Willey and McGimsey to be different from any other pottery in Panama except possibly that of the Cocalito site in Darien.

There follows a presumed gap in the sequence closed by the Santa Maria Phase characterized by inland sites and pottery with geometric designs in black on a red, buff, or occasionally white, ground.   Largely because of the shift in site location and the lack of extensive shell deposit, agriculture is postulated as the primary subsistence base. Stonework includes manos and celts with polished cutting edges but chipped polls, a type characteristic of the polychrome graves at Sitio Conte and He–4.   Santa Maria Phase ceramics, broken down in this report into the Girón, Escotá, and Red Line types, have been found at Sitio Conte (Ladd, 1957), and the Girón type characterized by open bowl forms with a predilection for concentric banding of the rim interior has been found at He-1 and He-2 along with Early Coclé poly-chromes. At the Girón site, the bulk of this Aristide group (Girón and Escotá types) underlay Coclé polychrome sherds. The use of black bands and solids in rectangular or triangular motifs on red or buff everted lips of open bowls is characteristic of the Banded Lip variety and, together with the ground color ovate in a black rectangle motif which appears sparingly at the Girón site, is a common occur-rence at Venado Beach and has been reported from Panamá Viejo. Vessels of this sort, called Black Line Geometric ware by Lothrop, but more often with white than buff ground were found in Early Period graves at Sitio Conte. It therefore appears that the Santa Maria Phase represented by both Escotá and Girón types predated the Coclé styles, but that the Girón type pottery continued to be produced well into the Early Coclé Phase.

The following sequences for the area are a bit more confused; phases are not as easily delineated as the earlier ones. At Sitio Conte a Late Period has been established based primarily on changes in design motifs and vessel shapes in the polychrome, Paneled Red and Smoked ware classifications. This is followed by what was presumably a brief period of decline represented by a few graves with minimal ceramic content. In the Parita Bay locale the sequence postulated by Willey and McGimsey begins with an Alvina Complex, followed by a mixture of El Hatillo, La Mula and Parita-Coclé, all of which would be contemporary with the polychrome periods at Sitio Conte. These in turn are followed by El Tigre and modern La Arena. As Willey and McGimsey point out, the Alvina Complex, consisting of about 460 sherds in the trough fill at the Monagrillo site and 4 probably associated chipped poll celts, is identified with certainty at only one site. The pottery consists of Alvina Plain collared jars, vertical sided bowls, and Alvina Red (50 sherds) with outflaring collars and deep bowls with outslanting rims. Willey and McGimsey see affinities to the Coclé tradition rather than Mona-grillo. In support of this, the similarity of shape between the collared jars with vertically-placed strap handles of the Alvina Complex and those of the Red Daubed variety encountered at He-1 with probable Early Coclé affiliations is significant. Vertical strap handles on collared jars occurred occasionally in the later red wares at He-4, but these few are on small jars. The large (4–5 cm. wide; total arc of 12–15 cm.) strap handles of Alvina Plain are characteristic of the Red Daubed variety wide-mouthed jars at He-1 and He-2. The five painted sherds in probable association with the Alvina Complex, three black on white, one black on buff, and one red and cream, are inconclusive. None can be definitely classified with a particular variety, but none would be out of place in the polychrome tradition of the region. I believe, then, that Alvina is probably a local variation of the same kind of complex found a short distance away on the Parita River at He-1 and He-2, but without the Girón type painted pottery. I have excluded it, therefore, from the chronological phase chart.

La Mula, like Alvina, was defined by Willey and McGimsey as a tentative complex, and they note its affinities to both Coclé and Azuero ceramics (Willey and McGimsey, 1954, p. 135). Later appraisal suggests even more strongly that it should be reclassified as Delgado Red. The pottery, characterized by globular collared jars with occasional vertically placed loop handles and globular collared jars with horizontal loop handles, occurs in a plain, a red-slipped, and a polychrome variation. Sherds of the latter were so badly eroded that designs could not be discerned beyond the use of parallel black bands and broad red bands. Chipped poll celts with polished blades were associated. As a complex, this could easily be lost in the material from He-4 and He-8, the La Mula Plain and La Mula Red considered together within the range of firing variation (dark brown to brick red) for Delgado Red. Certainly the shapes are shared by both groups, as are the chipped poll celts and the associated polychrome sherds with the exception of those painted in broad red bands. It therefore appears reasonable to absorb La Mula into Delgado Red, thus placing it chronologically with the Late Coclé Period at Sitio Conte, or later. La Mula was recognized at nine sites in the Parita Bay area and, considered as Delgado Red, would extend the geographical range of the latter to some extent.

The El Tigre Complex, consisting of several thousand sherds of massive heavy pottery with collared jar and open bowl shapes, has been described as probably the remains of salt boiling occupations along the coastal flats. The pottery was found in the upper layers at He-5 (the Monagrillo site) and at other sites in the same area. It resembles the modern pottery of La Arena, but with sufficient differences to be distinct from it, and has been tentatively placed by Willey and McGimsey as of colonial age, a chronological position supported by Cruxent's La Villa style in Darien.

As noted elsewhere in this report, the highly developed polychromes from the Calderon or El Hatillo site (He-4) are probably in part contemporary with Late Coclé, and in part postdate that Period (see chart 2 for chronology and Appendix 1 for ceramic type distribution). Macaracas type vessels have been found in Late Period graves at Sitio Conte, but Parita and El Hatillo types are apparently absent (at least in the graves) at that site and, from the meager stratigraphic evidence at He-4, appear to be later developments. This may be more of a geographical difference than one of time, however, but the suggested post-Coclé position is supported by the evidence from Trench 11 of Sitio Conte where Azuero style sherds (then called El Hatillo) increased in proportion in the upper levels as Coclé polychromes declined. Further discussion of these later phases in the Coclé region may be found on pages 221–225.

EL HATILLO (HE–4) SITE

SITE DESCRIPTION

The site known as El Hatillo (fig. 1), designated He-4 as the fourth
site surveyed and excavated in 1948 by Drs. Matthew Stirling and
G. R. Willey, lies on land owned by Sr. Juan Calderon about a quarter
of a mile from the Parita River, Herrera Province, roughly 3 or 4
miles south of the town of Parita. The site is located on a number
of what appear to be flat-topped mounds on a level elevation about
300 yards west of a hill named Cerro de la Mina (or Cerro de las
Minas). The mounds were covered with pottery sherds, and there
is record of at least one of them (designated here as Mound III)
having undergone partial excavation prior to the 1948 season. Probably before the 1948 season, and certainly since, the site has been
probed by huaqueros and members of the Archaeological Society of
Panama. The Dade collection specimens, at the Museum of the
American Indian, listed from the Finca Calderon undoubtedly come
from this site as well as many of those listed from Parita. Mr.
Philip L. Dade of the Society recently excavated a number of graves
at the site (personal communication from Dr. S. K. Lothrop), and
Dr. Russell H. Mitchell of the Society has purchased a fairly large
collection also from the same site (Mitchell, personal communication).

Drs. Stirling and Willey put down trenches in seven of the mounds
and three additional test pits in the flat. A discussion of these
excavations follows.

MOUND I; TRENCH 1

The mound is roughly circular, about 20 meters in diameter, and
was excavated to a maximum depth of 6.7 meters at the south end of
Trench 1, a 3 × 10 meter trench laid out on a north-south axis. The
northern end of the mound was faced with boulders at the mound
base, a facing about 50 cm. thick extending up the mound side about
1.0 meter and, in part, made up of irregularly shaped, relatively shallow mortar stones. Other special features of the mound include four
areas of distinct fill, and three ash layers located as follows: a trace
of one mixed with pink (burned?) clay at a depth of 1.0 meter, another
at about 1.5 meters in the south profile, and a third at 2.2 meters.
A "floor" of waterworn stones about the size of tennis balls was
noted at a depth of roughly 2.0 meters. Fragments of "burned floor"
were found at a depth of 1.2 meters. Two deep intrusions, Find 346,
a burial, and Find 384, a cache of pottery and stone, were encountered
in the southeast corner of the trench at depths of 3.5 meters and 6.7
meters respectively. Additional smaller finds of one or two vessels
were scattered through the trench.

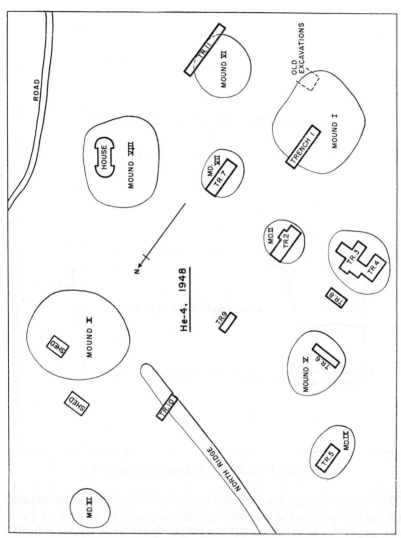

FIGURE 1.—He-4, 1948. (This map was made with a Brunton compass and chain.)

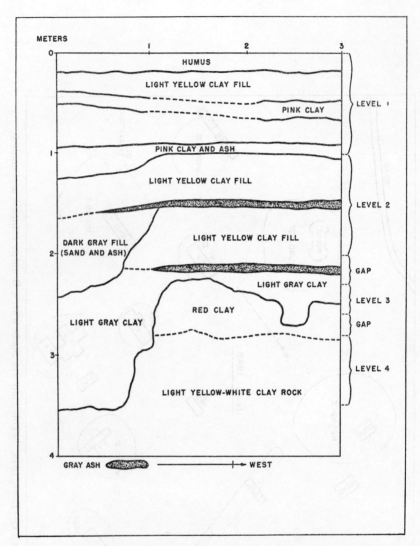

FIGURE 2.—He-4, Mound I, Trench 1, south face.

The lack of occupational refuse layers or indications of structures, with the exception of the floors, and the presence of clay fill and ash layers suggest that the mound may have been built up as a burial mound in a series of stages, each connected with a burial ceremony involving the use of fire—hence the ash layers. There is no evidence of cremation such as burned bones or burned vessel interiors. Although there was a relatively high number (about 1,350 sherds) of Red-buff or "utilitarian" ware sherds taken out of Trench 1, this need not represent an accumulation due to actual habitation of the mound, but rather incidental fill inclusion which may have come from adjacent habitation areas. A fuller discussion of the stratigraphy is presented in the section dealing with chronology, but it is worth noting here that even on the assumption that the mound was constructed in stages, there appears to be present the basis of a gross stratigraphy. If it is assumed that the fill of each successive stage was obtained from the surrounding surface areas, the ceramic culture of the builders of this particular stage and that of their predecessors should be reflected in the stratigraphy. Actually, as described in the chronological section, a definite rise in the frequency of the El Hatillo and Parita types is apparent in the upper levels, combined with a drop in frequency for the Macaracas type.

The mound as a whole contained significant numbers of Azuero group sherds of all types; Coclé and Aristide groups were not heavily represented. The main graves and caches were characterized by Macaracas type polychrome vessels and all were found below the lowest ash layer.

MOUND II; TRENCH 2.

Mound II was a small (14 meters in diameter), almost circular, low mound. Trench 2, a 10×3 meter cut on a north-south axis, was located near the center of the mound. Apparently built up of rubbish, the mound consisted of a single stratum of refuse mixed with red clay suggesting purposefully piled-up fill. Within the mound were found one large burial, Find 10, and three smaller burials, Finds 14, 16, and 18, and two caches which may have been deposited as one. All of the burials are of the same type and two of them contain Jobo variety polychromes. The two caches have large urns with modeled adornos which are rare for the site. Although the sherd material from the fill included all types except Calabaza, all of the find units are limited to one or two types and suggest that the mound was constructed to cover these particular burials.

MOUND III; TRENCHES 3, A, B, C, AND 4, A, B

Mound III, the most thoroughly excavated of all the mounds, was located on the edge of the plateau with a sloping base which followed the plateau contour. Oval in shape, the mound measured 20 meters long by 15 meters wide and reached a maximum height of 3 meters in its southern portion where the plateau slopes downward. The mound fill was amorphous in structure with no evidence of layering or intrusions of any kind except for pits excavated a few years prior to 1948 by a Columbian, and consisted of an "almost incredible" number of sherds, a large proportion of which were sizable pieces. There were no burned floors, fire pits, ash layers, or signs of structures,

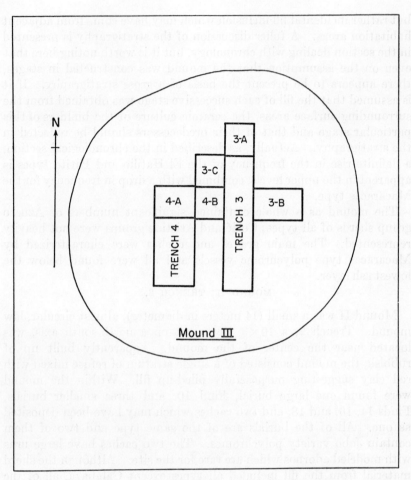

FIGURE 3.—Relationship of trenches in Mound III, He-4.

nor any sterile areas. Stone implements, except for a few manos, metate legs, hammerstones, and celt fragments were absent. Bone implements likewise were rare, but unworked animal and bird bones were present in some quantity. No human bone was found nor was there any evidence that the mound was used for burial. Very few complete pottery vessels were recovered, and those almost always occurred singly or occasionally in pairs, but there were few finds of more than one vessel. On the other hand, many almost complete vessels were found; that is, bottles with spouts broken off, bird effigy bowls and simple bowls with pedestals missing as if the vessels had been intentionally broken, or ceremonially "killed" without destroying the entire vessel. In fact, it seems probable that care was taken not to mutilate the vessels beyond a minimal amount. Almost all of the incomplete vessels from this mound appear quite "new" and show no signs of wear. The great majority of the incomplete polychrome vessels from Mound III were varieties of the Parita type or the Calabaza type. The El Hatillo variety was fairly heavily represented. No complete vessels of the Macaracas type were encountered, although there were numerous Macaracas type, Higo variety, and Coclé group sherds. The mound evidently was ceremonial in nature and apparently was erected during the space of time represented by the Parita type ceramics (i.e., probably a short period late in the sequence), but the nature of the ceremony is not apparent. It is possible that a major burial remained undetected in the mound or under it.

The mound was excavated by two main trenches which were extended until a considerable portion of the mound was excavated. Trench 3, an 11×3 meters cut, was first laid out on a north-south axis somewhat east of the center of the mound. Three additions were made to this trench: Trench 3-A, a 3×3 meters cut, on the north end of Trench 3; Trench 3-B, a 5×3 meters eastward addition to Trench 3; and Trench 3-C, a westward addition to Trench 3 near its northern end. The basal red clay of the plateau was encountered at a depth of 2.8 meters in the south end of Trench 3.

Trench 4, located 3 meters west of Trench 3 and extended parallel to it, was 6.5 meters long by 4.0 meters wide. It later was extended an additional 3 meters to the north by Trench 4-A and to the east to join Trench 3 by the addition of Trench 4-B.

In view of the completely unstratified nature of the mound, cultural material was, for the most part, not bagged by level and is treated in this study as material selected at random from the total mound.

MOUND IV; TRENCH 5

This mound, a relatively small one about 80 cm. high, is located on the edge of the plateau with its northern end extending down the plateau slope and its southern end on a small rise in the plateau. The mound is covered with the usual thin layer of humus about 20 cm. thick under which a layer of organic stained clay with refuse blends into a transition layer of clay and gray midden over the claylike rock of the mound base and plateau. Comments from the field notes state that the material looked very much like a living accumulation of rubbish.

Material from the mound, present at Peabody Museum, consisted of 218 sherds from the top level of 0–50 cm., and it is possible that these are selected sherds since only 24 of them are of monochrome (red-buff) ware. No burials, complete vessels, or significant features of any sort were recovered in the mound.

Trench 5, a 7×3 meters cut, was laid out on a north-south axis and carried down to the sterile clay rock of the mound base in all except the center section of the trench where it was continued into the clay rock for a total depth of 1.25 meters.

MOUND V; TRENCH 6

This is a small mound relatively close to the plateau edge about 1.4 meters in maximum height built over a slight depression in the plateau. Trench 6, an 8×2 meters cut laid out along the long axis of the mound (east-west), revealed the mound to be primarily of unstratified yellow clay fill with an intrusion of gray fill at the east end. Both fill areas contained a few sherds. The only find was a large stone ax (Find 219) from the center of the mound at a 20-cm. depth.

Material from this mound, present at Peabody Museum, consisted of 16 sherds from the top level of the mound.

MOUND VI; TRENCH 11

Mound VI is a small roughly circular mound, about 15 meters in diameter and 1.5–2 meters deep. Trench 11, a 15×2 meters cut, was laid out on the eastern slope of a north-south axis. Field observation suggests that the horizontally banded layers in the upper fill may be either occupational or purposeful fill, while the relative lack of sherds in the light layer below point more definitely to purposeful fill. The dirty brown and gray layer below this appeared to be the old weathered surface with refuse intrusion. No finds are reported from the mound nor were any features of significance noted other than a few lumps of red fired clay, one with white paint, which were present in the first and second levels.

MOUND VII; TRENCH 7

Although this is not a large mound, roughly 17×18 meters, excavation was carried down to a considerable depth, almost 5 meters, and the mound yielded a wealth of burials and find units of more than one vessel. Trench 7, a 10×3 meters cut, was laid out on a north-south axis. Field comments are scanty, but fragments of burned floors and scattered pieces of human long bones were reported from 60–100 cm. Level 1 (0–150 cm.), and the sherd analysis revealed that Level 2 (150–200 cm.) contained clay lumps or plaster fragments as well as considerable amounts of burned pottery. As may be seen from the profile, a series of ash deposits along with the line of demarcation between the upper layer of mottled-brown fill and the lower layer of light-brown fill runs roughly along the junction of Levels 1 and 2 and up into the lower portion of Level 1, thus corresponding generally to the burned plaster and pottery distribution suggested

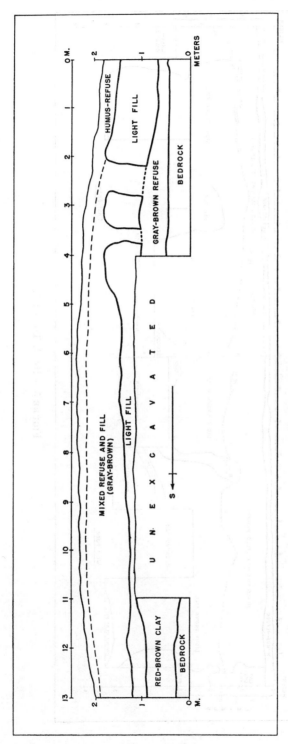

FIGURE 4.—He-4, Mound VI, Trench 11, west face.

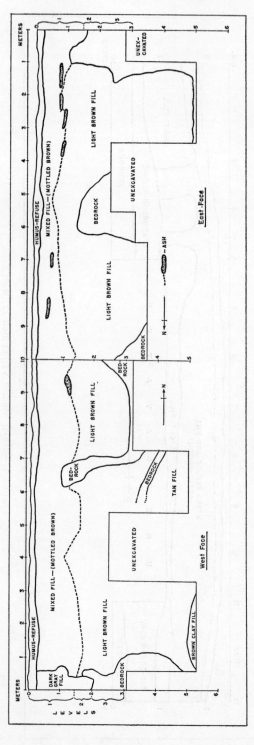

FIGURE 5.—He–4, Trench 7.

above. The relative lack of layering, combined with the presence of many burials, suggests that the mound was erected primarily for mortuary purposes, possibly in two stages; one represented by the lower light-brown fill, the other by the mixed fill of mottled brown.

MISCELLANEOUS TEST PITS

In addition to the trenches in the five mounds already described, three tests were made in other areas of the site.

Trench 8, a 5×3 meters test pit in the flat area between Mounds III and V and somewhat closer to the former, was excavated in 25 cm. levels to a depth of 1.5 meters in the northeast corner. The pit yielded abundant sherds, especially in the second 25–50 cm. level of yellow-gray fill. Because the refuse is much deeper at the eastern

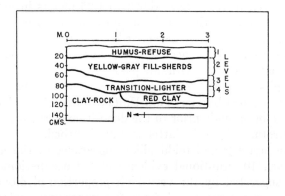

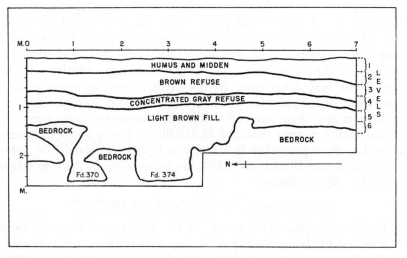

FIGURE 6.—He-4. *Upper*, Trench 8, east face; *lower*, Trench 10, east face.

end of the pit near Mound III, the stratigraphic results may be distorted by the presence of Mound III refuse. However, excavated as it was in 25 cm. levels, this pit probably offers the most reliable stratigraphic evidence from the site.

Trench 9, a 5×2 meters cut on a north-south axis, was located in the flat or "courtyard" about 20 meters north of Mound II. The upper 30 cms. of the pit consisted of humus with a few sherds underlain immediately by sterile gray-white clay rock and granite nodules. Level 1, 0–25 cms., the only level with cultural material from the pit, yielded 1 milling stone and 11 sherds of Red-buff ware. No distinctive features were noted.

Trench 10, a 7×2 meters cut on a north-south axis in the crown of the north ridge about 25 meters north of Trench 9, was also excavated in 25 cm. levels and yielded many sherds and at least three burials. The trench was carried down to 1.25 meters in most of its length, to 1.6 meters in the southern end and to 2.6 meters in the northern end. Excavations were carried down to the basal clay rock through an apparent midden accumulation consisting of layered bands of dry refuse honeycombed with ant passages. Beneath this midden a number of pits filled with loose dust penetrated into the clay rock; two of these contained burials (Find Units 370 and 374). These pits appear to have been made prior to the deposition of the concentrated gray refuse stratum, since the latter was undisturbed.

Besides the layering and middenlike appearance of the upper fill areas of Trench 10, additional evidence of the occupational nature of the fill is suggested by the very high proportion of monochrome to polychrome wares recovered from the uppermost meter of the trench, the primary refuse strata. In Level 5 (1.00–1.25 m.) a large lump of burned floor or wall plaster with a well-smoothed surface on one side was recovered. Of the three finds encountered in the trench, only one contained polychrome pottery (Find 374) and this was entirely of the Macaracas type, Cuipo and Higo varieties. If this burial was laid down prior to the layers above, as seems evident from the field observations, and if the layers above are true occupation midden rather than purposeful fill, the Macaracas type would be placed earlier in time than the El Hatillo or Parita types which are more heavily represented in the refuse layers. It should be noted that in this case Macaracas sherds are represented in the upper four levels by only 18 sherds.

CHRONOLOGY OF TYPES AND VARIETIES

The stratigraphic evidence at He-4 is scanty, and in many cases untrustworthy, because some of the mounds with the greatest number of sherds appear to have been completely unstratified and those excavations, such as Mound IV and Trench 10 in the north ridge, which showed fairly definite indications of occupational refuse yielded relatively few polychrome sherds, either as a total for the trench or in many of its levels. Nevertheless, a sherd count was taken on all trenches, and a general picture of relative chronology for the types and varieties emerges which has held up thus far in grave associations (with one or two exceptions) and which coincides with the conclusions which can be drawn from an evolutionary interpretation of some of the design elements shared by the types but expressed differently among them.

MOUND I

Only the upper three levels and the lowest level (Level 7) contained sufficient polychrome sherds to be statistically significant. Of these, Level 1 corresponds roughly to the upper ash layer and deposits above it and Level 2 includes all of the fill between the one upper and two lower ash layers. It is apparent from chart 3 that of the various Azuero types present, the El Hatillo and Parita types have their greatest popularity in the two uppermost levels; the former especially rises sharply above the upper ash layer. The Macaracas type and associated Coclé-like categories reach their maximum proportions in the third level, and drop sharply in the uppermost level. Cuipo variety is not represented in the trench. Calabaza has a very minor role in the second and third levels and is not represented at all below Level 4. Coclé Polychrome is barely represented. Red Daubed and the Girón type are both represented by small proportions, which, while continuing on into the upper levels, are at their highest in the fourth level. Smoked ware reaches two peaks, one in the fourth level and one in the first level.

Briefly recapitulating the typology of the grave ceramics encountered in Trench 1:

Find 1. A class "b" collared jar and sherds of an El Hatillo type (Achote variety) vessel. Sherds may be from fill; breaks are weathered and the vessel was only partially restorable.

Find 5. A large Delgado Red collarless jar, a Red-buff class "a" collared jar, and a Red-buff pedestal plate. Collar fragments of probable Ortiga jar may be associated.

Find 6. No polychrome vessels. A buff ware plate, a large Red-buff collarless jar or urn, a Smoked ware pedestal bowl, Sangre variety.

Find 8. Polychrome: A Macaracas type (Pica-pica variety, ray design) pedestal plate, questionable provenience. Class "a" Red-buff collared jars. Smoked ware or Buff plate with horizontally flattened lip.

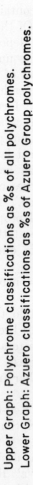

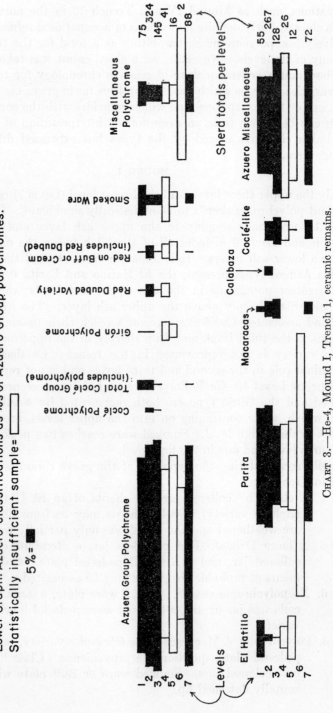

CHART 3.—He-4, Mound I, Trench 1, ceramic remains.

Find 9. No polychrome vessels. A large Red-buff collarless jar or urn and a Smoked ware plate with horizontally flattened lip.

Comment.—These five finds, on the basis of the monochrome wares, all resemble each other in the presence of either a large Red-buff collarless jar or Smoked ware plates or both. The polychrome associations are questionable either because they are in terms of sherds with weathered breaks which may have belonged in the surrounding fill rather than in the find unit proper, or because the field description does not jibe with the material present for study, e.g., the Macaracas pedestal plate (Find 8–1) is not mentioned in the field notes although the other vessels of the unit are. All were found above the lowest levels of the trench, that is at 2.4 meters or above, and all were caches, not graves.

Find 346. Polychrome: Two Macaracas type (Pica-pica variety) vessels. Monochrome: Large Red-buff collarless jar (fragments only). Red-buff class "a" collared jars. Red-buff ring-based plate. Miniature ring-based gray-brown plate. Find is a grave unit.

Find 364. Polychrome: Macaracas type (Pica-pica variety). Monochrome: Red-buff ring-based plate and a class "a" collarless jar. Find is a cache only.

Find 384. Polychrome: Three Macaracas type (Pica-pica variety) vessels. Cache only.

The only other complete vessels found in the trench were a Red-buff collared jar (class "a") and a small Red-buff collarless jar.

With the exception of Find 1, all the finds of this mound containing polychrome vessels are characterized by the Macaracas type. The association in Find 1 of an El Hatillo type vessel with the class "b" collared jar, is supported by a similar but more reliable association in Find 30. Without attempting to extract too much from insufficient evidence, one might reasonably postulate that the mound was built up in at least two main stages. The earlier stage covered the deepest Macaracas burials. The later one, in which were deposited the caches represented by Finds 1, 5, 6, 8, and 9, was characterized by higher proportions of El Hatillo and Parita sherds. This leaves unexplained the high proportion (43 percent of the total Azuero Polychrome for that level) of Parita type sherds in the lowest level. It could be argued that the Macaracas graves in levels bearing Parita sherds indicate a later date for the former. This thesis, however, is otherwise unsupported by the stratigraphy at He-4 and Sitio Conte, where Macaracas is associated with Late Coclé in graves and caches but Parita varieties are missing.

MOUND II

The mound is chronologically significant only in its grave association; that of the large globular urns of Finds 10, 14, 16, and 18 with the Jobo and El Hatillo varieties of the El Hatillo type. If the mound was constructed primarily to cover these burials, then the presence of all other varieties (except Calabaza) in the sherd fill of the mound would suggest that the Jobo variety is at least contemporary with, or later than, those varieties.

MOUND III

This mound does not provide stratigraphic evidence for chronological relationships but does give some clues through vessel association in caches. Find 19 associates a Red-buff collared jar, class "a," with a Calabaza variety bottle. Find 22 tentatively (because of possible confusion in labeling) allies a Níspero bird bowl with two El Hatillo variety bird effigy vessels. Find 24 combines an Anón variety vessel with an El Hatillo variety bird bottle. Find 30, a unit dominated by El Hatillo variety polychromes, includes an Anón variety vessel, and both class "a" and class "b" Red-buff collared jars. Individual finds, of which there were many, included El Hatillo and Parita types, and Calabaza variety vessels, but no Macaracas vessels, although Macaracas sherds occurred in the mound. On the assumption that most of the finds are of contemporary or later age than the fill in which they are found, the El Hatillo and Parita types and the Calabaza variety would be later than the Macaracas type.

MOUND IV

No significant chronological information.

MOUND V

No significant chronological information.

MOUND VI; TRENCH 11

This trench, presented here in levels of 0–1 meter and 1–2 meters, supports the thesis that the El Hatillo and Parita types and probably the Calabaza variety reached their height of popularity at He-4 later than the Macaracas type (chart 4). Total Azuero-style sherds increase in proportion in the upper level. Coclé polychrome, Red Daubed, Red Line wares, and Aristide group sherds are slightly more popular in the lower level. There were no find units in the trench.

MOUND VII

The only stratigraphic feature of significance present in the mound fill is the line of demarcation between an upper layer of mottled brown

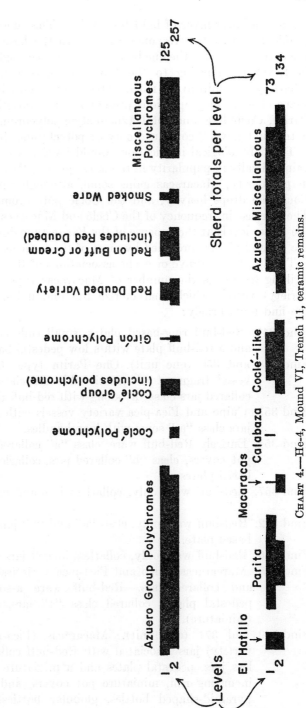

CHART 4.—He-4, Mound VI, Trench 11, ceramic remains.

fill, and a lower layer of light-brown fill. This line on the west face profile (see p. 32) corresponds roughly to the base of Level 1. On the east face profile, the line between different colored fills falls midway in Level 1. Turning to the table of relative sherd percentages (chart 5), this shift in the natural stratigraphy may be reflected in the sharp changes in proportions present in such varieties as El Hatillo, Parita, Coclé-like, and total Azuero style polychromes. It should be noted that Level 2 contained only 51 polychrome sherds of all types.

The chronological implications would be that the El Hatillo types gain radically in popularity in the latest period, Parita types drop off in popularity, Macaracas gains some, although the closely related Coclé-like drops heavily, and the Coclé polychrome gains slightly. The increase in frequency of the Coclé and Macaracas polychromes in the upper levels at the expense of the Parita type does not agree with the general picture provided by most of the trenches.

Turning to the grave or cache associations of the mound, the most striking feature is the number of Macaracas type (including Cuipo variety) vessels which characterize the find units. Recapitulating the find units briefly:

Find 347. Red-buff ring-based plates, small collared class "a" jars, and a red-buff plate with a low pedestal base.

Find 348 and 350 (one unit). One Parita type (Caimito variety) vessel fragment of questionable association and red-buff collared jars class "a" along with red-buff ring-based plates.

Find 351. Cuipo and Pica-pica variety vessels with red-buff collared jars class "a," some with loop handles.

Find 354. Entirely Red-buff ware, class "a" collared jars, miniature pot covers, class "b" collared jars, collarless jars, and ring-based plates.

Find 357. Red-buff ware only, collarless jars and collared jars class "a."

Find 362. Red-buff ware only, class "a" and "b" jars and an annular based plate.

Find 366. Red-buff ware only, collarless lugged jars and a pot cover.

Find 368. Marcaracas (Higo and Pica-pica varieties) pedestal plates and collared jars. Red-buff ware associated included pedestal plates, collared class "a" jars, and pot covers (miniature).

Find 369 and 371 (one unit). Macaracas (Pica-pica and Cuipo variety) jars associated with Red-buff collared jars, collarless jars, pedestal plates and a miniature open bowl with incurving rim, miniature pot covers, and small Red-buff pyramid-shaped bottles, globular bottles, and bird jars.

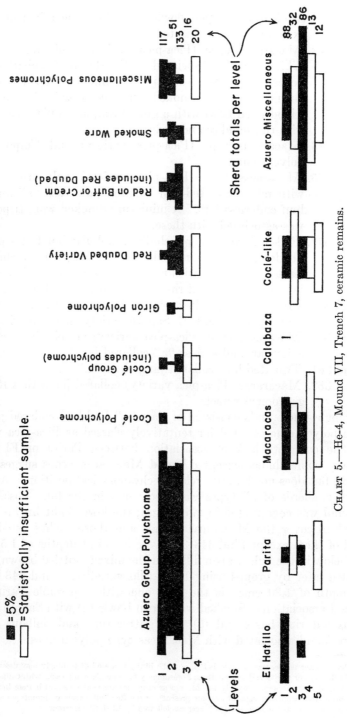

CHART 5.—He-4, Mound VII, Trench 7, ceramic remains.

Smoked ware open bowls, including one miniature tripod example, were associated.

Find 372. Macaracas type (Pica-pica variety) and Black Line on White vessels associated with Red-buff collarless jars, pedestal and ring-based plates, miniature open bowl with incurving rims. Smoked ware consisted of a miniature tripod open bowl with a gutter rim, and a plain-based plate with rim handles and nodes.

Find 373. Macaracas type (Pica-pica variety) and Cuipo variety polychromes.

Find 375. Macaracas type (Pica-pica variety) polychrome vessels with miniature Red-buff collared jars class "a" and Red-buff collarless jars. A miniature Smoked ware tripod bowl was associated with these.

Find 377. Red-buff ware only including: globular bottles; a pyramid bottle; collarless jars; collared jars class "a," including at least one example with rope handles; a reverse flare collared jar; pot covers; and ring and pedestal-based plates.

Find 378. Macaracas type (Pica-pica variety) vessels and two Smoked ware open bowls with Sangre variety rims, but ring bases.

Find 379. Macaracas type (Pica-pica variety) vessel with a Red-buff effigy jar, and a class "a" collared jar.

Find 381. Two Red-buff collared jars, class "a."

Find 382. Macaracas (Pica-pica variety) collared jar with a Red-buff gadrooned vessel.

Single whole finds consisted of class "a" Red-buff collared jars and one polychrome collared jar tentatively classed as Pica-pica variety.

The complete lack of association between Parita or El Hatillo types (some shapes excepted [7]) and Macaracas types suggests time gaps, but does not indicate relative chronological position. As noted earlier, sherds of all types were recovered in the fill. Possibly the mound was constructed in two stages; the lower light brown fill was used to cover the Macaracas burials and those caches listed above (all of them except Find 348–350 were found at depths of 1.5 meters or below in the light-brown fill), and the mixed mottled brown fill was added later by groups using El Hatillo varieties. Find 348–350, at a depth of 1.30 cms., is the only one with a possible Parita type vessel association. Smoked ware open bowls (a) with Sangre variety rims but ring bases and (b) with gutter rims and bulbous tripods were found associated with Macaracas type polychromes.

---

[7] The globular bottle, the pyramid bottle, and the bird jars are all disturbingly reminiscent of either El Hatillo type or Ceritó variety vessels, and presumably have no place in a cache with Cuipo and Pica-pica variety polychromes. Possibly the Macaracas examples are heirlooms which were included in a later burial (no exceptional signs of wear are present), or the Red-buff vessels are prototypes of later polychromes, or the postulated sequence of Macaracas followed by El Hatillo is wrong.

TRENCH 8

This trench, a test cut in the flat near Mound III, probably presents the most reliable stratigraphic data of any of the trenches in the excavation, since it was less disturbed by construction stages. The percentage trends represented in chart 6 are more definite than others from the site. According to this table, the El Hatillo type appears only in the uppermost level and then with a low frequency. The Parita type, Calabaza variety, and Azuero design style, all show a clear tendency to increase in popularity from the lowest to the uppermost levels. Macaracas and Coclé-like ceramics decrease in frequency in the upper levels. The Cuipo variety, represented by a very small proportion of total polychrome sherds, occurs only in the first and second levels, but is slightly higher in the latter. Coclé polychromes, Red-on-buff or Cream wares, and the Black-on-red technique all have greater frequencies in the lower levels than in the upper ones, while Smoked ware remains constant. The trench contained no graves or caches.

TRENCH 10; NORTH RIDGE

The stratigraphic picture of this trench (chart 7) is a confused one despite the fact that it appears to have been excavated in an area of occupational refuse and should have provided a picture clearer than that for most of the trenches. Discounting the lowest four levels, due to paucity of polychrome sherds (the greatest number was 17 in Level 5), we find that the El Hatillo type reaches its highest proportion in Level 4, then drops somewhat and remains constant to the surface. Parita Polychrome decreases from a fairly high percentage in the uppermost level to a low in Level 3 and then increases in the lowest statistically valid level, 4. The Calabaza variety is not represented in the upper four levels. The Macaracas type, absent in the uppermost level, has its greatest relative representation in Level 2 and then diminishes until it disappears in Level 4. Coclé-like and the Girón type are present in the first and third levels and absent in the second and fourth. Coclé Polychrome has its greatest frequency in the uppermost level. Thus, according to this trench, Coclé wares and the Parita type had their greatest frequency in the latest period, while the El Hatillo type was most popular in the earlier periods. These conclusions, with the exception of that for the Parita type, are not supported by the record in the other trenches nor by grave associations thus far discovered at other sites.

Only two find units were encountered in the trench:

Find 370. No polychrome. Red-buff collarless jars, collared jars class "a," and a Red-buff collared jar with vertical loop handles.

Find 374. The Cuipo variety and the Pica-pica variety (all in dull finish, many in black-on-red technique) polychromes are

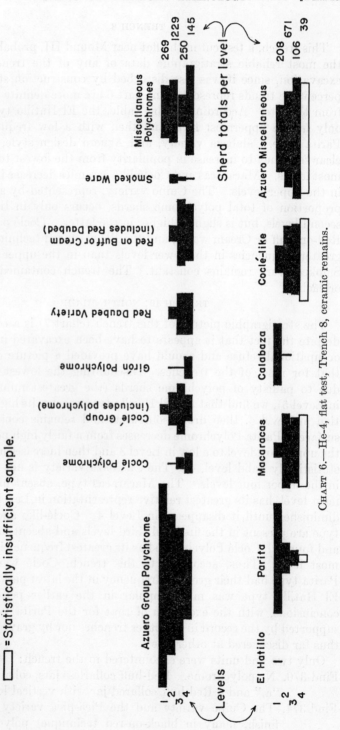

CHART 6.—He-4, flat test, Trench 8, ceramic remains.

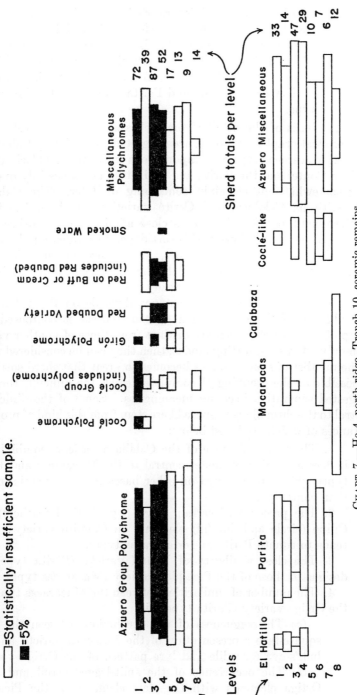

Upper Graph: Polychrome classifications as %s of all polychromes.
Lower Graph: Azuero classifications as %s of Azuero Group polychromes.

□ =Statistically insufficient sample.
■ =5%

CHART 7.—He-4, north ridge, Trench 10, ceramic remains.

associated with miniature Red-buff pedestal plates, ring-based plates, collared jars class "a," straight collared jars, and two miniature deep bowls. As was the case with Find 369, the Cuipo and Pica-pica varieties are associated in the same grave, but there is no association of the Calabaza variety or El Hatillo and Parita types with the Macaracas type.

On the basis of almost all of the caches and burials as well as the meager stratigraphy, the sequence suggested would be that shown in chart 2; Macaracas type contemporaneous with the Late Coclé Period at Sitio Conte, and the Parita and El Hatillo types possibly overlapping somewhat but certainly continuing on later. The Calabaza type with its Calabaza and Ceritó varieties, has been left in an indeterminant position due to its close affinities to the other three types. Since postulations of this sort depend as much on absence of association as on definite contact, and future investigation may change the proposed chronological scheme, it is in order to briefly recapitulate the inconsistencies already evident.

The chronology in the first instance depends on the validity or individuality of the types. If a type or variety is composed of a group of core vessels which are distinct from those of another variety with only a few crosscutting modes, then they can be considered valid. If the number of shared modes becomes so great that sherd sorting is impossible or the grouping of complete vessels too difficult, then the suggested separation becomes meaningless. Some of the difficulties central to the chronology proposed here stem from this kind of problem, instances of which are listed below:

1. The mere existence of the Calabaza variety, combining as it does a number of modes central to the Macaracas and Parita types which are assumed on other bases to be sequential rather than contemporary.

2. The presence of certain Higo (e.g., barbed feathers) and Cuipo (circle and dot fill) elements on Caimito variety vessels tends to equate Parita and Macaracas types.

3. The close similarity of Yampí variety (Parita type) ray designs to those of the Pica-pica variety (Macaracas type).

4. The number of similarities between the Macaracas type and the Ortiga variety (Parita type) viz,

(a) The vagueness of the distinction between the split-square-face representation of the Pica-pica variety and the bull's-eye crocodile and lyre pattern of the Ortiga variety.

(b) The occurrence of the split-legged scroll and other Ortiga elements with the claw elements of the Pica-pica variety.

(c) The appearance of the Cuipo seed pod element (although treated quite differently) on a vessel otherwise clearly assignable to the Ortiga variety (Lothrop, 1942, fig. 482, a).

(d) The combination of typical Cuipo negative dragon designs with Ortiga frog handles (Lothrop, 1942, fig. 480, a).

(e) The combination of typical Ortiga filler elements with a split-square-face design (Pica-pica) on a typical Pica-pica collared jar (Mus. Amer. Ind. cat. No. 22/9340).

Some of these difficulties can be explained by stylistic evolution or developments as in the case of the split-square-face developing into the bull's-eye crocodile, the claw scroll with circle and eye developing into the split-legged scroll, the progressive stylization or conventionalization of the seed pod from typical Pica-pica representations to that on the Ortiga vessel cited above, and the development of the ray motif. This stylization process, however, does not apply to the few cases of combinations of typical or core elements on the same vessel.

The other category of contradiction lies in the association of vessels which are chronologically separate. As far as I know at the present time, there are fewer examples of this, and these are indirect. If such associations are infrequent, they may mean no more than a slight overlap in time. The example I have in mind is that of Find 369 in which vessel shapes in Red-buff ware, which are very similar to El Hatillo and Ceritó variety shapes in polychrome (the globular and pyramid bottles and the bird jar), are associated with Pica-pica variety polychromes. This association is reinforced by the crossties between Find 369 and Finds 372 and 375, each with Pica-pica polychrome vessels. This may be explained by the assumption that the Red-buff ware shapes were actually earlier (they show some differences in proportion from the polychrome examples) and were prototypes for the later development in polychrome styles. No instances of direct associations of typical Macaracas and Parita or El Hatillo types have come to my attention.

CERAMIC REMAINS
POLYCHROME WARES

It seems best to preface the detailed discussion of polychrome types found at the El Hatillo site with a few general remarks concerning the decorative styles.

Two major divisions are apparent in the highly developed styles found at the site: a curvilinear style and an angular style. The latter, represented by the El Hatillo type, is characterized by the extensive use of frets and rectilinear elements. Even depictions of "natural" designs, such as faces or reptilian forms, seldom exhibit a curved line; the only conspicuous exception to this angularity occurs in the treatment of birds and bird effigy vessels. Designs are generally arranged in a series of panels around the closed vessel shapes, often with a broad black band below, but heavily banded panels framing the decorative area are far less frequent than in the curvilinear style. Ground color ranges from orange to a dark brownish red, and the light-cream slip so common in the curvilinear style appears here infrequently and is largely restricted to effigy bird bowls. The depictive colors are black or red bordered by black lines. The use of purple, a color characteristic of the curvilinear style, occurred in only one angular style variety of the site, and then was associated with a greater frequency of curvilinear elements. "Fillers," or small distinctive elements such as triangles or circles used to fill in vacant areas in the design pattern, are characteristic of only one angular variety but, for the most part, are absent. However, black dots, either grouped or scattered, are used as massive fill in another variety. Both styles have color-fast painted surfaces which show a definite luster. In one variety, however, the polish has been lost over time and colors wash off easily.

The shapes on which the angular style appears tend to be more varied than those of the curvilinear within each major shape category, especially in the case of bottles. Thus, there are globular bottles, bird bottles, and cylindrical bottles with sharply angled shoulders and bases. Other shapes include bird effigy jars of at least two types, plates and shallow bowls, and rare sherds of large closed vessels. With the exception of the one large vessel mentioned above, there was very little variation in gross size in the angular style, the vessels tending to be small or medium and ranging from 11–20 cms. in diameter. Although major shapes, such as the bottle category, are shared between the two styles, subshapes or a particular expression of form are seldom shared.

The curvilinear style (Parita, Macaracas, and Calabaza types) is characterized by a flowing, curving, design line, although the particular motifs are often enclosed in heavy black-banded rectilinear or triangular panels. This use of a broad black outline to frame individual designs may be taken as a diagnostic of this style of Azuero polychrome (Lothrop, 1942, p. 228). Considerable use is made of scroll elements, closed arcs or leaf-shaped panels, curving clawlike elements, concave-sided triangles, and color-filled circles or ellipses. Life elements such as crocodiles, rays or sharks, and turtles are rendered in the same curving line. Although rectangular patterns such as the panel are common, they almost always enclose curvilinear elements and their angularity is softened by the technique of extending the corners of the panel into long fine points. This technique of terminating corners, triangle points, and scroll points in finely graduated and often slightly curved hair thin lines is another highly characteristic trait of the style. The angular style exhibits the same trait, but the line extensions are short and stubby.

Ground color ranges from a light-cream slip (sometimes light gray) through an orange to a reddish-brown hue. Although, like the angular style, designs appear in solid black and in red outlined with black, there is a much more frequent use of purple in the curvilinear style, especially the alternate use of purple and red in repeating elements such as claws along a crocodile's plume or in alternate plumes. Dots are rarely used as a form of massive fill, but individual filler elements such as small triangles, double stemmed T's, circles with three radiating equidistant lines of dots, and small barred elements are frequent.

Shapes are less varied within the major categories than is the case with the angular style. In fact, the extreme regularity of the bird effigy bowl examples or the incurving bowls on pedestals is striking. Two vessels may appear almost identical in shape, size, and design, a pairing of vessels which is a characteristic of Coclé styles (Lothrop, 1942, p. 10). Among the most frequent shapes are pedestal plates, shallow pedestal bowls with incurving rims, globular and subglobular jars with flaring collars and rounded or angled shoulders, and gourd-shaped bottles. Effigy vessels are also present, and bird effigy pedestal bowls are extremely common at the El Hatillo site. Open bowls with straight or flared-out sides are represented by only a few sherds and no complete vessels. Relatively large open bowls with incurving rims and somewhat pointed bases are fairly common, but in most cases are known on the basis of rim sherds only, thus the base form is a matter of conjecture. The range of size from miniatures (5 cm. in diameter for example) to very large (e.g., 104 cms. in estimated diameter) vessels is a striking feature of this style, although the number of miniatures recovered far exceeds the examples of very large vessels.

Although the grace and fluidity of the curvilinear style creates a strikingly different impression from that of the angular, both styles share a highly developed sense of design balance and proportion and a mastery of decorative planning and technique. Each uses a continuous design on some shapes and a breakdown into panels on others, apparently depending on the area to be decorated, although the curvilinear style resorts to panels more often and emphasizes them by the use of the broad black band. Both tend to terminate corners in some sort of line extension; in the curvilinear a finely graduated point, in the angular a short and blunt projection. Both rely on black for delineation of design, and on black or red for solid fill. Red is never used by itself, either as a line or as solid design. Purple is always bordered with black. No designs in white were found in either style at He-4, nor have I noticed any in the literature. In both styles the artists favored an orange to a brownish-red ground color, although lighter and creamier shades were common in the curvilinear style. Finally, the styles shared some motifs, such as the crocodile, although expressed in quite different fashions.

Differentiation of the curvilinear style as expressed in Macaracas type design elements from the Late Coclé style is difficult and not always possible in sherd lots. The distinction depends on quality of line, combinations of pigment, and types of design (Lothrop, 1942, p. 118). There is generally a greater use of fine lines in the Macaracas type (hence Lothrop's Foreign Style A, Fine Line Style of Grave 5); claws on alligator plates may be both fine line or color filled on Macaracas vessels, but are seldom if ever fine line on Coclé vessels; barbed plumes are characteristic of Macaracas, but apparently absent in the Coclé style; etc.[8] As a general characterization, designs in the Coclé style appear less cluttered and more delineated than do those in the Azuero. The inclosure of designs in black-banded panels, a characteristic of all Azuero types, is absent in Coclé style polychromes. However, broad purple or red bands bordered by narrow black lines, used in geometric designs, or by themselves above or below the design area (e.g., Lothrop, 1942, pl. 2, e) are more common on Coclé vessels.

Other characteristics not specifically stylistic which are covered in other sections of this report are the following:

1. Ground color of the design area is commonly buff, salmon, or brown in the Azuero styles, although a cream white occurs fairly often. In the Coclé styles the cream white to dead white is much more common.

2. The design elements of the two ceramic groups are not shared, with the conspicuous exception of scroll elements and dragon motifs.

3. Paste color of the Azuero vessels and sherds at the El Hatillo site invariably fell within an orange to brick red, dark red or brown hue, never gray, whereas the latter shade occurs quite frequently in sherds with unmistakably Coclé designs.

4. Basic shape categories between the two styles are, for the main part, separate. About the only two shared by Late Coclé and the Azuero styles are the pedestal bowl or plate and the collared jar. However, pedestals of vessels decorated in the Coclé style are generally shorter in proportion to the vessel's diameter and more frequently are flanged at the foot, a mode which is absent on Azuero style vessels. Coclé collared jars are more apt to have straight rather than curving collars and the lips are more frequently horizontally flattened and

---

[8] These particular differences concerning the alligator motif are discussed more fully in that section dealing with the Higo variety. As noted, confusion generally is limited to scroll or alligator motifs and often other modes besides those of style must be included to differentiate the two polychrome groups.

everted, a characteristic which apparently occurs only on Cuipo variety vessels in the Azuero style.

It should be evident from the above that Coclé and Azuero styles (particularly those of the Macaracas type) are closely related, and sherds with fragmentary designs cannot always be differentiated. Because of this, a residual category of "Coclé-like" was established for sorting purposes in the study of the El Hatillo material (see Coclé polychromes under "Ceramic Typology"). Despite the sometimes frustrating similarities in design style, the two ceramic groups are sufficiently different to allow them to be considered as separate though related entities.

El Hatillo Polychrome

EL HATILLO POLYCHROME; EL HATILLO VARIETY

Sample.—22 vessels or large fragments; 57 sherds [9] (pls. 1, *d*; 2, *a–c*).

Paste.—The temper consists of crushed rock with occasional smooth particles of a reddish substance, probably hematite. Paste color is generally brick red (Munsell hue 2.5YR 4/6–8), though it is sometimes fired to a lighter orange hue (Munsell hue 2.5YR 6/6–8). Hardness rates at 3 on Mohs' scale.

Shapes.—One of the more striking attributes of this variety is the great variation in form which occurs within a general category. Shapes include globular bird bowls with short pedestal or collarlike bases (fig. 7, *n*, *s*), dovelike bird vessels with tall, straight spouts (fig. 7, *f*), angled shoulder bottles with varying proportions (fig. 7, *a–e*, *i*), globular and subglobular bottles (figs. 7, *g*, *h*). Although many of the bottle shapes listed above occurred only once at the site, some are common, especially the globular bird bowls, the dove-shaped bird bottles and the angled shoulder and globular bottles. Thickness ranges from 5–10 mm. depending on the vessel size; most vessels average 6–7 mm. for the wall at midheight. Maximum diameters of bottles average around 11–13 cm.; for the bird bowls about 18–20 cm.

Other forms are conspicuous either for their rarity or their absence. Only one collared jar fragment was found. This belonged to a small vessel, 11 cm. in diameter, which had a short out-curved collar but its base was missing. Shoulder sherds for another closed vessel, quite large (estimated diameter, 60 cm.), were found, but its base and rim areas were missing. One, probably spouted, effigy bottle with three small loop handles and typical El Hatillo variety design elements was found (fig. 7, *j*, *k*; pl. 1, *d*). Both spout (or collar) and the base are missing. Small open bowls are unknown for this variety

---

[9] The sherd sample count for this variety represents a minimum since it excludes sherds recovered under unstratified conditions in Mound III. Of the total of 559 El Hatillo type sherds recorded for Mound III, the majority was of this variety.

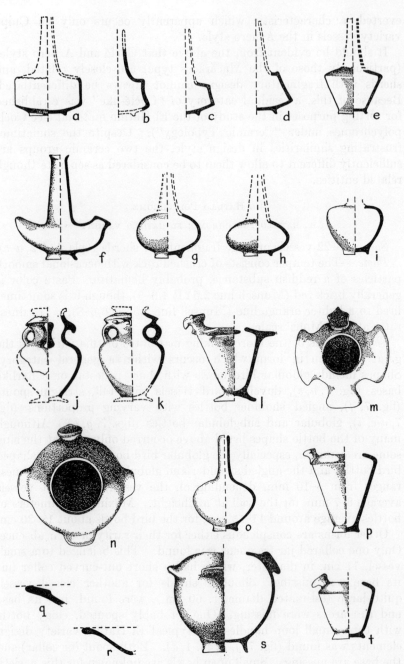

FIGURE 7.—El Hatillo type vessel shapes.

in the material from the El Hatillo site, and I know of no examples elsewhere. No whole plates were recovered, and plate sherds are very rare. Large open bowls with either a pear-shaped deep base or a shallower rounder base and sharply incurving rims (see fig. 35, c), a fairly common shape in the Parita and Macaracas Polychrome types, are also unknown as yet for the El Hatillo type and variety.

Bases.—Ring bases are by far the most common. Pedestals, apparently limited to the bird bowl shape, are very short and collarlike.

Rims.—On the globular bird bowls the rim and lip are simple, unmodified incurving continuations of the body wall. Only one collar was noted, on the small jar mentioned above, and it was short and curved outward. The plate sherds exhibit either a rounded lip with the rim an unmodified continuation of the body, or else a horizontally flanged rim with rounded lip (fig. 7, q). Spout lips on the bottles are either rounded or flattened horizontally, but never flanged or curled in as is often the case with the Calabaza variety.

Appendages and construction.—No handles (with the exception of the effigy vessel mentioned above) or adornos were noted. The only appendages assignable to this type are the wings, tails, and heads on the globular bird bowls. Very little significant information was apparent concerning details of construction, except the characteristic that the heads of the bird bowls clearly assignable to this variety are solid. Heads vary in shape; some are relatively large and flattened, others small and rounded (see fig. 10, f-i). Wings and tails tend to be short and stubby. The method of vessel construction, whether by coiling or paddle and anvil, was not apparent. Holes punched through the bottle necks or shoulders, a common feature of the Calabaza variety, are absent in the El Hatillo variety.

Surface.—The entire exterior surface is highly polished and the decorated area, although naturally varying with the vessel shape, is ordinarily restricted to the upper two-thirds or half of the vessel. The slip covering the undecorated area is generally a red-brown color. The ground slip of the design area is lighter, usually ranging from orange to a dark orange, although a lighter shade, almost a cream, also occurs. One example of a light-gray slip was found. Occasionally the lighter ground color of the design area will be used to cover the entire exterior of the vessel including the base. More often, two broad black bands, barely separated from each other by a very thin line of ground color, will be used to divide the design area from the darker basal portion.

Colors used in delineation are red and black, the red invariably bordered by a narrow black line. As may be seen, the designs are primarily geometric and angular (fig. 8). When life designs are employed, they are usually angular. Thus, faces are in the form of triangles (fig. 9), bodies take a massive rectangular outline, and crocodiles appear in highly conventionalized angular form. Notable

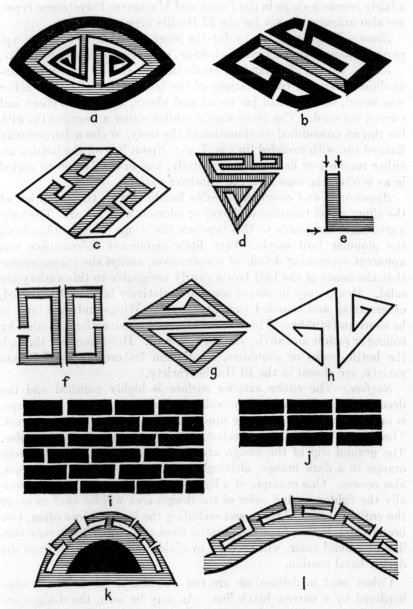

Figure 8.—El Hatillo type, El Hatillo variety, design elements. *a*, P-10; *b, d, j*, P-9; *c*, P-41; *g*, Find 30-1; *i*, Find 29; *k-l*, P-43. Horizontal (vertical in *d*) lines indicate red.

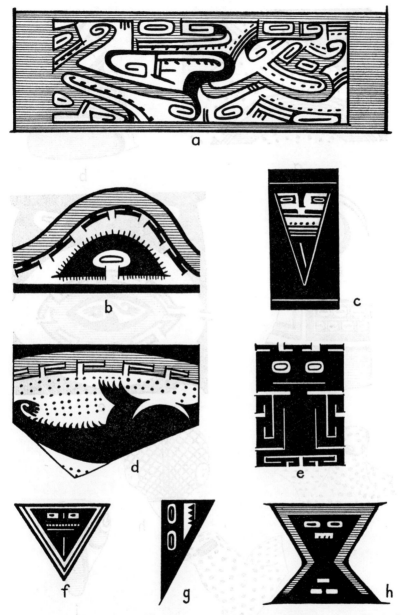

FIGURE 9.—El Hatillo type, El Hatillo variety, design elements.   a, c, P-12; b, d–f. Mound III sherds; g, P-42; h, P-10.   Horizontal lines indicate red.

FIGURE 10.—El Hatillo type, El Hatillo variety, design elements. a, P-19; b, d, Trench 5 sherds, 0–50 cm.; c, e–g, Mound III sherds; h, Find 22-1; i, Find 30-5. Horizontal lines indicate red.

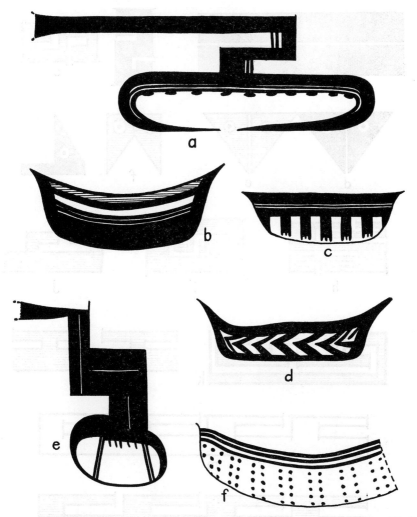

FIGURE 11.—El Hatillo type, El Hatillo variety, design elements. *a, c,* Find 22-1; *b,* Find 39-*a; d–e,* Find 30-5; *f,* Mound III sherd. Horizontal lines indicate red.

exceptions to this general practice are the graceful birds, probably pelicans, of figure 10, *c,* a few sherds with alligator decoration, bird bowl claws, and occasionally a curving geometric design. No small filler elements were noted for this variety, but black dots are frequently used as massive fill on the globular bird bowls (fig. 10, *a, f, g*). Occasional instances of negative technique occur, as illustrated by figure 12, *i.*

Variations from other sites.—I know of none at the present time.

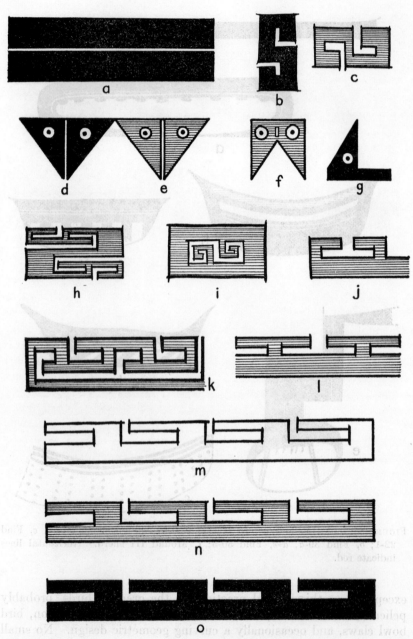

FIGURE 12.—El Hatillo type, El Hatillo variety, design elements. *a–c*, He-4 miscellaneous sherds; *d–e*, Find 30-1; *f*, P-9; *h*, Find 30-4; *i*, Find 20; *j*, P-11; *k*, P-13; *l*, P-42.   Horizontal lines indicate red.

Geographical range.—I know of no definite examples outside of the Parita area. Two possible examples from the Pearl Islands are illustrated by Linné (1929, fig. 25-*B*, 18-*A*). Lothrop (1950, fig. 55) illustrated an undecorated bottle with a typical El Hatillo variety bird effigy bottle spout. Examples of the variety in the Heye Museum (Nos. 22/9334, 22/9452, and 22/9499) are all from the Parita area; two from the Finca Calderon or El Hatillo site.

Chronological position.—Believed to be late on the basis of scanty stratigraphic evidence at the El Hatillo site.

Relationships of variety.—Related in form and design elements to other varieties in the type. Related by choice of colors and surface finish to both Parita and Macaracas types, and to the Ceritó variety.

Bibliography.—Stirling, 1950, p. 239, 2d row from top, left.

EL HATILLO POLYCHROME; ESPALÁ VARIETY

Sample.—Neither vessels nor large fragments; 30 sherds.

Paste.—Same as the El Hatillo variety.

Shapes.—At the El Hatillo site this variety shares most of the shapes of the preceding variety with the notable exception of bottles. Since the variety is known by sherds only, shapes are not always determinable. They include, however, closed vessels with rounded shoulders, sharply angled shoulders, and bird bowls. In addition, two shapes not noted for the previous variety are the pedestal plate and a dish with outcurved flaring sides (fig. 7, *r*). A few of these sherds indicate large vessels; one sharply angled shoulder sherd is 8 mm. thick and has a projected diameter for the whole vessel of about 60 cms. In general, however, the size appears to be close to that of the El Hatillo variety.

Surface.—The surface color, polish, and general technique of decoration is the same as that of the preceding variety. Actually, the Espalá variety is distinguished from the El Hatillo solely on the basis of the use of "teeth" projections along what appear to be the mouths and snouts of rectangular alligator motifs (fig. 13) and the occurrence of double or even triple black lines bordering the red. Although occasional rectangular alligator motifs are found on the vessels assigned to the El Hatillo variety, the toothlike projections and the more frequent use of double line are absent. This motif with tooth projections does occur, however, on Ceritó variety vessels. Whether these slight decorative differences, as well as some shape variations, are a sufficient basis for setting up a variety will only become apparent with further investigation and excavation.

Variations from other sites.—Lothrop illustrates two additional shapes decorated in the style of this variety; one a sharp-angled-shoulder cylindrical jar fragment which has a short flare collar (Loth-

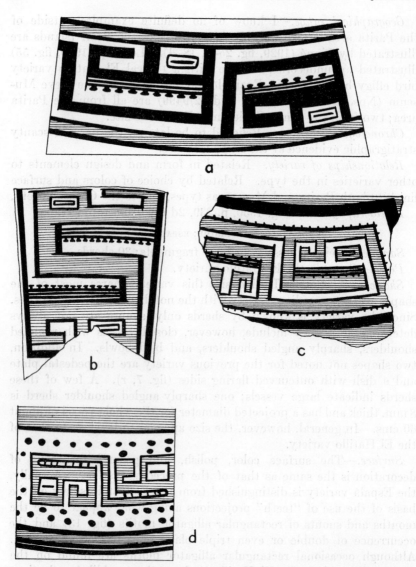

FIGURE 13.—El Hatillo type, Espalá variety, sherds from Mound III. Horizontal lines indicate red.

rop, 1942, fig. 229) and the other, a spouted barrel-shaped vessel with the "barrel" alined horizontally on a ring base (Lothrop, 1950, fig. 134-a). Both of these vessels are from the Espalá district of south-west Veraguas near the Bubí and Lovaina Rivers, and neither shape is known at He-4.

The Heye Museum of the American Indian exhibits a bird effigy bowl from the Finca Calderon site at Parita, which combines the dot fill of the El Hatillo variety with the toothed line and double line elements of the Espalá variety (cat. No. 22/9452). In this case the wings and tail are represented by painted decoration only, not by modeling. Another vessel at the same museum (cat. No. 22/8384) listed from Parita combines the Espalá alligator motif with the characteristic shape and arc with pendent triangle motif of the Achote variety.

Geographical range.—As noted above, two vessels with Espalá design patterns are illustrated by Lothrop (1942, fig. 229; 1950, fig. 134–*a*) from Espalá, Veraguas, and one vessel combining Espalá and Achote design elements was present in the Heye collection from Parita. I know of no other examples in the literature.

Chronological position.—Same as El Hatillo variety.

Relationships of variety.—Same as El Hatillo variety.

Bibliography.—See *Geographical range.*

EL HATILLO POLYCHROME; ACHOTE VARIETY

Sample.—Three whole vessels or large fragments, four sherds (pl. 2, *d*).

Paste.—Same as the El Hatillo variety.

Shapes.—Vessels assigned to this variety are limited in shape to a sharp-angled-shoulder jar with a small bird head projecting from the constricted orifice rim (fig. 7, *p*). The lips are rounded and the vessels have ring bases. As may be seen in figure 7 from a comparison of *p* with *t*, this shape is very similar to one of those assigned to the Jobo variety and might be treated as a minor variation of the latter if the differences were not so consistent in the few vessels so far recovered. The Achote variety jar always appears to be taller and slimmer than those of the Jobo variety due to the smaller base diameter in proportion to the diameter of the shoulder.

Surface.—The entire surface is polished as is the case in the El Hatillo variety, but here the polishing marks are usually more apparent. Decoration is limited to the shoulder and extreme upper body, and usually consists of a single design motif (fig. 14, *a*), a split or semiclosed arc with fretted ends and, often, triangles pendent from the arc roof.

The semiclosed arc element is shared with the Macaracas varieties, but in this case the element is expressed in an angular style. One sherd from Mound III at the El Hatillo site combines the semiclosed arc with the pendent triangle motif and the toothed angular crocodile of the Espalá variety, a combination which also occurs elsewhere.

Variations from other sites.—As noted above, a vessel from Parita, now at the Museum of the American Indian (cat. No. 22/8384), combines Espalá design elements with Achote shape and design motifs.

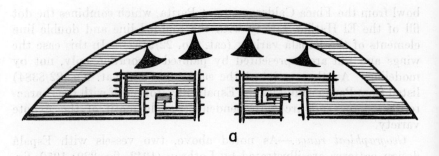

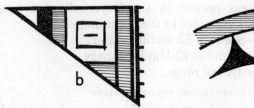
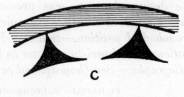

FIGURE 14.—El Hatillo type, Achote variety, design elements from Find 35-a. Horizontal lines indicate red.

Geographical range.—One other example of this variety from the Parita area is present in the Dade Collection at the Museum of the American Indian (cat. No. 22/8384). Otherwise, I know of no other specimens.

Chronological position.—Same as El Hatillo variety.

Relationships of variety.—Same as El Hatillo variety.

Bibliography.—None.

EL HATILLO POLYCHROME; JOBO VARIETY

Sample: 18 vessels or large fragments (mainly from one grave lot) and 52 sherds (pl. 3, *a, b*).

Paste.—Fired to the same color range as the El Hatillo variety, but there appears to be a higher incidence of black particles in the crushed rock temper. The slip is considerably softer than that of the El Hatillo variety and has a rating of 2 on Mohs' scale.

Shapes.—Two basic shapes are apparent (fig. 7, *o, t*): a globular bottle with a narrow straight spout and a ring base, and a ring-based jar with a high angled shoulder and incurved rim. The latter shape occurred in the collection in three variations:

(*a*) with a solid, flattened bird head attached to the rim (fig. 7, *t*),

(*b*) with a hollow bird head, solid wings and tail appended to the shoulder (fig. 7, *l, m*), and

(*c*) an apparently similar shape (known only from sherds) but with solid head.

Jar lips are rounded; spout lips are generally rounded although occasionally flattened horizontally. All the bottles and "a" type bird jars are supported by ring bases. The one example of the "b" type vessel had a shallow widely flared pedestal base; no bases of "c" were recovered.

Surface.—The most striking aspect of the surface treatment and one of the variety's distinctive features is the faded and flat appearance of the colors, a quality accompanied by a distinct tendency for colors to wash off and probably related to the softness of the slip. It is clear from the gloss retained on part of one vessel, however, that the surface originally had been either polished or treated with some organic material to provide a lustrous effect. Whether the entire exterior surface or only the decorated area was polished is not known. The ground slip in all cases is a light-cream color. Design colors are predominantly black and red with purple occurring on only one sherd, a bottle spout. As usual at the El Hatillo site, red and purple are bordered by black lines. The design area on the bottles and wingless jars is limited to a band encircling the vessel, on the bottles along the lower portion of the shoulder and on the jar rims from shoulder to lip. The spout, upper shoulder, lower body, and base of the bottles are covered with a red slip (the polychrome spout example excepted). On the other hand, in the case of the wingless bird jars, the cream ground extends over the shoulder and down to the bottom fourth of the body where a narrow black band separates it from the red slip of the lower body and base. Design on both the wingless birds and the bottles is very similar (figs. 15, 16, *a*, *b*), consisting of angular panels formed by black bordered red bands. A feature which distinguishes this variety from the El Hatillo variety is the use of narrow black lines alone (without the use of red fill) for the formation of filler elements such as straight-sided triangles, "T's" and dashes (fig. 15, *a–d*, *h*, *i*).

The one example of "b" shape is decorated rather crudely on each wing with a solid black egg-shaped area (fig. 16, *e*). The tail is solid black.

It is with "c" shape that the main evidence of curvilinear design appears, in this case a red-filled scroll nested in black lines (fig. 16, *c*). Along with this possible subvariety, I have grouped the polychrome spout mentioned above (fig. 16, *d*). The cream slip, lack of polish, and red-filled rectilinear designs with dash fill all place the spout in the variety, but the use of purple suggests affinities to the Parita and Macaracas types.

Variations from other sites.—A vessel of the De Zeltner Collection from Chiriquí and illustrated by both MacCurdy and Lothrop (MacCurdy, 1911, fig. 256; Lothrop, 1942, fig. 280-*e*) displays a use

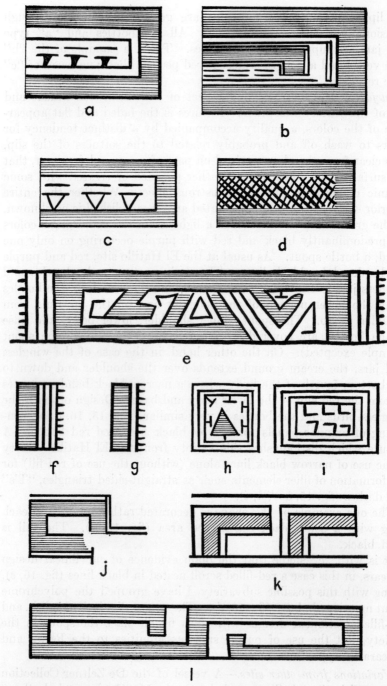

FIGURE 15.—El Hatillo type, Jobo variety, design elements. *a*, Find 10-11; *b*, 10-1; *c*, 10-2; *d*, 10-13; *e*, 10-14; *h–i*, 10-5. Horizontal lines indicate red; diagonal lines indicate purple.

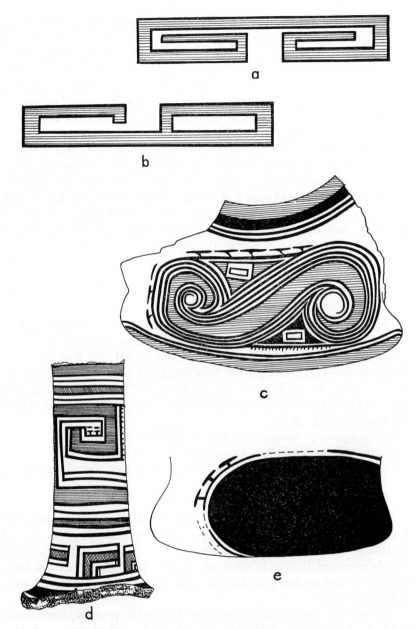

FIGURE 16.—El Hatillo type, Jobo variety, design elements. c, Trench 2; d, Trench 7, Level 1; e, Find 10-17.   Horizontal lines indicate red; diagonal lines indicate purple.

of purple with the fret motif, but surface quality and ground color are not clearly described. As pointed out by Lothrop in his discussion of this vessel (Lothrop, 1942, p. 346), the row of arc elements around the lower body is almost identical to that on a pedestal plate (Lothrop, 1942, fig. 485) which in turn is a typical example of Parita Polychrome, Yampí variety, but the shape of the De Zeltner vessel, a concave-sided cylinder jar with ring base, is unlike any found at the El Hatillo site.

Another variation is demonstrated by a vessel from Rio Grande, Coclé, now in the Dade Collection at the Museum of the American Indian (cat. No. 22/8409). The shape may be described as a spouted barrel lying horizontally on a ring base (similar to one of the Espalá specimens), and decorated with the "S" scroll element (similar to fig. 16, c) and dot fill. Surface treatment, that is, the lack of polish and chalky cream slip, is identical with the Jobo variety.

An example of the bottle shape typical of this variety, but in this case undecorated and treated with a plain red slip, was excavated near Bubí in Veraguas and is illustrated by Lothrop (Lothrop, 1950, fig. 55).

Geographical range.—I know of no definite examples of this variety in the literature. Possible examples include a cylinder jar from Chiriquí (Holmes, 1888, fig. 213; MacCurdy, 1911, fig. 256; Lothrop, 1942, fig. 280-e), and a spout or base fragment from the Pearl Islands (Linné, 1929, fig. 18-b; Lothrop, 1942, fig. 442). I believe that the main center of production for this variety was Veraguas, but this is no more than a guess.

Chronological position.—Same as El Hatillo variety.

Relationships of variety.—Same as El Hatillo variety.

Bibliography.—Stirling, 1949, p. 376, bottom row, right, Find 10.

PARITA POLYCHROME

This type includes at least five varieties and was represented in relatively high quantity in all the mounds and trenches at the El Hatillo site. Naming the category presented some difficulty since sherds or complete vessels which clearly fit within the type have been illustrated and reported in the literature from various areas and with different labels.

The earliest reports, and therefore those with priority, were made by Holmes in 1888 and MacCurdy in 1911, but all of their examples came from the Chiriquí area and, in view of the general paucity of the type in that area, may be considered imports. Lothrop (Lothrop, 1942, pp. 225–230, 233–240), the next writer to deal with the type, illustrates sherds and vessels from both Parita and Macaracas. Since the type was apparently more plentiful at the former site, Parita was selected for the type name. Other published examples are listed either under the sections dealing with variations or the bibliographies listed with each varietal description.

All of the varieties discussed here, except the bird bowl, are easily distinguished from the El Hatillo polychrome. However, as will be noted below, the type shares a number of elements with the Macaracas type and is closely allied to it. Designs represent life forms more frequently than do those of the angular style and their depiction tends to be more naturalistic. Favorite subjects are birds (especially the vulture), fish, turtles, and frogs. In addition, one variety contains the only unmistakable representations of human beings found at He-4, in this case appearing as small figurines attached to large collared jars between rim and shoulder alongside the neck of the vessel. The designs are beautifully executed with fine control of line and a graceful proportion. Very few crudely or hastily done examples were found. Design colors are black, red, and purple with the red and purple invariably bordered by black lines. Corners and points are terminated in finely graduated points as is the case with the Macaracas type. The preferred forms of the Parita type include pedestal bowls with and without bird appendages, pedestal plates, and large collared jars with high angular or rounded shoulders and pear-shaped bodies. Unfortunately, the latter was found in sherd form only, and the total shape must be inferred from illustrations of similarly decorated vessels found at other sites.

PARITA POLYCHROME; NÍSPERO VARIETY

Sample.—40 vessels or large fragments, 857 sherds (pl. 4, *a, b*).

Paste.—The temper is crushed rock, the white particles of which are easily visible without magnification. Paste is usually fired a brick red (Munsell Hue 2.5 YR 4/6–8), though this may vary from orange to dark-brown red (Munsell Hue 2.5 YR 6/6–8 to 2.5 YR 3/4–6). Occasional smooth lumps of hematite occur. Hardness rates at 3 on Mohs' scale.

Shapes.—Basically, the vessels are pedestal based subglobular bowls with incurving rims and rounded lips (fig. 17, *a*). Occasionally the lip will have a slight upward flange, and the depth of the bowl may vary from those which are fairly deep with a relatively gentle curve in the wall profile to those shallow examples with an almost angular wall profile. Added to this basic bowl form are flat wings extending well around the body on each side, a tail, and a vulturelike head with hooked beak and a modeled crop on the neck or on the chest (vessel wall). The diameter of the bowls averages about 20 cms. and the bowl height about 9 cms. The only example with pedestal attached measured 21.5 cms. in total height. Pedestal bases are generally

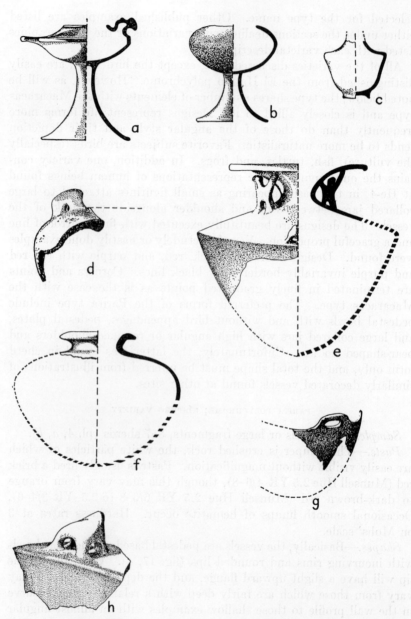

FIGURE 17.—Parita type vessel shapes. *a*, Níspero P-6; *b*, Anón; *c*, Caimito, P-3; *d*, *h*, Ortiga; *e*, P-33; *f*, P-39; *g*, Mound III Ortiga.

fairly tall in proportion to the total vessel and have a distinct flare or outward curve as they descend from place of attachment to base rim. The basic shape described above was varied at the El Hatillo site on two occasions; once by the addition of a second head close to the first, and a second time by the addition of a spout (missing in this instance, but indicated by the jagged rim condition) or some type of constricted opening converting the vessel into a bottle.

Appendage and construction notes.—The method of construction is not apparent. Wall thickness ranges from 4–8 mm., with the average about 6 mm. Heads of all vessels clearly assignable to this variety are hollow in contrast to those of the El Hatillo Polychrome, and the practice of roughening or gouging the surface of the bowl with a stick or reed (not with shell as occurred at Venado Beach) before applying tails and wings was generally followed. Eyes and crops occasionally may be slightly flattened.

Surface.—Design colors are red, black, and purple applied to a ground color ranging from cream to an orange or light-red brown. The recovery of some entirely cream, presumably unfinished, vessels suggests that the entire exterior surface was first covered with the cream slip. Design colors were then applied and the design area alone was polished after firing, a process which tends to deepen the ground color in the polished areas, sometimes giving it a light brownish hue. Actually, it is not clear whether the high gloss attained was produced by polishing or by the application of a varnish, since the extension of the glossed area beyond the design in some cases gives the appearance of having been accomplished by a polishing stone, and in others as if by brushing. Interiors below the lip are undecorated and unslipped.

The vessel lips are almost always red slipped and bordered on the shoulder by one or two black bands encircling the orifice. Various polychrome elements, generally bars and ellipses (figs. 18, *a–f;* 19, *b, c*), are arranged along the shoulder between the lip band and the wing design. Occasional filler elements characteristic of the Yampí and Ortiga varieties also occur (fig. 18, *a–h*). Wings, for the most part, are decorated in a highly conventional manner with either straight or chevronlike bands running out from the body to the outer wing edge and presumably indicating feathers (fig. 19, *d, e*). Tail elements show somewhat more variation and are usually of rectangular pattern (fig. 18, *i, j*).

On either side of the head a painted black leg extends down below the neck and wing level to terminate in a claw. It is in the depiction of the claws, often extremely graceful and complex curvilinear designs, that the greatest individuality of design expression is demonstrated. Figure 19, *f–h*, gives a necessarily meager indication of the range of

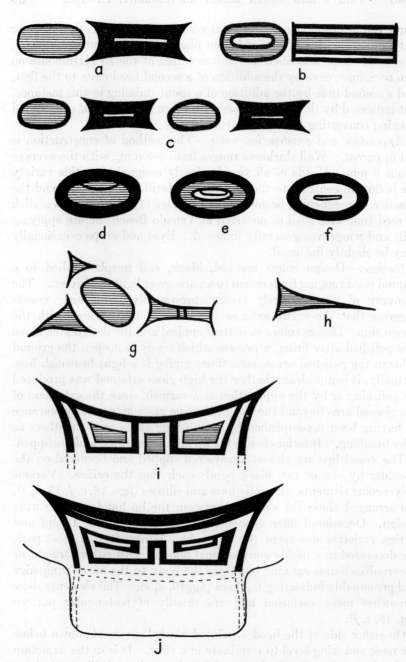

FIGURE 18.—Parita type, Níspero variety, design elements. *i*, Find 140 (?); *j*, Find 121. Horizontal lines indicate red.

FIGURE 19.—Parita type, Níspero variety, design elements. *a*, Find 22-1; *d*, P-5; *e*, Find 112; *f*, Find 221; *g*, Find 90; *h*, P-6. Horizontal lines indicate red.

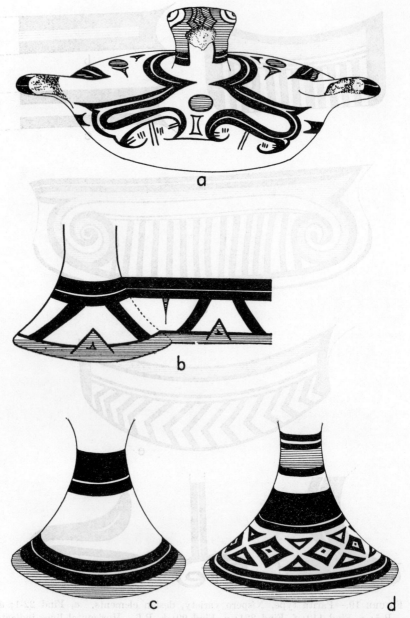

FIGURE 20.—Parita type, Níspero variety. a, P-5; b–c, Mound III miscellaneous; d, Find 162 (fits P-6). Horizontal lines indicate red.

variation here. Arrangements of designs on the birds' heads also showed considerable variation, and no attempt was made to record these. Below the wings a black or black and red band (fig. 19, *b*, *c*) generally extends horizontally around the vessel from claws to anus, the latter normally represented by a black or black and red egg-shaped motif (fig. 18, *d–f*).

Despite a core of quite similar vessels within this type, it blends to some extent into the El Hatillo globular bird bowl; i.e., occasional vessels were found which might be classified as variants of either type. Other variations present at the El Hatillo site include a plain red slipped counterpart, and a predominantly red slipped vessel with decoration of the head and claws only.

The pedestal bases of this variety and the following Anón variety are generally decorated by broad black bands horizontally encircling the base (fig. 20, *c*), although "pointer" bases with red triangular motifs extending vertically from the horizontal bands are also noted (fig. 20, *b*). Though this latter base is very similar to the "diamond base" of the Macaracas type (see fig. 38, *b*), and sherds with only part of the design present could be classed with either type, no diamond bases were found attached to vessels of either the Níspero or the Anón varieties. An additional base pattern of alternating diamond and pyramid elements is illustrated in figure 20, *d*.

Variations from other sites.—MacCurdy (MacCurdy, 1911, fig. 246) illustrates a globular bird effigy jar from Divalá, Chiriquí, with wings, tail, and decoration similar to this variety, but with a ring base and a short straight collar.

A vessel with still a different shape, but sharing the tail elements of this variety and the triangle and zigzag element of the Ortiga variety, is present in the Dade Collection at the Museum of the American Indian (cat. No. 22/8375). The shape is reminiscent of a plump pigeon perched on a ring base; the head and neck form the collar or neck of the jar. Measuring 25 cms. in length and 18 cms. in width, the vessel is listed from Parita.

Geographical range.—As noted above, a straight collared jar of this variety from Divalá, Chiriquí, is listed by MacCurdy. Otherwise, all examples I know of come from the Parita area, and probably the same site (Lothrop, 1942, fig. 449); a red-buff example (ibid., fig. 472), Museum of the American Indian (cat. No. 22/8374; cat. No. 22/8375, a variant shape). The vulture bowl shape in plain or red ware has been reported extensively in Veraguas, however (see Lothrop, 1950).

Chronological position.—On the basis of the meager stratigraphic evidence at the site, as well as grave associations, I believe that the variety is late, possible contemporary with El Hatillo Polychrome.

Relationships of variety.—Related to other varieties of the Parita

Polychrome type; also, in shape, to Veraguas "double rimmed" vessels (Lothrop, 1950, pp. 41–43).

Bibliography.—See "*Geographical range*" section above, also Stirling, 1949, p. 376 upper row (Find 121, left; Find 173, right), and Stirling, 1950, p. 239, bottom row, right.

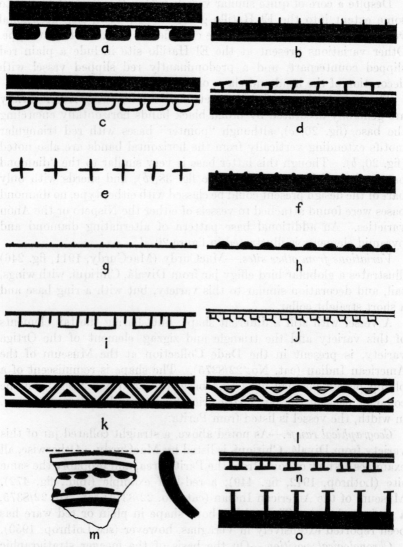

FIGURE 21.—Parita type, Anón variety, design elements. *a–h*, Miscellaneous vessels, Mound III; *i*, Find 35; *j*, Find 168; *k*, P-1 (Mound III); *l*, Find 333; *m–o*, Miscellaneous vessels, Mound III. Horizontal lines indicate red.

Sample.—41 vessels or large fragments and 331 sherds (pl. 3, *c*).
Paste.—Same as the Níspero variety.

Shape.—Shallow incurving bowl on a pedestal base, thus the same shape as the Níspero variety shorn of its wings, tail, and head (fig. 17, *b*). As with the latter variety, variations occur in the shallowness or globularity of the bowls and occasionally the lip of a vessel will be slightly flanged upward. Pedestals and overall vessel dimensions are also similar to those of the preceding variety. Shallow open bowl rim sherds with typical Anón decorations were recovered in Trench 1 and Trench 7, but no complete vessels of this shape were found (fig. 21, *m*).

Appendages and construction.—Method of construction not apparent and no appendages noted for this variety. Scoring of the under surface of the bowl for the attachment of the pedestal bases takes place fairly frequently as with the Níspero variety.

Surface.—Design colors are primarily black with an occasional use of red fill between the black bands. No purple was noted for this variety at the El Hatillo site. Ground color ranges from cream through orange to a reddish brown. Again, only the decorated area is polished and it therefore has a darker hue than the remaining vessel surface even though the slip is the same. One vessel was extensively scratched on the exterior wall in a manner similar to the Calabaza variety bottles or rattles and may have been used as a rattle.

The primary area of decoration is restricted generally to the upper exterior half of the bowl (sometimes decoration extends somewhat below this point) and to the pedestal base. The lower half of the bowl remains unpolished in the solid ground color. Interiors are not decorated below the lip, nor are they slipped. The lip is almost always red slipped, and the shoulder below is decorated in a series of horizontal concentric black bands of varying width to which may be appended a number of elements such as dots, "T's," perpendicular dashes, hemispherical blobs, and rectangular elements (fig. 21). Although there is considerable variation between vessels in the use of these elements, the total impression of the type is one of great consistency and similarity of overall appearance. Pedestal bases are decorated in a fashion similar to those of the preceding variety; that is, with either horizontal bands or the pointer motif.

This variety, while being clearly allied to the Níspero variety in shape and surface treatment, also shows some affinity to the Ortiga variety discussed below by its occasional use of the same decorative elements (fig. 21, *j*, *l*).

Variations from other sites.—Lothrop (1942, fig. 471, *d*) illustrates an open bowl from Macaracas with interior designs similar to those illustrated in figure 21, *a*, *k*.

Geographical range.—I know of no examples in the literature other than the open bowl with interior Anón design elements from Macaracas mentioned in the section dealing with variations at other sites. One distinct example of this type, from Parita, is present in the Museum of the American Indian (cat. No. 22/9382) and a variant shape with Anón design elements from Rio Grande, Coclé, is also in the Museum of the American Indian (cat. No. 22/8405). Dr. Russell Mitchell reports (personal communication) typical cross and blob or scallop decoration in Veraguas at Quebrada Honda, Mamey, and Piedra del Sol.

Chronological position.—Same as Níspero variety.

Relationships of variety.—Other varieties of the Parita Polychrome type.

Bibliography.—Lothrop, 1942, fig. 471, *d*; Stirling, 1950, p. 239, second row from bottom, left, Find 334.

PARITA POLYCHROME; CAIMITO VARIETY

Sample.—2 whole vessels, 15 sherds (pl. 4, *c*, *d*).

Paste.—Same as preceding two varieties.

Shapes.—One example (vessel P-3) is presumably a bottle (spout missing but indicated by jagged rim) with a high and sharply angled shoulder and a ring base (fig. 17, *c*; pl. 4, *c*, *d*). The only other example (Find 348-2) in the He-4 material at the Peabody Museum appears to have the same shape although it is too fragmentary to permit definite comparison. A third vessel from the site, which remained in Panama, is an angular shouldered pedestal-based bowl (pedestal missing) with an incurved rim similar to the two preceding varieties. Included in the sherds are two plate fragments and two handles.

Surface.—The treatment is the same as that for the Níspero and Anón varieties; i.e., a cream base slip polished in the decorated areas only. The cream ground color shades to light brown in the polished areas; the delineating colors are black and red. The style of painting is very similar to that of the Níspero variety, and the body elements of egg and band (fig. 22, *c*) are identical on both examples studied. The main design on one specimen (vessel P-3) consists of an undulating reptile body around the spout, with a mustached mouth at one end (hammerhead shark?) and a stingray tail at the other (fig. 23, *a–c*). Interspersed in the undulations are elements which evidently indicate scales or turtle shell segments (fig. 23, *a*, *b*). Shoulder decoration on the other vessel studied (Find 348-2) consists of fish or reptilian ele-

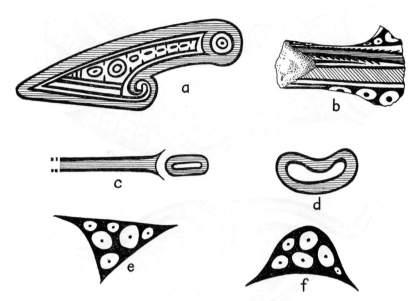

FIGURE 22.—Parita type, Caimito variety, design elements.   *a, d, e,* Find 348-2; *b,* Mound III sherd; *c,* P-3; *f,* Mound III miscellaneous.   Horizontal lines indicate red; diagonal lines indicate purple.

ments of dotted circles on a black ground (fig. 22, *e, f*) combined with barbed feathers (see fig. 40, *l*), an element frequently found in the Higo variety, Macaracas Polychrome.   A white ground circle and dot motif (fig. 22, *a*), common in the Cuipo variety, is present on the shoulder, and the body of the vessel exhibits a mouth motif (fig. 22, *d*). The photograph of the Panamanian example (Find 334) shows the scale or turtle shell elements of figure 23, *a,* interspersed in the undulations of a red-filled black-bordered band combined with what appears to be a wing element.

One of the handle fragments (fig. 22, *b*) combines the black ground circle and dot element with a barbed feather.   The other (fig. 23, *d*) exhibits the black ground circle and dot element alone.   The plate sherds are decorated with the hammerhead shark motif and the undulating line turtle element.

Variations from other sites.—The Museum of the American Indian possesses three vessels which may be assigned to this variety.   One (cat. No. 22/9455) from Veraguas is a "double rimmed" type bowl on a pedestal base generally similar in overall shape to the unpainted vessels illustrated by Lothrop (1950, pp. 41–43) as typical of Veraguas. It is decorated with a hammerhead shark motif, a stingray or barbed tail, a mouth, and the fish scale element described above (fig. 22, *f*). The base is banded.   Another vessel (cat. No. 22/9450), from the Finca Calderon, Parita, is a small rendition of the vessel described

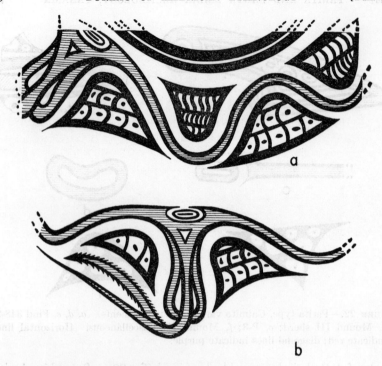

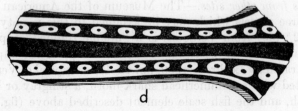

FIGURE 23.—Parita type, Caimito variety, design elements. a–c, P-3; d, Mound
III sherd.   Horizontal lines indicate red.

above complete with banded base, but adds to that design an egg and bar motif on the body.   Finally, a third vessel at the Museum, again from the Finca Calderon at Parita (cat. No. 22/9451), has a shape similar to the Peabody specimens, in this case with a short spout intact, but differs in its froglike head.   Again, the circle and dot on a black ground scale element occurs.

Geographical range.—The variety at present knowledge is limited to Parita (El Hatillo site), one vessel from an unknown part of Veraguas (Mus. Amer. Ind. cat. No. 22/9455) and another in the Museo Nacional de Panamá from Catine, Las Palmas, Veraguas (G. R. Willey photograph).

Chronological position.—Same as Níspero variety.

Relationships of variety.—Same as Níspero variety.

Bibliography.—None.

PARITA POLYCHROME; YAMPÍ VARIETY

Sample.—10 vessels or large fragments, 198 sherds (pl. 3, *d*).

Paste.—Same as the previous varieties of this type except that unslipped areas of the vessel tend to be slightly softer (Mohs' scale rating of 2.5) and darkened cores are more frequent in the paste.

Shapes.—All examples at the El Hatillo site were pedestal plates ranging from 24–26 cms. in diameter.   In all cases the pedestals were missing.   However, a fragmentary base matched with a plate was relatively short with a wide diameter.   Holmes (1888, figs. 211, 212; also Lothrop, 1942, fig. 485) illustrates another example, this time with a somewhat taller and more flaring base similar in proportion to many of the Níspero and Anón variety vases.   Rims are either unmodified extensions of the plate body with rounded lips (these tend to fall in the larger diameter range), or are slightly flanged with a flat horizontal surface and rounded lip.   The latter tend to cluster around the lower pole of the diameter range.

Appendages and construction.—Mode of construction is not apparent. Vessels tend to be fairly thick, ranging from 8–10 mm., and at least one example of surface scoring or jabbing at the point of base adhesion was noted.   The only appendage noted, but a characteristic one on the flanged rim plates, is a small headless "frog" effigy lump, generally two or three in number and spaced equidistantly around the upper surface of the flat rim.   This feature is also characteristic of the Ortiga variety described below.

Surface.—The upper surface of the plate is generally covered with an orange or orange-red slip on which the design in black, red, and purple is delineated.   Both upper and lower surfaces of the plate are highly polished and the underside, in all instances noted, has been covered with a plain red slip without decoration.   The flat rimmed

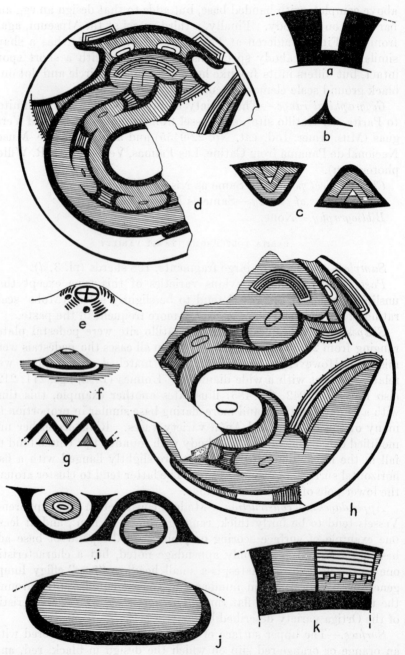

FIGURE 24.—Parita type, Yampí variety, design elements. *a, d, j*, P-24; *b–c, k*, Mound III; *e–i*, Mound II. Horizontal lines indicate red; diagonal lines indicate purple.

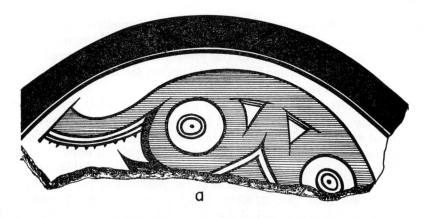

FIGURE 25.—Parita type, Yampí variety, Mound III miscellaneous sherds. Horizontal lines indicate red.

plates give the impression of greater delicacy of style, although the same elements appear on both types of plates. These include ovals, semiclosed arcs, and boxlike elements all executed in broad black lines (often with red or purple fill) on the plate rims (fig. 24), while the central area of the plate is filled with a ray or sharklike fish (fig. 24, *d*, *h*). The latter motif definitely occurs on the flanged rim plates. The nature of the motif on the unmodified rim plates is not as clear, although at least one instance of a hammerheaded element (fig. 25, *a*), similar to the preceding variety, occurred. It may be noted that the oval or ellipse elements are the same as those which appear on the effigy birds of this type.

In those instances where pedestal bases are definitely known for this variety, the design was of the horizontal band type. However, a typical specimen of this variety at the Museum of the American Indian (cat. No. 22/9514) from Veraguas had a pointed base.

Variations from other sites.—Two atypical examples of this variety are present in the Dade Collection at the Museum of the American Indian. One (cat. No. 22/8349) listed from Santiago, Veraguas, while maintaining the typical flat rim with frog effigy lumps and other decorative motifs characteristic of the Yampí variety, has as its primary motif a full face, rectangular mouthed monster in the "dancing crocodile" pose so characteristic of the Higo variety of Macaracas Polychromes (see fig. 42, *c*). The vessel under discussion also shares the barbed feathers motif (see fig. 40, *l*) of the latter variety. The style of drawing and general "feel" of the design is so similar to the typical Yampí flat rimmed plates that this consideration, combined with the other Yampí elements, suggests a copy of a Higo variety plate by a potter normally working with the Yampí variety.

The other (cat. No. 22/8372), a typical Yampí plate shape listed from La Peña, Veraguas, contains a profile dragon or crocodile head on a ray body. The execution of the design is somewhat cruder than usual for this variety, but the vessel seems justifiably assigned to the Yampí variety. Additional variations in execution of the ray design motif are discussed in the section dealing with the Pica-pica variety.

Geographical range.—Examples range from Chiriquí (Holmes, 1888, figs. 211, 212; same vessel illustrated by Lothrop, 1942, fig. 485) through Veraguas (Mus. Amer. Ind. cat. Nos. 22/8362 Soná; 22/8349 atypical from Santiago; 22/8372 atypical from La Peña; and 22/9514 unspecified area of Veraguas, similar vessel at Mamey reported by Dr. Russell Mitchell, personal communication) to the Parita sites, He-4, He-1, He-8, and Co-2 on the Santa Maria River.

Chronological position.—Same as Níspero variety.

Relationships of variety.—Same as Níspero variety with the addition of a similarity to the ray motif of the Pica-pica variety and to the Cuipo variety.

Bibliography.—See above.

PARITA POLYCHROME; ORTIGA VARIETY

Sample.—No whole vessels, 1,236 sherds (pl. 5, *a–c*).

Paste.—Similar to the Níspero variety although black cores occur more often and color is more variable.

Shapes.—The predominant shape (fig. 17, *f*) represented in this variety is a large jar with either angled or round shoulders high on the vessel and collared neck with flaring rim. Often the lips are flattened obliquely on the upper surface (fig. 17, *f*). Although no

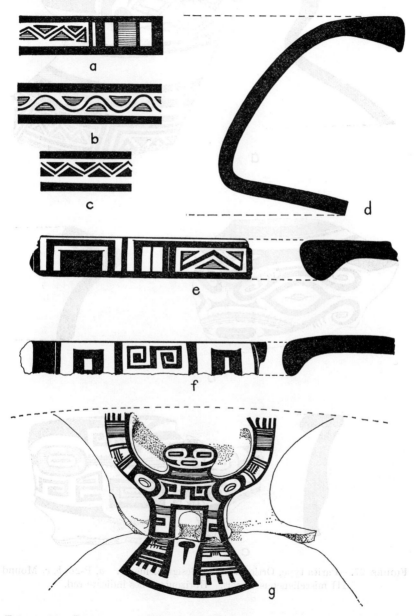

FIGURE 26.—Parita type, Ortiga variety, design elements. *a–f*, Mound III miscellaneous vessels; *g*, P-33. Horizontal lines indicate red.

FIGURE 27.—Parita type, Ortiga variety, design elements.   a, P-26; b, c, Mound
III miscellaneous vessels.   Horizontal lines indicate red.

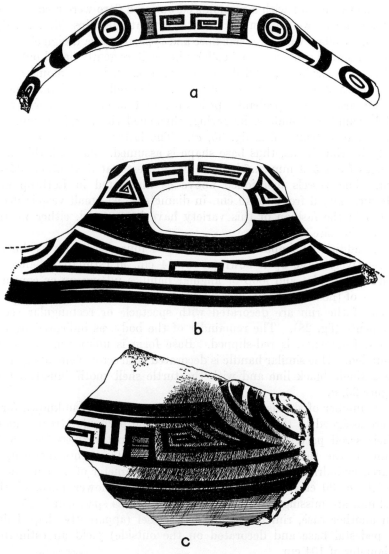

FIGURE 28.—Parita type, Ortiga variety, Mound III sherds.   Horizontal lines
indicate red.

complete vessels were present in the Peabody collection, it is probable
that they were similar to specimens illustrated by Holmes and also by
Lothrop, in which the body is shaped somewhat like a fat pear with
a rounded, unmodified base (Holmes, 1888, figs. 207–8; Lothrop,
1942, figs. 483–4).   Holmes also illustrates a vessel of this variety
with a high, slightly flared collar and a ring base.   High collars

similar to this but with a pronounced outward flare were recovered at El Hatillo as well, often with vertically flattened lips (figs. 26, d-f, 17, e). Collars with a reverse flare and typical Ortiga design elements were found as well as "face" collars; i.e., collars gently flared outward with an incurving lip and decorated with painted eyes, mouths, and painted and modeled noses (fig. 27). The only additional shapes noted are plates (probably pedestal), and deep open bowls with high rounded shoulders, incurving, thickened rims, and presumably pear-shaped bodies (see fig. 35, c). The latter form is represented only by rim sherds, thus base shape is assumed. Jar wall thickness ranges from 5–9 mm., and diameters are estimated at about 35–50 cm. The vessels mentioned above as illustrated in Lothrop and Holmes ranged from 35–40 cm. in diameter. No small vessels decorated in the fashion of this variety have been noted, either at the El Hatillo site or elsewhere.

An additional shape known by three or four sherds only is that of a relatively large open bowl (about 34 cm. in estimated diameter) with steep sides and loop or angular handles jutting up as continuations of the rim (fig. 17, g). The handles and immediately adjacent area of the rim are decorated with spectacle or rectangular scroll elements (fig. 28). The remainder of the body, as indicated by the sherd fragments, is red-slipped. Base form is unknown. Lips are rounded. One similar handle is decorated with scroll elements ending in a single black line and with the turtle shell motif illustrated in figure 23, a.

A number of sherds from extremely large vessels of unknown form were assigned to this variety because of the particular treatment of their scroll patterns. These sherds ranged in thickness from 8–25 mm. at the thickened lip. In one case the fragments make up a flared cylindrical column with a minimum diameter of 19 cm. and a height of 30 cm. although both the upper and lower parts of the column are missing. The wall thickness of this specimen is 15 mm. In another case, rim fragments of a vessel (apparently shaped like a pedestal base and decorated on the outside) yield an estimated diameter of 104 cm.

Appendages and construction.—Though the method of construction was not apparent, two main types of appendages were obvious: (a) a small "atlas" human figure standing on the shoulder of the vessel and supporting the high flared-out collar above him (fig. 17, e) and (b) froglike appendages which suggest handles because of their four-pronged shape (fig. 29, e). These frog handles occur on both collared jar shoulders, and the open pear-shaped bowl rims (fig. 17, d). The presence of the atlas figure can often be inferred, when the effigy is missing, by the rectangular feet painted on the vessel shoulder (fig.

26, g).   The frog handles occur at this site with three main decorative motifs: an elliptical shaped element, generally red filled (fig. 29, d); a cruciform element with a circle (fig. 29, a); and a scroll within either a rectangle or a circle (fig. 29, b, c).

FIGURE 29.—Parita type, Ortiga variety, design elements.   a–d, Mound III miscellaneous vessels.   Horizontal lines indicate red.

These scrolls may have "earlike" projections from the outer edge of the swirl as in the Calabaza variety (fig. 29, *f*) or may be "split-legged," i.e., with a forked extension from the swirl edge, the triangular aperture of which is filled with bar elements and an ellipse (fig. 29, *c*).

As noted earlier, these frog handles reduced to mere lumps with a faint suggestion of legs or none at all appear on the rims of pedestal plates in both the Yampí and Ortiga varieties and occasionally on the collared jar shoulders. The only other instance of modeling noted is the previously discussed face collar.

Surface.—The entire surface is polished. Ground slip in the design area varies from cream to salmon to a reddish brown while delineating colors are primarily black and red, although purple is also used, particularly in the type "a" design noted below. Design area is limited to the shoulders, collar, and rims of the collared jars, and to the shoulder of the open pear-shaped bowls. The remainder of the body is separated from the design area by a black band and is normally covered with a red-brown slip. The only plate examples recovered were decorated on the upper surface only. Tall, flaring pedestals decorated with Ortiga variety elements, especially the triangle in a zigzag or the undulating ribbon, also were recovered (fig. 26, *a–c*).

Lips and collars of the sharply flaring or curved type are decorated with simple concentric bands of black or black and red in a fashion similar to that of the globular jars of the Pica-pica variety, Macaracas type (see fig. 41, *a*). Those of the tall, flared type are generally decorated in the interior of the collar with concentric bands of black or black and red and the triangle in a zigzag or undulating line motif. The flat vertical section of the lips usually is covered with rectangular scroll or spectacle elements similar to those on the tails of the Níspero effigy bird bowls.

Three, possibly five, main design patterns are apparent in the collection for this variety. One, pattern "a," consists of what might be called a "ribbon scroll" in a black banded rectangular panel (fig. 30, *a*). The same motif may occur in a circular panel on plates (Lothrop, 1942, fig. 479; and sherds from Trench 1, He-4). The motif is usually accompanied by a characteristic set of fillers in the shape of distorted rectangles or leaning boxes, triangles, and filled circles (fig. 31). Both red and purple are often used for fill color with these. Pattern "b," which is extremely frequent at the El Hatillo site, especially on collared jars, consists of a series of rectangular and interlocking panels which contain triangular elements (fig. 30, *b*). The third pattern, "c" or "lyre" element (fig. 30, *c*), again framed by a rectangular black panel and probably representing an alligator, combines a large "bull's-eye" element with an element which suggests a lyre or harp. Characteristic filler elements of barred triangles, boxes and "carpet

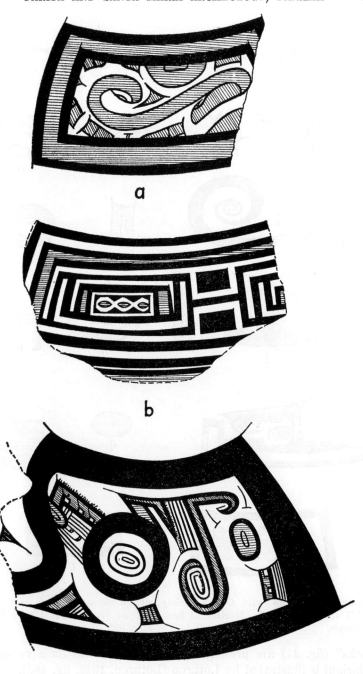

FIGURE 30.—Parita type, Ortiga variety, design elements. a, P-38; b, Mound III sherd; c, P-39. Horizontal lines indicate red; diagonal lines indicate purple.

FIGURE 31.—Parita type, Ortiga variety, design elements. *a–k*, *m–t*, Mound III sherds; *p*, P-37. Horizontal lines indicate red; diagonal lines indicate purple.

tacks" (fig. 31) are present. An example of this on a vessel from Chiriquí is illustrated by Lothrop (Lothrop, 1942, fig. 483).

These bull's-eye and lyre panels may be joined by an elliptical element as on the Chiriquí vessel mentioned above and vessel number 22/9340 in the Museum of the American Indian, thus forming a split-

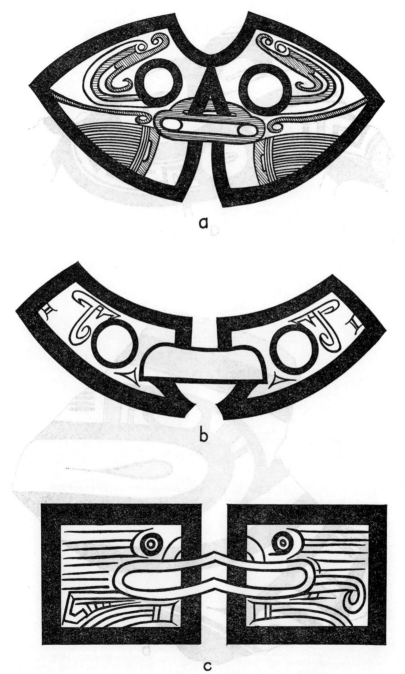

FIGURE 32.—Pica-pica to Ortiga design element development, from c, Pica-pica, through a to the highly conventionalized Ortiga, b. a, Trench 8, level 24–50 cm.; b, P-39; c, Find 372-1. Horizontal lines indicate red; diagonal lines indicate purple.

a

b

FIGURE 33.—Parita type, Ortiga variety, design elements. *a*, P-37; *b*, Mound III sherd. Horizontal lines indicate red.

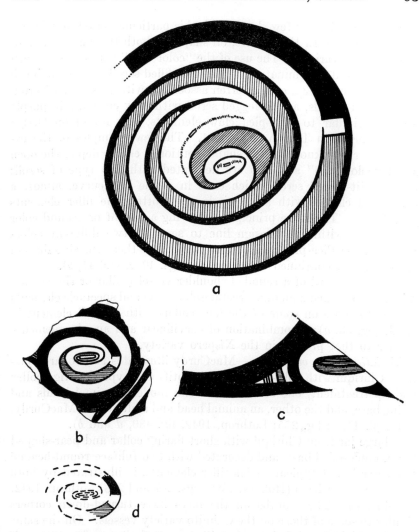

FIGURE 34.—Parita type, Ortiga variety, design elements.   *a*, P-34; *b–d*, Mound III sherds.   Horizontal lines indicate red; diagonal lines indicate purple.

square-face motif similar to that of the Pica-pica variety (see fig. 37, *e*).   A schematic representation of these two patterns is shown in figure 32 along with a crocodile motif like those of the Higo variety. If, as indicated by the stratigraphy at He-4, it is true that the Ortiga variety is a later ceramic development than the Macaracas varieties, then the Ortiga bull's-eye and lyre panels could be interpreted as a highly stylized version of the Macaracas motifs.

An additional possible primary motif is the split-legged scroll, often ladder-filled and combined with a color-filled ellipse as in figures 33, *b*, and 34, *c*. Only a few sherds with this particular scroll motif were recovered at the El Hatillo site, on shapes of both this variety and of the Calabaza variety. The use of the "color stop" with one side open (fig. 34, *d*) and a termination of the color-filled scroll in a single black line or ellipse (fig. 34, *a*, *b*) is often associated with this type of scroll. A variation of this, a split-legged scroll with claw elements in purple and red similar to Pica-pica claw elements, was found on Ortiga shaped sherds in Trench 8, Level 1. The few examples of the extremely large unknown vessel shape mentioned earlier depict the open sided "color stop" and also are decorated with this type of scroll; i.e., a split-legged scroll which ends in a fine line curve, almost a completed ellipse, with small circle and dotted line filler elements (fig. 34, *a*). The same principle of leaving a vacant or ground color filled space within the design line to separate two different colors occurs in the Pica-pica variety claw scroll, but there the side lines of the design are continued unbroken (see figs. 40, *c*, and 41, *b*).

One large sherd of a rounded shoulder vessel (collar or rim section missing) combined a modified rectangular scroll and spectacle elements similar to those on some of the face collars with a scroll element in black (fig. 33, *a*); a combination of curvilinear and angular elements similar to that present in the Níspero variety.

Variations from other sites.—MacCurdy illustrates two collared jars from Chiriquí with split-legged scroll motifs and typical Ortiga collar and lip treatment, one of which has two modeled animal heads and a ring base, and the other, an animal head and a blunt tail (MacCurdy, 1911, pl. 44, *b*; fig. 255; Lothrop, 1942, fig. 480, *d* and *b*).

A large jar from Chiriquí with short flaring collar and pear-shaped body, unmodified base, and decorated with two fullface round-headed "monsters" and typical Ortiga filler elements, is illustrated by both Holmes and Lothrop (Holmes, 1888, figs. 207 and 208; Lothrop, 1942, fig. 482, *a*). The mouths on the faces have turned-down corners similar to some of those on the Caimito variety vessels. On the same vessel, a highly modified "seed pod" element similar to figure 44, *g*, is present, an element characteristic of the Calabaza and Cuipo varieties at the El Hatillo site.

Another vessel with typical Ortiga elements, e.g., frog handles and type "b" designs but with a ring base and high flaring collar, is illustrated by Holmes and by Lothrop (Holmes, 1888, figs. 209 and 210; Lothrop, 1942, fig. 482, *b*). This vessel, also found in Chiriquí, is significant primarily for the high collar and ring base associated with Ortiga decoration.

An additional vessel from Chiriquí characterized primarily by Cuipo variety designs, but with frog handles, is illustrated in MacCurdy and in Lothrop (MacCurdy, 1911, figs. 257 and 258; Lothrop,

1942, fig. 480, *a*) and will be described in greater detail in the section dealing with the Cuipo variety.

A globular jar, listed from Parita, with a short flaring collar, a rounded base which combines design type "c" and typical Ortiga filler elements with the split-square-face design and a characteristic shape of the Pica-pica variety, Macaracas type, is present in the Dade Collection at the Museum of the American Indian (cat. No. 22/9340). Besides constituting a good example of the blending of these two design patterns as discussed earlier, this is the only example I know of which combines an Ortiga design with the globular jar shape. As with the Yampí variety plate with a square-faced, dancing crocodile drawn in Yampí style, this vessel may be a copy of a Pica-pica variety vessel, but created by a potter working in the Ortiga style.

Geographical range.—Vessels either definitely of this variety or with marked similarities to it have been reported from the following areas: Chiriquí (Holmes, 1888, figs. 183, 207, 208, 209, 210; Lothrop, 1942, figs. 480, *a*; 482, *a* and *b*; 483, 484; McCurdy, 1911, fig. 257); from Soná, Veraguas (Lothrop, 1942, fig. 479); from Macaracas (Lothrop, 1942, fig. 473, *e*); and from Parita (Lothrop, 1942, pl. 3, *f*; figs. 446, *a*; 448, *d*; Mus. Amer. Ind. cat. No. 22/9340). A few Ortiga sherds occurred at He-1 and He-8.

Chronological position.—Same as Níspero variety.

Relationships of variety.—Related to other varieties of the type. Also related through the bull's-eye crocodile design to the Pica-pica variety of the Macaracas type. Related through various other elements to the Calabaza variety.

Bibliography.—See above section on geographical range.

MACARACAS POLYCHROME

This type, the second main representative of the curvilinear style at El Hatillo, consists of three varieties: the Pica-pica, the Higo, and the Cuipo, the first two of which are fairly clear-cut groups with numerous associated typical decorative motifs and vessel forms. In each of these the preferred shapes are pedestal plates and globular or subglobular collared jars ranging in size from miniature to large. The favored design motifs are clawed scrolls, closed arcs with claw elements, and various alligator forms. The Cuipo variety shares vessel form with the other two varieties and adds another form, an angled shoulder collared jar, generally with a flattened area at the collar base (fig. 35, *j*). Characteristic design attributes include the rendering of the primary design motif in negative fashion and the frequent use of a "seed pod" or highly conventionalized alligator motif.

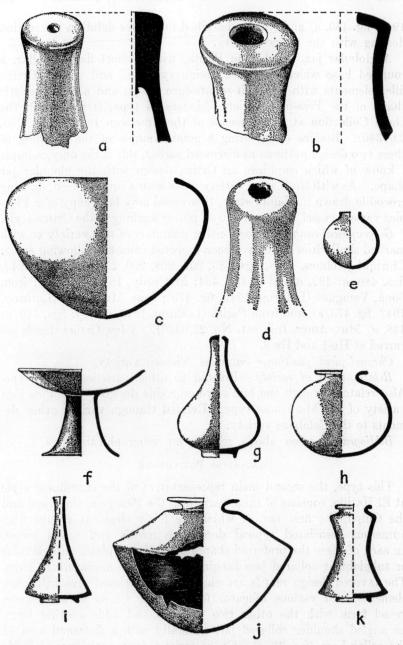

FIGURE 35.—Macaracas and Calabaza types vessel shapes. *a–b, d*, Mound III Calabaza; *c*, Find 346-1, Pica-pica; *e*, Pica-pica and Higo (?) from Mason collection photograph B-11-33; *f*, Find 368-1; *g*, Find 136; *h*, Find 368-4; *i*, Mitchell slide of Zelsman vessel; *j*, Find 373-3 (Cuipo); *k*, carafe bottle with flanged neck, Pica-pica from Rio de Jesus, 12 inches high, 9 inches maximum diameter.

As in the Parita Polychrome, the style of decoration in the Macaracas varieties is predominantly curvilinear. Design layouts are well proportioned and general decorative technique is highly developed. All three colors, black, red, and purple, occur frequently, especially the alternate use of red and purple in repeating elements. Line or corner terminations are delicately graduated lines, often curved in a fashion similar to that of the Parita type.

MACARACAS POLYCHROME; PICA-PICA VARIETY

Sample.—33 vessels or large fragments; 118 sherds (pls. 5, *d*, and 6).

Paste.—The temper is crushed rock with both black and white particles which are easily visible to the naked eye. Paste like that of Níspero variety, Parita Polychrome, is usually fired a brick red (Munsell hue 2.5YR 4/6–8), ranging from reddish orange to a brown red (Munsell hue 2.5YR 6/6–8 to 2.5YR 3/4–6). Thickness ranges from 4–8 mm. and averages around 6 mm. even in the larger vessels. Hardness rates as 3 on Mohs' scale.

Shapes.—The shapes include plates on tall pedestals, collared globular jars, and deep pear-shaped bowls with high shoulders and incurving rims (fig. 35, *f*, *h*, *c*). Of the latter shape, most are assumed on the basis of rim sherd only, thus some of the original vessels may have been shallower than the one illustrated. Both this variety and that which follows are noted for the number of miniatures produced and provide a wide range in size for the type. Miniatures as small as 6 cm. in diameter are fairly common, while the largest complete vessel, a pear-shaped bowl, was 45 cm. in maximum diameter. Between these two extremes are pedestal plates and collared jars ranging from 22–26 cm. in diameter.

Other shapes found at the He-4 site in 1957 by Dr. Russell Mitchell, John W. Acker, and others include straight collared jars with constricted orifices (fig. 35, *e*), which are almost snub-nosed bottles, the same shape with three loop handles appended vertically and equidistantly about the shoulder, and cylinder jars with angled shoulders and bases (fig. 35, *k*) (Russell H. Mitchell, personal communication).

At the El Hatillo site all jar bases are rounded and plate bases are pedestaled. Plate lips and rims are rounded but otherwise unmodified. Jars have short outcurved collars with rounded lips, or lips slightly flattened horizontally. Lips on the pear-shaped bowls are rounded and thickened (fig. 35, *c*).

Appendages and construction.—The method of construction is not apparent. One significant characteristic noted was the occurrence of wedge-shaped or cuneiform slits, usually two or three in number, about two-thirds of the way up on a few of the pedestal bases. This feature is shared by the Higo variety.

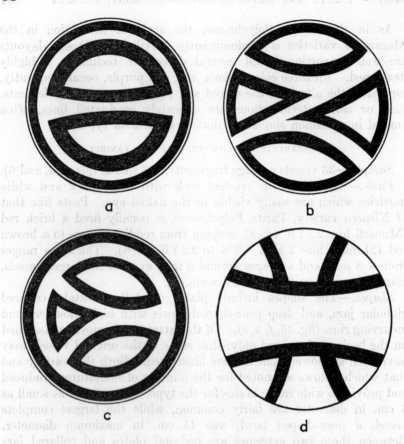

FIGURE 36.—Macaracas type, Pica-pica variety, design elements. *a*, Find 375-3; *b*, 368-4; *c*, 372-9; *d*, 372-10; *e*, 372-2.

Surface.—All exterior surfaces except for the extreme base areas of the collared jars are highly polished. Undecorated areas are covered with a red slip. Decorated sections have a lighter ground slip which may range from an almost white or gray cream to a salmon color. The design is delineated in black; red, black, and purple are used as fill colors. On occasion (Find 374 and sherds from Mound III) black alone is used on a red ground, a decorative mode also character-

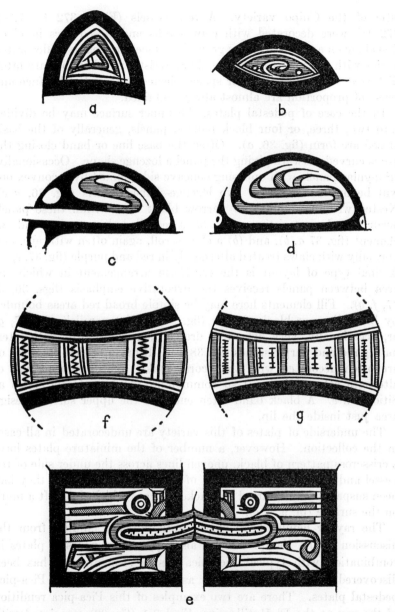

FIGURE 37.—Macaracas type, Pica-pica variety, design elements. *a*, Find 368-10; *b*, 375-3; *c*, 372-6; *d*, 372-8; *e*, 372-1; *f*, 372-10; *g*, 375-2. Horizontal lines indicate red; diagonal lines indicate purple.

istic of the Cuipo variety. A few vessels (Finds 372–4, 372–5, 372–18) were decorated with claw scrolls and closed arcs in black line alone on a white to cream ground. Since the area to be decorated varies with the vessel form, the characteristic panel shapes are often distorted to fit the particular space selected, although a balance and sense of proportion are almost always retained.

In the case of pedestal plates, the upper surface may be divided into two, three, or four black banded panels, generally of the basic closed arc form (fig. 36, a). Often the base line or band closing the arc is curved outward giving the panel a lozenge shape. Occasionally, triangular panels with opposing concave sides joined by a convex one will be opposed between two lozenge-shaped panels (fig. 36, a–c). Nested within a number of narrow black lines within these panels occur two characteristic motifs: (a) a red-filled claw or claw and eye element (fig. 37 a, b), and (b) a claw scroll, again often with eye, and normally with claws treated alternately in red and purple (fig. 37, c, d). A final type of layout is the cruciform arrangement in which the area between panels receives the decorative emphasis (figs. 36, d; 37, f, g). Fill elements here may be simple broad red areas bounded by black lines or black zigzags (fig. 37, f), "monorails" (fig. 37, g) or, occasionally, very delicately drawn "spindle" motifs with alternating red and purple spines (fig. 38, a). Rims are either plain red or are often decorated with the "coral snake" motif (another use of alternate color technique) so common in the Late Coclé styles at Sitio Conte. A black band often encircles the upper surface design area just inside the lip.

The underside of plates of this variety are undecorated in all cases in the collection. However, a number of the miniature plates have a crisscross pattern of black, uneven lines across the under side of the vessel and around the upper part of the pedestal base as if they had been suspended by a tarred or blackened cord which then left a mark on the surface (pl. 9, b, c).

The ray or hammerhead shark motif, already familiar from the discussion of the Yampí variety, also appears on pedestal plates in combination with typical Pica-pica design elements and has been discovered in a Veraguas site in association with typical Pica-pica pedestal plates. There are two examples of this Pica-pica rendition of the ray at the El Hatillo site: Find 8-1 (fig. 39) associated with class "a" red-buff collared jars, and Find 373-1 associated with Pica-pica and Cuipo variety vessels. Characteristic of this style of ray, as represented by these two vessels and three from the V-5 site in Veraguas, is the depiction of the body with a central channel which may be either vacant or filled in with dots and dashes (this channel

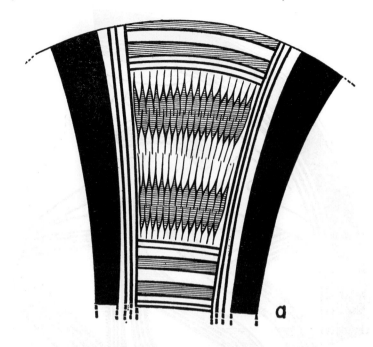

FIGURE 38.—Macaracas type, Pica-pica and Higo design elements. *a*, Find 368-2; *b*, Find 368-1. Horizontal lines indicate red; diagonal lines indicate purple.

FIGURE 39.—Find 8-1; Macaracas type, Pica-pica variety. Horizontal lines indicate red.

is not present in the Yampí variety), the rendition of eyes usually in circular form and separate from any horizontal barring (eyes of the Yampí variety are generally elliptical with a horizontal long axis, the eye resting on a horizontal bar or band across the face, see figure 24, *d*, *h*), and the more frequent appearance of more than one ray in

FIGURE 40.—Macaracas type, Pica-pica and Higo varieties, design elements.
a, Find 372-1; *d–e*, *g–k*, Mound III sherds; *f*, Find 368-2; *l*, Find 368-1;
m, Lothrop, 1942, fig. 149.   Horizontal lines indicate red; diagonal lines indicate
purple.

FIGURE 41.—Macaracas type, Pica-pica variety, design elements. a, Find 368-3;
b, 346-1; c, 368-2.   Horizontal lines indicate red; diagonal lines indicate purple.

the design area. Characteristic Pica-pica elements associated on the same vessels with these are diamond bases, coral snake lips, and claws. Yampí elements normally associated with the ray motif, such as frog adornos on the rim and large rectangular and elliptical elements on the rim (fig. 24, *f*, *i*), are conspicuously absent.

Pedestal bases are generally decorated with the diamond motif on a cream base (fig. 38, *b*), or are treated with a plain red slip. Cross-hatching and the diamond in a ribbon motif (fig. 40, *e*, *g*) also occur on bases.

The design area of the globular jars, with its cream to salmon colored ground slip, usually extends well down over the side of the vessel stopping just short of the base area especially on the miniature and smaller jars where space is limited. On the larger jars, the decorated portions may be limited to the shoulder and upper body. Bases are either red slipped or, more often, unslipped. Designs are generally arranged in three or four panels around the entire vessel, although claw scroll motifs may be laid out either in a continuous interlocking pattern around the shoulder (fig. 41, *b*) or placed in rectangular or closed arc panels. The latter are often arranged in alternating postures so that an undulating band of ground color is achieved between them (fig. 36, *e*). Regardless of interior motif, distortion of the closed arc panels into lozenges, and curved triangular shapes and rectangular panels into trapezoidal forms, occurs. Rectangular panels generally enclose "rectangular claw scrolls" (fig. 41, *c*), usually nested within a series of narrow black lines. Color-filled circles may be interspersed between panels. An interesting motif which occurs fairly frequently is the "split-square-face" (fig. 37, *e*) or two rectangular panels, enclosing black band eyes, joined horizontally by a mouth. Sometimes the eyes will have horizontal lines extending from the lower portion forming an element which might be called the "tearful eye" (fig. 40, *a*) similar to the "weeping eye" motif in the Southeastern United States. Definite face motifs are not common in the Azuero styles at the El Hatillo site, although they do occur sparsely in both the angular and curvilinear styles. The relationship of the "split-square-face" motif and "bull's-eye" and "lyre" motifs of the Ortiga variety has already been discussed.

The collar and rim area are also generally decorated with simple, narrow, black bands or two black bands separated by red fill applied over the cream slip. As shown in figure 41, *a*, a black band generally encircles the outer surface of the lip, the main portion of the rim remains in the cream ground slip, and the inner surface of the rim is again banded. Below this, on the interior of the rim, a red slip is applied for a short distance although the deeper interior portion of the neck is left unslipped with the color of the fired paste evident.

The deep pear-shaped bowl with high shoulder and incurving rim is represented at He-4 by only one whole vessel and a number of sherds. Sherds of this form assigned to the Pica-pica variety (others were assigned to the Ortiga variety on the basis of frog handles and design) were decorated either in continuous claw scrolls with alternating purple and red claws, or with a series of closed arc elements in black on a red ground. In all cases the area of decoration was limited to the upper portion of the vessel between shoulder and lip. The scroll technique often included use, in this case, of the "color stop," i.e., the practice of leaving a portion of the claw blank so that the ground color shows through (fig. 40, c), and the "color shift," i.e., treating one section of the claw first in black and then in red or purple (fig. 40, b).

Other decorative elements occurring in the Pica-pica variety include the diamond in a ribbon motif (fig. 40, e, g), shared by the Higo and Cuipo varieties and very similar to the triangle and zigzag pattern of the Ortiga variety, and the color-filled chevron (fig. 40, d).

Variations from other sites.—A collared jar with a fairly typical Pica-pica variety claw scroll and what is probably a deer's head attached to the shoulder is present in the Museum of the American Indian (cat. No. 22/8378).

Cylinder jars on ring bases and with short outcurved collars have been recovered at the El Hatillo site (Dr. Russell H. Mitchell, personal communication). A Veraguas example of this shape, decorated with spindle motifs in panels, is present in the Dade Collection at the Museum of the American Indian (cat. No. 22/9448).

Lothrop (1942, fig. 188, a–b) illustrates two high flare-collared subglobular jars on ring bases from Cache 5 at Sitio Conte. Both have plain red bodies, but the collar of one is decorated in the typical base diamond motif of the El Hatillo site, and the other in the chevron motif mentioned above. Another similarly shaped vessel with claw scroll was recovered in Grave 26 at Sitio Conte (Lothrop, 1942, pl. 2, f; fig. 192, c).

Various bird designs associated with clawed elements or claw scrolls have also occurred at other sites and could be placed equally well in either this or the Higo variety. The Dade Collection includes two pedestal plates (cat. Nos. 22/8350 and 22/9514), both with coral snake rims and cuneiform slits in the base, which combine typical claw elements with profile bird patterns as the primary design. In both specimens the tails are spread out like a turkey's or peacock's and are depicted checkerboard style in alternate squares of red, ground color, and purple. Both plates exhibit the fine line feet of the Higo variety. Provenience for these vessels is listed as Santiago, Veraguas, and this same checkerboard motif occurred in Mound III at He-4 on the under side of a plate sherd the upper surface of which was decorated with the Higo crocodile motif (fig. 40, *k*).

Lothrop illustrates a Grave 5, Sitio Conte, globular collared jar which bears a profiled bird of a different type; the body cavity encloses a claw scroll utilizing alternate color and color stop (Lothrop, 1942, figs. 194 and 225, *b*). A vessel with this bird motif and barred scroll collar was also found at La Peña (Mahler, 1961, fig. 3, *d*). The Sitio Conte vessel is one of a group of four jars from the same grave which are almost identical in shape, style of decoration, and in collar treatment (with one exception), and which include a number of motifs characteristic of the Pica-pica and Higo varieties at the El Hatillo site. The use of barred scrolls in black line on the collars of three of the vessels, however, is known at He-4 in only one instance (Find 346–5), although black figured designs (in contrast to bands alone) are present on vessels from Macaracas (Lothrop, 1942, fig. 466, *a*) and on a specimen from He-1 at Parita (Find 16–17–*d*).

As mentioned earlier in this section, four pedestal plates with ray motifs were recovered by Dr. Russell Mitchell at the V-5 (Piedra del Sol) site near Santiago, Veraguas (personal communication). Two of these require no comment as they are typical Pica-pica ray pedestal plates. The fourth, done in negative technique, will be discussed under the Cuipo variety. The third is notable primarily for the addition of Cuipo circle and dot fill seed pods on the under surface of the plate to Pica-pica elements such as the closed arc with claw base panels and two Pica-pica style rays on the upper surface.

Jars which, with straight collars and quite constricted orifices, could almost be described as short-spouted bottles (fig. 35, *e*) with both Pica-pica and Higo variety designs were recovered by Dr. J. Alden Mason at Sitio Conte in Coclé (Univ. Pennsylvania Mus. cat. Nos. B-11, B-11-33, and 40-15-470) and at the He-4 site by Dr. Russell H. Mitchell (personal communication).

Geographical range.—Many vessels of this variety and the following Higo variety are illustrated in the literature or are present in museum collections. Some of the vessels listed below have been treated in greater detail in the section dealing with variations at other sites.

Chiriquí: MacCurdy, 1911, pl. XLIV, fig. 255; Lothrop, 1942, figs. 480, *b* and *d*.

Veraguas: La Peña, near Santiago (Wassén, 1960, figs. 12, 13, and 14) (Mahler, 1961, fig. 2, *c*).

Cerro la Vigia, Caseria Culantro, Soná, Veraguas: Lothrop, 1942, fig. 477, *b* and *b'*; 1950, fig. 132; another vessel, Lothrop, 1942, fig. 477, *a'*).

Santiago, Veraguas (Mus. Amer. Ind. cat. Nos. 22/8348 and 22/8350).

Catine, Las Palmas, Museo Nacional de Panamá, G. R. Willey photograph.

"Cocuyal," Las Palmas, Museo Nacional de Panamá, G. R. Willey photograph.

Piedra del Sol (Finca Gonzales) near Montijo, Veraguas (vessels Nos. 9, 11, 14, 17, 18, 20, 21, 24, Dr. Russell H. Mitchell, personal communication).

Veraguas: Veraguas in general (Mus. Amer. Ind. cat. Nos. 22/8390, 23/200, 23/202, 22/9448).

Herrera: Parita: Lothrop, 1942, figs. 444, e, and 446, i (Mus. Amer. Ind. cat. Nos. 22/9340 and 22/8382); Stirling, 1950, p. 239, upper row left and center right vessels, second row from top, right, Find 346–5, and sherds at He-1.

Los Santos: Los Santos: a typical vessel shape with possible Pica-Pica design elements (Lothrop, 1942, fig. 455, a).

Macaracas: Lothrop, 1942, figs. 461, a, 462, e, 464, c.

Coclé: Potrero Requelme, Rio Coclé (Lothrop, 1942, fig. 418, a), Sitio Conte, Rio Grande de Coclé, a number of vessels from Late Period graves and caches, and sherds from the trenches:

> Grave 5 vessels (Lothrop, 1942, figs. 152, a, b, and 172; these appear as atypical variants) (fig. 193, a, also figs. 224 and 225, c); variant bird motif with Pica-pica elements (Lothrop, 1942, figs. 194 and 225, b, and fig. 178, b).

> Grave 24 (Lothrop, 1942, fig. 179, a, b) Coclé variants of rectangular claw scroll, diamond in a ribbon, and split closed arc.

> Grave 26 (Lothrop, 1942, pl. II, f; fig. 192, c).

> Cache 5 (Lothrop, 1942, fig. 188, a, b).

> Sherds, Trenches 5 and 11 (Lothrop, 1942, fig. 228, b).

Mason excavations: Excavations of J. Alden Mason at Sitio Conte, material now at the University Museum, University of Pennsylvania; from photographs and notes of G. R. Willey.

Burial 10–b: one collared jar.

Burial 11: at least three small flare-collared jars and two small straight-collared jars including cat. No. B-11-33.

Burial 14: at least three vessels, two small flare-collared jars and one pedestal plate including cat. Nos. 40-15-71 and 40-15-87.

Burial 16: at least three small pedestal plates including cat. Nos. 40-15-339, 40-15-341, and, probably, 40-15-354.

Burial 18: at least two small pedestal plates, cat. Nos. 40-15-498 and 40-15-496.

Burial 23: at least one small flare-collared jar, cat. No. B-23-21.

Co–2: Sherds.

Chronological position.—Both Pica-pica and Higo varieties of the Macaracas type are probably coeval with Late Coclé, and earlier than either the El Hatillo or Parita types.

Relationships of variety.—The close relationship to the Higo variety is demonstrated repeatedly by the appearance of Pica-pica and Higo elements on the same sherd or vessel. Closely related also to the Cuipo variety, again through shared elements on the same vessel. Related also to the Calabaza variety.

Bibliography.—See geographical range above.

MACARACAS POLYCHROME; HIGO VARIETY

Sample.—2 whole vessels; 232 sherds (pl. 7, *a*, *b*).

Paste.—Same as Pica-pica variety.

Shape.—Same as the Pica-pica variety with the exception of the pear-shaped high-shouldered bowl. The crocodile motif has been noted at El Hatillo on pedestal plates (both miniature and large) and on collared jars. Plate lips are rounded, pedestals are generally tall with the cuneiform slit present. Jar bases are rounded and unmodified.

Surface.—The surface is smoothed and polished over the entire exterior. In this variety, designs appear on both the upper and lower surfaces of the plates as well as on the pedestals. As in the Pica-pica variety, the major portion of the jar body is decorated, collars and lips are banded, but no instances of black line figured collars were noted.

The crocodile motif, as it appears in this variety, generally occurs in one of three characteristic poses, apparently depending on the space to be filled. Thus the "crouching crocodile" appears in triangular panels (fig. 42, *b*), the "galloping crocodile" in rectangular panels (fig. 42, *a*), and the "dancing crocodile" (fig. 42, *c*) when the design area is large and circular, e.g., on the upper surfaces of plates.[10] An example of an apparently rare variation on the crouching crocodile theme, in which two irregularly shaped panels are joined by a "mouth" element and heavy black bull's-eyes are added to the crocodile motif within each panel, is schematically presented in figure 32, *a*. This combination of an Higo style crocodile with the split-square-face layout was found on shoulder sherds of a large closed vessel (top and base missing) from Trench 8, the only instance of this particular combination of which I know.

Various crocodile or alligator motifs are widespread throughout the Panama area, from the alligator motifs of Chiriquí to the crocodile motifs of the Coclé styles at Sitio Conte. As mentioned earlier, they occur in highly stylized form in the El Hatillo Polychrome type.

---

[10] The terms "galloping crocodile" and "dancing crocodile" are from Lothrop's discussion of the motif at Sitio Conte and elsewhere (Lothrop, 1942, pp. 81–83, 103–105, 118–123).

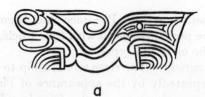

FIGURE 42.—Macaracas type, Higo variety, crocodile poses. *a*, Lothrop, 1942, fig. 193, b; *b*, He-4, Find 368-2; *c*, Lothrop, 1942, pl. 2, b.

They also occur on gold work and on the unpainted pottery of Veraguas. Very often the style of representation is clear cut as in the El Hatillo type. At other times the styles appear to blend as is the case between the Coclé and Azuero styles, where poses, general layout and, sometimes, smaller design elements are often shared. At the El Hatillo site as represented by the material at the Peabody Museum, one particular style showed considerable consistency, especially in its smaller elements. For example, crocodile heads in the Higo variety are shown in profile with a barbed nose which is curled upward (fig. 40, *f*). Feet (hind legs) and, generally, "hands" (forelegs) are represented by many narrow, parallel black lines (fig. 40, *h*, *i*) in contrast to the treatment frequently found in the Coclé style in which the feet are given color-filled claws (fig. 40, *m*). In the "dancing crocodile" pose hands may be treated as bird claws (fig. 40, *j*), that is, depicted with an opposed talon. The plumes or feathers streaming from the head and back of the figure are barbed in the Higo variety (fig. 40, *l*); in the Coclé style this barbed effect is achieved by color-filled claws. In the Higo variety representations at the El Hatillo site, the body of the figure is treated with solid red fill as against the tendency at other sites to elaborate the body cavity with clawed scrolls. Finally, the Coclé-style "dragon belt" motif, a secondary, smaller crocodile motif occurring alongside the larger figure, appears to be lacking in this variety.

Other elements characteristic of the Higo variety, and in most cases shared with the previous variety, include the color-filled spindle (fig. 38, *a*), the diamond-in-a-ribbon (fig. 40, *e*, *g*), rectangular claw scroll motifs in panels (fig. 41, *c*), and the checkerboard motif (fig. 40, *k*). Plate rims or lips are either treated with a plain red slip or are decorated with the coral snake motif. Of the two attached bases in the Peabody material, one was decorated in a modified rectangular panel pattern enclosing rectangular claw scrolls and spindle patterns, and the other was decorated with the diamond base pattern. One of these vessels is apparently exactly duplicated by a second vessel, from the same grave lot, which remained at the Museo Nacional de Panamá.

Variations from other sites.—Occasionally, a crocodile motif executed in the style of this variety is represented in full face view rather than profile. An example of this representation, with solid red body and barbed feathers but color-filled feet, is present in the Dade Collection (cat. No. 22/8347) and is listed as from La Peña, Veraguas. As noted earlier, the Dade Collection also contains a plate from Santiago, Veraguas, depicting a full face square-headed "crocodils" monster represented in the Yampí style.

Many variations of the basic crocodile motif, Higo motif with others, especially the "dancing crocodile," are illustrated in the literature. These appear to center around the treatment of the plumes or feathers, the feet, the body cavity, and the presence or absence of the secondary crocodile motif or "dragon belt." Examination of 19 examples of the crocodile motif in either Azuero or Coclé styles represented in the literature and the collection at the Museum of the American Indian revealed little in the way of a consistent pattern of relationships between these various elements. For instance, barbed plumes, claw plumes, claw feet, and claw fillers occurred about evenly with both solid body and claw-filled body. On the other hand, fine line feet, in all instances except one, correlated with the solid red body, while only one instance of a dragon belt was noted in conjunction with the solid red body. Of the 10 examples of solid body, 5 were from east Veraguas, 1 from Parita, 2 from Coclé, 1 from Los Santos, and 1 from Chiriquí. Only four examples of the claw-filled body were noted; one from Los Santos, two from Coclé, and one from Macaracas. Unfortunately the sample is so small that the few indications listed above can hardly be treated as conclusive.

The straight-collared jar or bottle, examples of which were found at Sitio Conte, Coclé, by Dr. J. Alden Mason, has already been noted in the section dealing with the Pica-pica variety.

Geographical range.—As with the preceding variety, there is a

plethora of museum specimens and illustrated examples of this variety
in the literature; every Province in Panama is represented:

Chiriquí: Holmes, 1888, figs. 214 and 215 (also in MacCurdy,
1911, frontispiece and pl. XLV; Lothrop, 1942, fig. 223).

Veraguas: Cerro la Vigia, Caseria Culantro, Soná, Veraguas
(Lothrop, 1942, fig. 477 c, c'; also Lothrop, 1950, fig. 132 c, c').

La Peña, Santiago, Veraguas (Wassén, 1960, fig. 8, a, a',
9, a, a'; another vessel fig. 11, a, a'; another vessel Mus.
Amer. Ind. cat. No. 22/8347).

Soná, Veraguas (Mus. Amer. Ind. cat. No. 22/9513).

Santiago, Veraguas (Mus. Amer. Ind. cat. No. 22/8348).

Rio de Jesus, Veraguas (Mus. Amer. Ind. cat. No. 22/9302).

Piedra del Sol, Montijo, Veraguas (vessels Nos. 5, 6, 10, 12,
15, 19, 23; Russell H. Mitchell, personal communication).

La Peña (Mahler, 1961, fig. 2, b).

Veraguas in general (Wassén, 1960, fig. 10; another vessel
Mus. Amer. Ind. cat. No. 22/8390).

Herrera: Parita, Herrera (sherds illustrated in Lothrop, 1942,
fig. 444, a, a', b; two vessels Mus. Amer. Ind. cat. Nos.
22/8379 and 22/8383); Stirling, 1950, p. 239, second row from
bottom, right, Find 368-17.

Los Santos: Los Santos, Los Santos (Lothrop, 1942, fig. 454, a, b)
variant.

Macaracas, Los Santos (Lothrop, 1942, fig. 463, sherd fig.
462, b).

Coclé: Sitio Conte, Coclé (Lothrop 1942, Grave 5 one vessel,
figs. 193, b, and 225, d; another vessel figs. 225, c, 224, 193, a;
another vessel fig. 225, a; another vessel fig. 149; Cache 5,
pl. II, a). All done in Coclé style.

Mason excavations: Excavations of J. Alden Mason at Sitio Conte,
material now at the University Museum, University of Pennsylvania;
information recorded here is based on photographs and notes of
G. R. Willey.

Burial 11: at least one small straight-collared jar (or short spouted
bottle) cat. No. B-11.

Burial 14: at least four vessels; one small flare-collared jar, one
large flare-collared jar, and two small pedestal plates.

Burial 16: at least one small flare-collared jar cat. No. B-16-12.

Burial 17-a: probably one medium sized straight-collared jar.

Burial 18: at least two vessels; one pedestal plate and one straight-
collared jar, cat. Nos. 40-15-483 and 40-15-470.

Co-2: Sherds

Chronological position.—Same as the Pica-pica variety.

Relationships of type.—Same as the Pica-pica variety.

Bibliography.—See geographical range above.

MACARACAS TYPE; CUIPO VARIETY

Sample.—13 vessels or large fragments, 11 sherds (pls. 7, *c*, *d*; 8, *a*).

Paste.—Temper is crushed white and black rock easily visible to the naked eye against the brick-red paste color. The color is the same as that for the Pica-pica variety. Hardness is 2.5 on Mohs' scale.

Shapes.—Vessel forms represented at He-4 include round based collared jars with angled shoulders (fig. 35, *j*) and pedestal plates. Size on both shapes ranges from miniature (plates 8 cm. tall, 8–9 cm. in diameter; jars 6–7 cm. in diameter) through small to medium (plates 19 cm. in diameter; jars 11–13 cm. in diameter) to one large example, Find 373-3, with a diameter of 38 cm. Wall thicknesses vary somewhat with overall size, ranging from 6–8 mm., but on the large vessel mentioned above were surprisingly thin, averaging about 5 mm. Plate lips are rounded and otherwise unmodified. Pedestals, like those of the Pica-pica and Higo varieties are generally relatively tall and slim. Jar collars are short with a tendency toward horizontal flattening of the lip. Adjacent to the collar base there is often a flattened area of shoulder, which may be horizontal or slant slightly down toward the shoulder angle. In some cases the shoulder angle is high on the body, giving a pear-shaped appearance to the total. In others, the angle is located about the midpoint of body height.

Appendages and construction.—Although the method of construction is not apparent and no appendages are known for this variety at the El Hatillo site, a short description of the rattle base mentioned above is in order. The pedestal interior is closed over near the foot, about one-fifth of the way up the pedestal, by a layer of paste. This layer is perforated by small holes and by two intersecting center cuts similar in appearance to a pie crust cut into quarters (see fig. 53, *k*, for a comparable Red-buff base). Forty-five small fired clay pellets were placed in the hollow area of the base between the paste layer and the point of juncture with the plate. Two narrow, opposed slits perforate the pedestal wall midway between the base rim and the point of juncture with the plate.

Surface.—Of the 13 whole vessels in the collection assigned to this variety, 10 came from one grave, Find 374, and it is this lot with a uniform surface appearance which will be described first. The surface is smoothed and polished, but the colors remain dull. Ground color in most of the specimens is a dark red similar to the paste color; only a few of the plates exhibited a dull cream or almost buff shade. Decorative zones vary with the vessel form. On pedestal plates both upper and lower surfaces of the plate and the exterior of the pedestal base are decorated. On the high-angled shoulder jar form the zone of decoration is limited to the upper two-thirds of the body and thus extends somewhat below the shoulder on both miniature and larger examples of the shape.

The three other whole vessels of this variety but not from the same Find Unit do not share the subdued coloring described above but make extensive use of a light cream ground color, thus providing a contrasting background to the design colors and a brighter appearance. That the subdued coloring of the Find 374 vessels is not due to the earth of that particular grave is suggested by the occurrence of similar sherds in three different trenches. Colors in both groups of vessels are black, red, and purple, the latter two used only as fill.

One of the striking characteristics of the Find 374 Unit is the use of negative design presentation in which the design is carried by the ground color. In the He-4 collection, the only motif executed in this negative technique is a dragon or crocodile element (fig. 43, *j*). Other elements occurring on the vessels with the negative dragon are the diamond-in-a-ribbon motif (fig. 40, *e*, *g*) shared by the Higo variety, and "seed pod" elements, usually enclosing circle and dash filler or other fine line designs (fig. 44, *a*, *b*, *g*).

In the case of the lighter-hued jars of other Find Units, all three examples combine various design elements (described below) on the shoulder with representations of turtle heads, tails, and feet on the body just below the shoulder (fig. 44, *d*, *f*). On two of the vessels (Finds 373-3 and 369-1) the area between these head and tail motifs on opposite sides of the vessel is decorated by a band of what may be turtle plastron motifs (fig. 43, *c*). Shoulder elements vary. One vessel (Find 373-3) combines circle and dot seed pods (fig. 44, *g*) with the color-filled spindle of the Higo variety. Another (Find 351-1) combines dot-filled seed pods with crosshatched square panels (fig. 44, *c*). The third (Find 369-1) is decorated in a series of color-filled triangles and ellipses each enclosing a circle or a series of concentric circles (fig. 43, *h*) and the turtle head is embellished with a crosshatch element. These concentric circle elements are somewhat similar to a "pointed eye" motif (fig. 43, *d–g*) which appeared on sherds in combination with the plastron element described above. On all three of the vessels, the lips and collars are banded in the fashion described for the Pica-pica variety.

Pedestal bases of this variety (represented at the El Hatillo site by the Find 374 vessels only) were decorated with the pointer motif or with two horizontal bands separated by crosshatching (fig. 43, *b*). Jar bases were either unslipped or red-slipped.

Variations from other sites.—Examples from other sites include at least two additional shapes, a shallow open bowl and a flat plate, and a number of instances in which typical Higo or Pica-pica elements are

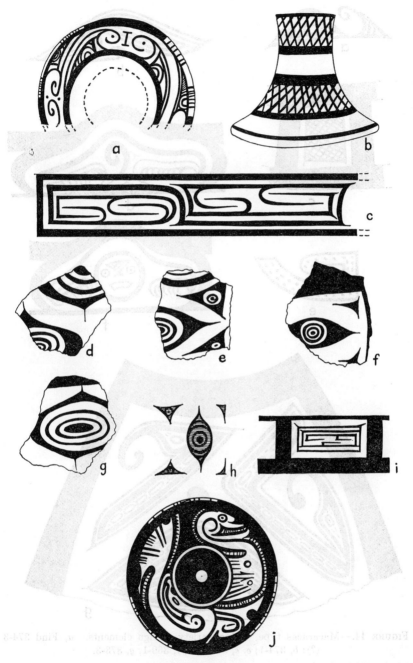

FIGURE 43.—Macaracas type, Cuipo variety, design elements. *a–b,* Find 374-6; *c,* 373-1; *d–g,* Mound II and trench 9, level 59–75 cm. sherds; *h–i,* 369-1; *j,* 374-4. Horizontal lines indicate red.

FIGURE 44.—Macaracas type, Cuipo variety, design elements. *a*, Find 374-3 (?); *b*, 374-1; *c, e*, 351-1; *d, f*, 369-1; *g*, 373-3.

combined with either the circle and dot seed pod or the negative technique motifs of the Cuipo variety. Lothrop illustrates both additional shapes: the open bowl with seed pod elements arranged about the upper exterior of the vessel (Lothrop, 1942, fig. 418, *b*) from the Potrero Riquelme site on the Rio Coclé, and a plate with flat base, slightly convex upper surface, and a flat rim decorated with the negative dragon motif, from Macaracas (Lothrop, 1942, fig. 461, *b*).

A negative style design not found in the He-4 collection, in this case a profile bird, is present along with the diamond-in-a-ribbon motif of the Higo variety on a pedestal plate listed from Veraguas in the Dade Collection (cat. No. 22/9303). In this case the ground slip is a light cream, and cuneiform slits are present in the pedestal base. Other instances of Higo or Pica-pica variety elements in combination with those of the Cuipo variety include a plate sherd from Parita with the seed pod motif on one side and a color-filled crocodile claw on the other (Lothrop, 1942, fig. 444, *a*, *a'*) and a pedestal plate in the Dade Collection listed from Veraguas combining the negative dragon with circle and dot seed pods, and a diamond motif base (Mus. Amer. Ind. cat. No. 22/9512). A simple form of the split arc is also present on this plate (fig. 45, *c*) and is reminiscent of the Yampí variety (fig. 24, *i*; also Lothrop 1942, fig. 485).

A more specific tie with the Ortiga variety is illustrated by both MacCurdy and Lothrop from the De Zeltner Collection of Chiriquí vessels (MacCurdy, 1911, figs. 257 and 258 and Lothrop, 1942, fig. 480, *a*). In this case, a vessel of typical Cuipo turtle jar shape, except for its short straight collar, combines seed pod and negative dragon elements with frog handles on the shoulder. These frog appendages are closely associated with Ortiga variety of the Parita type. To further complicate matters, the seed pods are not the typical circle and dot type, but apparently correspond more closely to the solid black or solid black with ladder element types of the Calabaza variety. In addition, Lothrop (1942, fig. 462, *a*, *a'*) illustrates a sherd from Macaracas with a possible Ortiga lyre element on one side and a fine-lined seed pod on the other.

Two examples of the Cuipo turtle jar, but with variant seed pod elements, are present in the Dade Collection. One (Mus. Amer. Ind. cat. No. 22/8391) listed from Veraguas is almost a duplicate of an He-4 specimen in shape, size, use of turtle elements along the vessel side including head, tail, and plastron motifs, and use of the color-filled spindle element. It differs by adding the diamond-in-a-ribbon motif and by arranging the circle and dot seed pod elements into Z patterns and split arc patterns (fig. 45, *a*). The color-filled circle is also present. The other vessel (Mus. Amer. Ind. cat. No. 22/9501),

FIGURE 45.—Macaracas type, Cuipo variety, design elements. *a*, Museum American Indian cat. No. 22/8391, Veraguas vessel, height 11 inches; *b*, Museum American Indian cat. No. 22/9501, Veraguas vessel, height 6 inches; *c*, Museum American Indian cat. No. 22/9512, Veraguas vessel, diameter 10 inches.

also listed from Veraguas, is similar in shape but somewhat smaller and combines the "monorail" element (fig. 37, *g*) of the Pica-pica variety with a slightly different Z-shaped circle and dot seed pod (fig. 45, *b*). Both of these vessels have cream to buff-cream ground coloring and the colors are bright.

Crosshatching similar to that occurring on the two turtle effigy jars mentioned earlier (Finds 351-1 and 369-1) also occurs on the large effigy jars at the Venado Beach site (Peabody Mus. cat. No. 51-25-20-20418) but without other specific similarities in design elements.

An example of the black on red technique, in this case black fine-line seed pods arranged around the orange slipped shoulder of a medium sized (14.4 cm. diameter) collared jar, was recovered by Dr. Mitchell at the V-5 or Piedra del Sol site between Montijo and Santiago in Veraguas (Vessel No. 7, Grave No. 1, personal communication from Dr. Mitchell) in association with Pica-pica and Higo variety vessels.

The ray or hammerhead shark motif also appears in negative technique; e.g., a pedestal plate recovered by Dr. Mitchell at the Piedra del Sol site near Santiago, Veraguas (Vessel No. 8, Grave No. 1, personal communication from Dr. Mitchell). In this example, two rays are represented on the upper surface of a pedestal plate; both are executed in the fashion typical of the Pica-pica variety, i.e., with circular, unattached eyes and channeled bodies. Colors are bright and sharp, the vessel has a coral snake lip, and the base is finished with a typical Pica-pica diamond pattern.

Still a further motif occurring in negative style is the bat, represented by a bowl found in a La Peña grave along with other Macaracas type vessels (Mahler, 1961, fig. 2, *d*). The same motif also was on a small straight-collared or "bottle jar" from He–4 found by Dr. Russell H. Mitchell (personal communication).

Geographical range:

Chiriquí: MacCurdy, 1911, figures 257 and 258.

Veraguas: La Peña, near Santiago, Veraguas (hearsay) (Wassén, 1960, fig. 2) (Mahler, 1961, fig. 2, *d*).

Piedra del Sol, Montijo, Santiago, Veraguas (Grave 1, vessels 2, 7, 8, 13, 22) (Russell H. Mitchell, personal communication).

Rio de Jesus, Museo Nacional de Panamá, G. R. Willey photograph.

Veraguas in general (Mus. Amer. Ind. cat. Nos. 22/9303, 22/8391, 22/9512, 22/9501).

Herrera: Parita, Herrera (sherd, Lothrop, 1942, fig. 444, *a*).

Los Santos: Macaracas, Los Santos (Lothrop, 1942, fig. 462, *a*, and pl. III, *d*, fig. 461, *b*; Stirling, 1950, p. 239, bottom row, left, Find 369–1).

Coclé: Potrero Riquelme, Rio Coclé, Coclé (Lothrop, 1942, fig. 418, *b*).

Co-2: sherds.

Chronological position.—The Cuipo variety, on the basis of grave association (Piedra del Sol, Grave No. 1, El Hatillo, Find 374 and others) and shared elements, is contemporary with the other varieties of the Macaracas type, and thus presumably earlier than either the Parita or El Hatillo types.

Relationships of variety.—Related closely to other varieties of the Macaracas type; also related in some elements to the Calabaza variety.

Bibliography.—See section above on geographical range.

CALABAZA POLYCHROME

CALABAZA TYPE; CALABAZA VARIETY

Sample.—18 vessels or large fragments, 516 sherds (pl. 8, *b–d*).

Paste.—The paste is fired an orange to brick-red color (see Parita Polychrome for Munsell rating) and is tempered with crushed white and black rock, the particles of which are easily visible without magnification. Occasional pebbles of hematite occur. Hardness rates at 3 on Mohs' scale.

Shapes.—This variety includes one basic shape, that of a squat, gourdlike bottle with a ring base (fig. 35, *g*). Diameters of these vessels vary from 12–20 cm. (of the 18 vessels measured, 16 fell within the range of 14–19 cm.), and heights (minus the spouts) range from 10–15 cm. Thus, gross size is relatively constant. In general the shape is quite uniform, although variations occur in the degree of globularity or squatness of the vessel body.

Very few spouts were found attached to bodies, but an examination of detached spouts with surface treatment similar to the main portions of the vessels indicates a considerable variation in the shape of the mouth. Some appear as though the aperture in the top of the spout was made by knocking a hole in the sealed spout after the vessel was fired (fig. 35, *d*). In others, the mouth was clearly made before firing but still is extremely small as though punched through with a stick or reed (fig. 35, *a*). Still others flare outward just below the lip, which then turns inward to form a small aperture (fig. 35, *b*). In all cases the spouts do not appear to have been designed for pouring liquids, either because the spout hole is too small, or the lip is turned in such a way that some liquid would remain in the vessel.

Appendages and construction.—The presence of nonfunctional spouts coupled with the extensive scratching along the shoulders and sides of many of the examples suggest that they may have been used as rattles rather than as bottles. Holmes and MacCurdy (Holmes,

1888, pp. 156–157; MacCurdy, 1911, p. 169) both illustrate and describe Lost Color ware rattles from Chiriquí which are very similar in shape to the present variety. They differ in construction in that the Lost Color specimens as described by Holmes normally had spouts which were closed off at their bases allowing them to be used as whistles, and vessel bodies were perforated with slits around the shoulder. Both the Lost Color rattles and the Calabaza variety share the presence of two opposing perforations in the base of the spout wall, which may have been used for suspension. No appendages are known to be associated with this variety.

Surface.—The surface is smoothed and highly polished in the design area; i.e., the upper part of the body and the spout. Below the point of greatest diameter the body wall is seldom, if ever, polished although it carries the same slip as that of the decorated portion, a treatment similar to the Níspero and Anón varieties. Color of this ground slip varies from cream through orange or salmon to a brown, the latter occurring especially in those areas where polishing has given a darker hue to the slip. Design colors are in almost all cases limited to black or black and red. On the basis of inspection, the most frequent designs include the seed pod element (fig. 46, *a*) and the closed and split arcs (figs. 47 and 48). Both of these patterns show considerable variation in expression and both may occur on the same vessel. As is usual within the Azuero style, the major patterns or elements are arranged around the vessel so as to achieve an overall balanced effect.

The simple closed arc is characteristic of the Pica-pica variety (fig. 36, *a*) but seldom occurs with claws in the present variety. Simple split arcs with red fill are also found (fig. 47, *a*, *b*). This basic split arc pattern also occurs in scroll forms and with additional various appendages (fig. 47, *c*, *d*). Scrolls of either red or black fill are often terminated in a single line and may occur with a particular type of color stop, both characteristic of the Ortiga variety (figs. 46, *b*, and 48, *a*, *b*). Various embellishments within the arc include "ears" (fig. 46, *c*, *d*), "tongues" (fig. 46, *e*) and "closed tongues" (fig. 46, *f*), "ladder" fill (fig. 46, *g*) and circle and dot fillers (fig. 46, *h*), the latter also found in the Ortiga variety. If the split arc with scroll is turned upside down and viewed so that the arc becomes a chin, the entire pattern takes on a facial aspect (fig. 48, *c–e*), a treatment which was present in some of the Early Period Coclé-style scrolls at Sitio Conte (Lothrop, 1942, pp. 25–28).

The seed pods also are embellished with ears, make use of the scroll ending in a single line and, in addition, are often associated with "carpet tack" fillers (figs. 31, *f*, and 47, *d*) of the Ortiga variety. Generally, the seed pods are predominantly solid black, and no

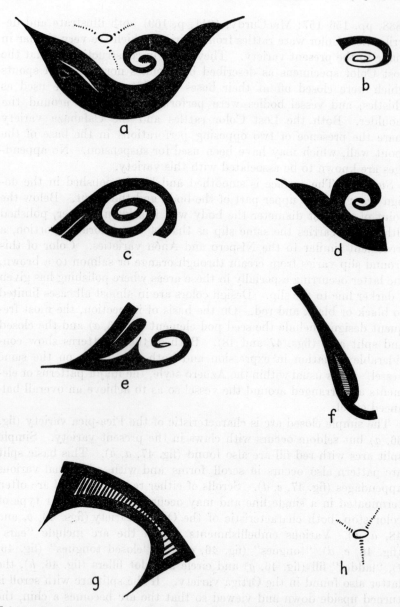

FIGURE 46.—Calabaza type, Calabaza variety, design elements. *a, d, h,* P-16; *b, g,* Find 136; *c,* P-21; *e,* Find 218; *f,* P-7 (?). Horizontal lines indicate red.

examples of the circle and dot filled seed pods associated with the Cuipo variety were found on the gourd bottle form.

Besides the seed pod and closed arc patterns, eared scrolls with color shift, ladder fill, and single line termination were also found on one specimen in the collection (Find 210). One example of the ribbon

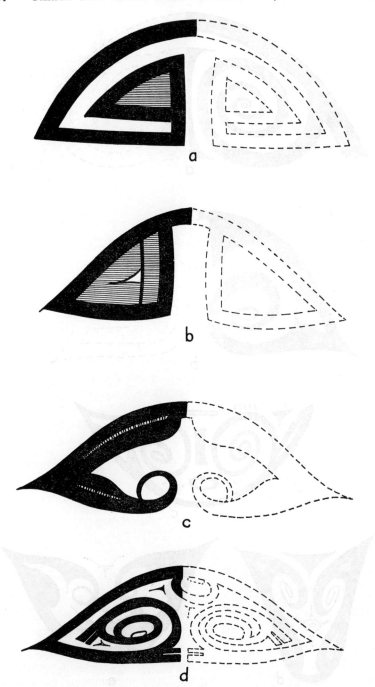

FIGURE 47.—Calabaza type, Calabaza variety, design elements. *a*, Find 59; *b*, 172; *c*, P-7; *d*, P-21. Horizontal lines indicate red.

FIGURE 48.—Calabaza type, Calabaza variety, design elements. a, Find 45; b, 136; c, 144; d, 59; e, 218. Horizontal lines indicate red.

scroll (a characteristic of Ortiga sherds), this time in a split arc panel, was noted on the gourd bottle shape (Vessel P-40).

One vessel (Find 45) (pl. 8, c, d) combined a single square face element with a split arc with scroll pattern. The face closely resembles a design on a gold plaque found in Grave No. 26, a Late Period grave, at Sitio Conte (Lothrop, 1937, fig. 92).

As mentioned earlier, very few spouts were found attached to the bottles, so that much of what follows is based on the assumption that the patterns described belong with this particular bottle form. The few spouts found intact were decorated with simple banding, and complete vessels with chevron design spouts have also been found (by Dr. Russell Mitchell, personal communication) (fig. 49, f). Other patterns found on spouts which clearly do not belong to the El Hatillo type bottles and bird bottles and, therefore, probably are valid here, include the following: triangle in zigzag elements (fig. 49, g), barred rectangles (fig. 49, h), both of which occur in the Ortiga variety, crosshatching, pointer elements (fig. 49, d), spectacle or paneled elements similar to the tail patterns of the Nispero and Ortiga varieties (fig. 49, c), a toothed element alternating red and purple (fig. 49, b), and various blob or dot on line elements (fig. 49, e) again similar to the Parita type, Anón variety.

General comment.—It is evident from the above that this vessel form with its characteristic decoration straddles two types and, in this sense, is a perfect example of one of the primary difficulties encountered in establishing a typology. In any case, the Calabaza variety shares paste, filler, and scroll elements, as well as the distinctive division of polished design area ground slip and lower body unpolished ground slip with the Parita type; while simultaneously sharing major elements or patterns such as the closed arc, split arc, and seed pod (with different fill) with the Macaracas type. Since almost no Calabaza variety sherds were found outside of Mound III, and none were found in grave associations, there is no information available at present on the temporal affinities of the variety.

Geographical range.—I know of only one other example of this variety (Mus. Amer. Ind. cat. No. 22/4823), but its provenience is unknown.

Chronological position.—No grave associations are known for this variety and its stratigraphic occurrence is too meager to be helpful. On the basis of surface treatment, including design elements, it is probably closer in time to the Parita type than to the Macaracas.

Relationships of variety.—Related to both Macaracas and Parita types, but more closely to the latter. Also related by form to the El Hatillo type, El Hatillo variety.

Bibliography.—None.

FIGURE 49.—Calabaza type, Calabaza variety, design elements. *a, c–g*, Mound III sherds; *b*, Trench 8, Level 2. Horizontal lines indicate red; diagonal lines indicate purple.

CALABAZA TYPE; CERITÓ VARIETY

Sample.—Fragments of 5 vessels (pl. 9, *a*).

Paste.—Large particles of crushed rock, much of it quartz, constitute the temper. The paste is fired to a red hue similar to that of the Calabaza variety, but the interior half of the vessel wall cross section in three out of the four vessels at the Peabody Museum varied from a light gray-brown to a dark gray-brown (Munsell 10YR; 5/1 to 3/1). Thickness ranges from 6–10 mm., averaging about 8 mm. Hardness rates at 4 on Mohs' scale and thus is fairly high.

Form.—A tall spouted bottle with a sharp basal angle and a ring base (fig. 35, *i*). Unfortunately, no complete vessels were present in the Peabody collection; thus heights cannot be given, but diameters estimated from the fragments ranged from 15.5–18 cm.

Appendages and construction.—Underside of body is deeply scored for attachment of ring base.

Surface.—Judging from a photograph of Dr. Mitchell's specimen, the design area is limited to the lower third or half of the vessel while the upper portion or spout is covered with a solid red slip. Likewise, the basal portion below the angle is red-slipped to the ring support.

The design area is set off from the red slipped areas above and below by a broad black band and two black lines. Within these the ground color varies from cream buff to a light brown. Design colors are apparently limited to black and red. On four of the fragments and on the complete vessel, the primary design motif is flanked above and below by four triangular elements combined with a row of dots (fig. 50, *c*) which act as dividers between repetitions of the primary

a   b

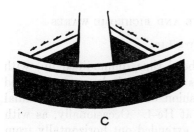

c

FIGURE 50.—Calabaza type, Ceritó variety, design elements. *a*, Find 30-9; *b*, ? 15; *c*, P-15. Horizontal lines indicate red.

motif (on two examples this is repeated three times; the other specimens are too fragmentary or eroded to provide this information). The complete vessels and two of the fragments exhibited a characteristic S scroll (fig. 50, *b*) as the primary motif. That of the third fragment with decoration remaining (Find 30-9), however, was an atypical rectangular scroll (fig. 50, *a*) reminiscent of the El Hatillo type. An additional vessel recovered at He-4 by Mr. Zelsman of the Canal Zone combines two design motifs, each apparently repeated twice—an Espalá variety rectangular dragon and a split-legged scroll design.

Comment.—Like the Calabaza variety, this variety also appears to straddle two types; in this case the El Hatillo and the Ortiga. The vessel form with its sharp basal angle is reminiscent of the various angled bottles of the El Hatillo variety and also resembles the "pyramid" bottle shape in red-buff ware of Finds 369 and 377.

Another mode resembling the El Hatillo variety is the rectangular scroll motif mentioned above. The paired triangular elements projecting from a border band also occasionally occur in the El Hatillo variety (e.g., Find 30-1, Vessel P-43). The S scroll motif or something very similar to it with split-legged elements containing circles in black line is found on both Ortiga and Calabaza variety vessels. Under these circumstances, and in view of the design consistency in at least three of the vessels, it seemed advisable to set up a varietal status in the Calabaza type even though the total number of examples is so small.

Geographical range.—The only examples I know of all came from the He-4 site.

Chronological position.—Grave associations in Find 30 indicate that the Ceritó variety is contemporary with the El Hatillo variety and thus probably coeval with, or later than, the Parita type and probably later than the Macaracas type.

Relationships of variety.—Related to the El Hatillo, Espalá, Calabaza, and Ortiga varieties.

Bibliography.—None.

MISCELLANEOUS POLYCHROME AND BICHROME WARES

BLACK-ON-WHITE LIP

Thirty-one sherds of small open bowl rims (unmodified lip) with white-slipped lips on which a series of black dashes are arranged radially around the bowl in the fashion of the Girón type, radial banded subvariety, were recovered at He-4. Occasionally, as with the Smoked ware bowls, small lobes extended out horizontally from the rim exterior, and one example has a modeled "frog" effigy face on the rim exterior. Interiors and exteriors of these vessels are red-slipped.

Chiriquí Alligator Ware

Five sherds of Alligator ware were recovered from Trench 7, Level 1, from a closed vessel of unknown rim or base characteristics. In addition, a small number of gray to gray-buff Chiriquí tripod legs were recovered.

Coclé Polychromes
(108 sherds)

As mentioned earlier, Late Coclé Polychrome and Azuero styles are often difficult to distinguish between, especially in sherd form, where only minute portions of design may be present. Both styles share design colors, often share cream to white ground slip color, and numerous elements such as claws and coral snake lips on plates. In sorting, a definite attempt was made to be conservative in assigning sherds to the Coclé group, and it was done only when the sherds showed typical Coclé design, distinctive lip shape, or the light gray paste color (Munsell Hue 10YR 8/1 to 7/1–2), which apparently never occurs with unmistakable Azuero-style designs, but does occur frequently with Coclé-style designs. A category labeled "Coclé-like" was set up for the sorting process. That is, sherds with the typical brick-red paste of the Azuero polychromes, but with, for example, clawed elements, which could be either Late Coclé or fragments of an Higo variety design. This category was later included in the Azuero style count and percentage determination on the basis, again, that only those sherds which were clearly Coclé should be assigned to that classification. In all cases except one, the design was too fragmentary to permit a distinction between Early and Late Coclé, in this case a large fragment of an Early Coclé "turtle" design. Most of the 108 Coclé-style sherds fell into the "indeterminate" category, although many of these are undoubtedly Late since a number of them have rounded lips. A number of plate sherds with the characteristic "drooping lip" were recovered, but this distinctive lip shape, while occurring very frequently in the Early Period at Sitio Conte, is also present in three out of the four classes of Late Period Polychrome plates at that site (Lothrop, 1942, p. 76), albeit common only in the beginning of the Late Period. In Trench 1, 3 out of 7 Coclé polychrome sherds had drooping lips; in Trench 2, 1 out of 6; in Trench 8, 5 out of 30; in Trench 10, 1 out of 4; and in Trench 7, 1 sherd with an Early design (mentioned above) out of 8 Coclé Polychrome sherds. No carafe or spouted jar sherds were recovered, but some closed shapes were indicated and sherds of a Paneled red ware vessel similar to a bowl from Grave 43, Late Period, at Sitio Conte (Lothrop, 1942, fig. 300, b) were recovered from Trench 7, Level 3 and Level 1. Out of a total of 43 Coclé-style sherds in

Mound III, 2 were classified as Early on the basis of concentric color-filled band design (Lothrop, 1942, fig. 74) and 16 as Late on the basis of coral snake lip combined with what was probably a dancing crocodile, other Late Period designs, and pedestal bases.

ARISTIDE GROUP POLYCHROMES

No Escotá type sherds or vessels were recovered, but the Girón type is represented by 49 sherds, all from Interior Banded open bowls with ski-tip rims and circumferential banding below the lip similar to those which characterize the He-1 and He-2 sites.

RED LINE WARE TYPE
(207 SHERDS)

This type, already described by Lothrop (Lothrop, 1942, pp. 131–134, and as Purple on Buff, p. 169) and also described in its Red Daubed variety by Willey and Stoddard in 1954, was found at He-4 in sherd form only. In the sherd analysis at He-4, three tentative categories were established: a Purple Line category (72 sherds), a Red Daubed category (182 sherds), and a Red Line category (16 sherds). The three were totaled in the final analysis as Red on Buff or Cream on the basis that the distinctions between them are not significant. As Lothrop pointed out, the same designs, generally teardrop or dribble elements, occur on both a buff ground (Red Daubed) and on a cream to white slip (Red Line), while the red may vary in hue from red to purple (Purple Line).[11] Thus the same designs noted by Lothrop, Willey and Stoddard, and in this report for the Girón site, He-1, and He-2, appear in either purple or red on the usual shapes, i.e., unmodified lip plates (incensario fragments?) and collared jars with or without strap handles. Both of these occurred frequently at He-4, but additional rare forms included loop handles with purple line decoration (Trench 8, Level 4), a dish fragment with a loop handle on the rim decorated in Red Daubed fashion (Trench 8, Level 3), and two Red Daubed buff fragments of an open bowl or dish (Trench 2) with an obliquely flattened lip, inclined and flanged toward the interior similar in shape to Smoked ware type, Platanillo variety rims.

RED AND WHITE WARE

This category (a few sherds from Mound III) did not become apparent until late in the analysis and undoubtedly should include a number of the rim and handle sherds which were classified as cream slip. Although the white shade may and often does vary to a pinkish cream, the Red and White ware is distinguished from creamed slipped

---

[11] If the 32 sherds of the Red Daubed Buff category (discussed below under Red-Buff wares) are added, the total for Red Line wares reaches 239 sherds.

Red Line vessels on the basis of decoration (design elements in red are absent in the Red and White ware) and, in some cases, size, shape, and handle type. Temper, like that of the Red Line ware, is crushed rock, but there appears to be a higher incidence of black particles in the Red and White ware, and the paste is more often fired to a dark red hue (Munsell 2.5YR, 4/6–3/6). Two shapes at He-4 were recognized on the basis of rim sherds; one, a large collared jar or urn with loop handles, and the other, an open bowl with sharply incurving rim as illustrated for the Red-buff ware sherd of the same shape (see fig. 51, *l*).

The collared jars must have been large, heavy vessels. The rim diameter alone of one representative fragment is estimated at 50 cm. and the handles, placed horizontally on the shoulder, had a diameter of 4 cm. and a length of 22 cm. Wall thickness averaged 1 cm. The rim, upper shoulder, and handles are covered with an unpolished cream to white slip, and the handles are often decorated with an applique lizard which in turn may be embellished with reed punctations (see fig. 51, *a*). The lower shoulder is covered with a thick, bright, polished red slip; the remainder of the body and base are unknown.

One typical example of the open bowl form rim sherds has an estimated diameter of 38 cm. and a thickness of 6–8 mm. A cream slip extends from the angle of the shoulder down to the base, but both the entire interior and the exterior of the lip and shoulder are red slipped. Another sherd of the same shape has a loop handle horizontally placed on the rim above the shoulder with a slashed node at either end. In this case, the handle and adjacent shoulder area are cream slipped (the remainder of the fragment is red slipped), a treatment which is analogous to that employed in Red-buff angled shoulder bowls where the handle and adjacent area are left unslipped. Since the number of sherds recognized as Red and White ware is so small, and its relationship to the Creamed-slip category discussed briefly below is unclear, I have hesitated to set it up on a formal varietal status. I do not know of any published examples of it, nor is its chronological position clear. It is definitely related in shape, handle treatment, and placement of slipped areas to the Red-buff open bowls with incurved rims. Likewise, the collared jar sherds are similar in shape and manipulation of slipped areas (the white slipped area of the Red and White vessels corresponds to the unslipped, or buff-cream-slipped areas of the Red-buff) to the Red-buff class "e" collared jars of Mound II. The upper shoulder (including the handle and, in the case of collared jars, the collar) was frequently differentiated from the main body exterior, either by leaving those upper portions unslipped, or by adding a buff, cream, or white slip.

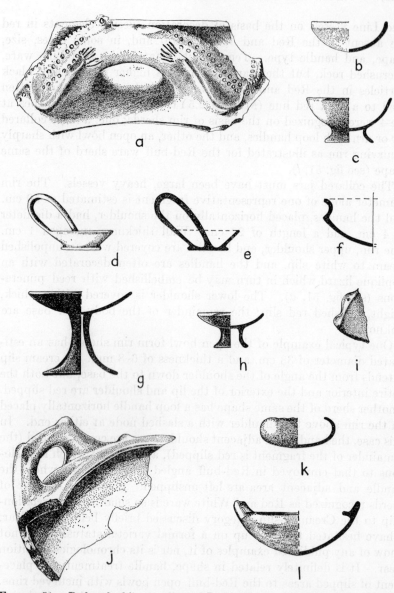

FIGURE 51.—Red and white, cream, and Red-buff ware vessel shapes. *a*, Lizard
handle on Red and white ware, Mound III; *b*, Find 344, Red-buff ware; *c*, *f*,
Mound III Red-buff ware; *d–e*, Find 354-1 and Mound III Red-buff ware; *g*,
Find 146, Red-buff ware; *h*, Red ware miniature plate, Find 369-4; *i*, Trench
5 Red-buff ware; *j*, Red and white and Red-buff ware Mound III sherd; *k*,
Find 372-15, Red-buff ware; *l*, vessel a-1 Red-buff ware and Red and white
ware.

CREAM WARE

This group (207 sherds), set up as a sorting category for sherds slipped in cream or white alone, undoubtedly includes fragments from a number of vessels which belong in the Red and White classification above. One complete vessel (Find 344) and a few large fragments of pinkish creamed slip shallow bowls with short vertical walls or upturned rims (fig. 51, *b*) were found. The diameter of Find 344 is 18.5 cm. and its height is 6 cm. Slips are unpolished and often rather rough or gritty. Other fragments of the same shape in cream slip but with shorter rims occurred with loop handles extending more or less vertically from the lips similar to the Red-buff examples (see fig. 52, *d–f*), and one of these also was decorated with an applique worm along the outer edge of the rim similar to those (see fig. 52, *b*, *c*) illustrated for Red-buff open bowls. The spacing of the handles on the rim fragments mentioned above (Trench 7, Level 1) indicates that there were four handles evenly spaced about the lip. Other cream-slipped handles recovered were of the loop type, and varied in size from medium (10 cm. long) to large (roughly 20 cm.). Other shapes in cream slip include plates, collars with a median flange or angle (similar to the Red ware shape illustrated in figure 53, *d*), and constricted orifice jars with horizontally placed loop handles on the shoulder. These are known from rim sherds only.

The following miscellaneous appendages or supports in cream slip also occurred: a large, heavy loop leg (the worn area at the exterior apex of the loop is clearly visible) with an oval cross section (Mound III), a small conical lug (Mound III), and a hollow bulbous foot with short parallel line incisions at the "toe" and two perforations on either side of the bulbous upper area.

As noted above, this category appears to be too vague to warrant varietal status. Many of the fragments which comprise it belong either to Red and White vessels, or probably to other, unclassified, vessels. It is also possible that Find 344 and some of the other large fragments of similar shape are unfinished examples of vessels which were to have had a red slip added. This is pretty definitely the case in Find 182, a clear and typical example of a Níspero bird effigy bowl entirely covered with a buff-cream slip without additional decoration of any kind.

MONOCHROME WARES

As distinct from the method used with the polychrome wares in which varieties and types were established primarily on the basis of whole vessels, the analysis of the monochrome wares is based, in part, on previous categories such as Lothrop's Smoked ware and Plain Red

ware (Lothrop, 1942, pp. 158–166) or Willey and Stoddard's Delgado
Red (Willey and Stoddard, 1954) and, in part, on the sherd lots at the
El Hatillo site.   Complete vessels, when available, naturally were
included in the analysis, but definition of categories rests primarily
on the material in sherd form.   As a result, four main groups of sherds
were distinguished: Red-buff (including Delgado Red shapes);[12] Coclé
Red; Red Daubed Buff; and Smoked ware.   A smaller group of thin,
buff unsmoothed vessels, as well as other miscellaneous unslipped
shapes, was also distinguished.   Of these, the Red-buff group is by
far the largest (about 12,000 sherds) and the loosest, for it may include
within it a number of paste and vessel form correlations, or categories
based on fine distinctions which were not attempted in the present
analysis.   Temper was noted for all whole vessels (in all cases it was
crushed rock), but not in the sherd analysis.   In the latter, the sherds
were divided into the four groups mentioned above on the basis of
gross distinctions.

Thus, sherds were classified as Coclé Red if they had a light gray
paste, because paste fired to this gray hue (Munsell 10YR, 8/1 to
7/1–2) is consistently associated with polychrome sherds of unmistakable Coclé design and is not present in those of the El Hatillo,
Macaracas, Parita, or unassigned varieties discussed earlier.   Additional diagnostics for Coclé Red were the "drooping lip," the "gutter
rim," and other distinctive rim shapes discussed by Lothrop in his
second volume on Sitio Conte.   Sherds with a cream-buff slip, a brown
or tan paste (Munsell 7.5YR, 5/4–4/4), and often with interior brushing
were classified as Red Daubed Buff, again on the basis that these characteristics are associated with the Red Daubed variety.   Finally,
chocolate brown or black sherds with polished surfaces (not sherds
heavily carboned by exposure to fire other than that used in the firing
process of manufacture) were classified as Smoked ware.

Within each of these groups, shapes as indicated by rim sherds,
appendages such as handles, lugs, feet, ring or pedestal bases, and
plastic surface treatment (incision, punctation, etc.) were noted.

RED-BUFF TYPE

Sample.—12,002 sherds; 80 whole vessels or large fragments.

Paste.—The temper is crushed rock, white and black, similar to the
polychrome wares with occasional inclusions of hematite.   The paste
is generally fired to a brick red, although darker cores occasionally

---

[12] These shapes as defined by Willey and Stoddard for He-8 include collarless jars with constricted orifice
and often with loop handles; collared jars; small open bowls; and plates or shallow bowls.   All of these in
addition to a number of others were represented in Red-buff Ware at He-4.   Red-buff shapes at He-4 which
are not included in the Delgado Red category are collared jars classes "d" and "e," median flange collars,
bottles, and bird effigy jars.

occur as do lighter shades, especially on jar bases. The Munsell range is the same as that for Parita Polychrome.

Surface.—The surface is red slipped and polished, generally over the entire exterior. Exceptions to this statement will be noted below in the discussion of the different shapes.

Form.—Shapes include plates or shallow bowls with plain, ring, or pedestal bases, deep open bowls with and without incurving rims, jars with and without collars, bottles, bird effigy jars, and miscellaneous shapes such as pot covers.

1. Plates.—(*a*) *Unmodified base.*—Only two certain examples of plain or rounded based plates were recovered at the site. One of these, Find 372-27, was 10 cm. in diameter, had two opposed loop handles extending horizontally out from the rim, and nodes along the lip. A similar shape, but with loop handles projecting vertically from the rim, occurred in Smoked ware (Find 372-28). The other was a miniature (5.8 cm. diameter) dish with unmodified lip. Numerous plate lips or rims were recovered in the sherd lots which gave no indication of the base and therefore could be classified either with this group or with the ring or pedestal based groups to follow.

(*b*) *Pedestal based plates.*—These vessels range in size from small or miniature (approximately 7 cm. in diameter) through medium (14 cm. in diameter) to large or about 24 cm. in diameter. The entire exterior is generally covered with a polished red slip although in some of the smaller examples the underside of the plate may be unslipped. Lips are unmodified.

On the basis of the occurrence of whole vessels it is possible to break this group down into two subgroups: (1) medium to large plates with tall slender bases which flare out markedly at the rim or foot (fig. 51, *g*), and (2) smaller to miniature plates with broader shorter pedestals (fig. 51, *h*).

(*c*) *Ring-based plates.*—As represented by a number of examples from Find 347, a grave unit, ring-based plates at the site are small to medium in size (13–15 cm. in diameter) with unmodified lips and a polished red slip usually over the entire exterior except for the extreme basal portion. Numerous ring bases, presumably belonging to plates, were present in the sherd lots.

A rather unusual form, a ring-based plate with a loop handle (often oval in cross section) extending from the center of the plate to the rim (fig. 51, *d, e*) and with a diameter of 18 cm., is represented by Find 354-1. In this case the lip is unmodified and the handle missing, although locations of attachment are present. A few handles and base fragments of larger vessels of the same type were present in the sherd lots from Mound III.

2. Shallow open bowls.—Plain rimmed shallow bowls on pedestals are rare in the collection. One whole vessel, a medium-sized bowl with a short pedestal was found in Mound III (fig. 51, *c*), and occasional shallow bowl rims with flattened lugs on the exterior just below the lip occurred. One bowl sherd with a lobed rim was recovered in Trench 5 (fig. 51, *i*).

Open bowls with median flanged rims (fig. 51, *f*) and either pedestal or tripod bases (actually small lugs) were represented in both the sherd lots and in Mound III. This shape also occurs in Smoked ware. Slashed nodes on the rim exterior are present on one example.

3. Open bowls with angled or incurved rims.—These vessels are known by photographs of two complete vessels, both in Panama, and by a number of large rim fragments from Mound III and two miniatures (Find 372-15, 19) which are in the collection at Peabody. Vessel size varies from medium to large for the most part; the diameter of one complete vessel (A-1, Peabody photo file) is 19 cm., the height 7 cm. Diameters estimated from the fragments in the collection at Peabody range from 26–36 cm. Thicknesses range from 6–9 cm.

The form (fig. 51, *l*) is generally that of a relatively shallow open bowl with rounded base, an incurved rim, and two opposed loop handles horizontally placed on the shoulders. Rims may curve in rather gently, producing a rounded shoulder, or may be angled in sharply. Lips generally are rounded and otherwise unmodified, but may also be thickened and even flanged slightly upward. The two miniatures (fig. 51, *k*, diameters 7–7.5 cm.) lack handles entirely or any form of modeled decoration.

Handles are looped or angular (figs. 51, *j*; 52, *a*), frequently are grooved on the outer or upper surface, and usually project from the shoulder just below the lip at an approximately 45° angle from the horizontal. Slashed nodes or applique "worms" with or without reed punctation often are present on the shoulders and/or the handles. The entire interior of the vessel is red-slipped. The exterior, including handle, may be red slipped, or the area with handles and decoration may be left unslipped.

Comment.—This relatively shallow "casuela" shape with sharply incurved rim occurs also in the Red and White ware, although handles may or may not be included. A much deeper open bowl shape, somewhat similar in its gently incurving rim, was decorated with Pica-pica polychrome design elements (Find 346-1).

4. Deep bowls.—This form is known primarily by rim sherds, hence total shape and base are a matter of conjecture. All rim sherds so classified had rounded lips. Two opposed loop handles attached either at the outer edge of the rim, extending outward at a slight angle, or directly to the rim as an extension of it, are common. The handles may be either slipped or unslipped and are occasionally punctated (fig. 52, *d–f*). The only whole vessels of this kind in the collection are two miniatures, Finds 374-30 and 374-31, both without handles.

5. Globular and subglobular jars (except bird effigy).—There are two main types of jars within this category; those without and those with collars. In the latter, there appear to be at least three characteristic rim types which correspond to those found in the polychrome pottery.

(*a*) *Collarless jars* (*fig. 52, h*).—Dimensions include miniatures (8 cm. in diameter); many examples of jars 18–26 cm. in diameter; and large urns, somewhat less globular and more pear-shaped, up to 44 cm. in diameter. Lips are slightly thickened and usually rounded except for the occasional appearance of a slight upward flange. Bases are rounded. A red slip is applied to the major portion of the exterior, but bases are often left unslipped as are the handles and an area just below the lip including the handle (fig. 52, *g*). Lips themselves are slipped. The handles looped with circular cross section are placed horizontally on the shoulders so that they oppose each other. Usually two in number, they may be punctated, slashed, or modeled to give a ropelike appearance. Slashed nodes occasionally are placed on the handles, one at each end. A number of miniature or small collarless jars were recovered in which one of the horizontally placed loop handles was replaced by a vertical loop handle (Find 372-17) or by an effigy lug (Finds 366 and 377-28), or in which flat horizontal lugs (Find 377-3) or one vertical and one horizontal flat lug (Find 368-19) were substituted for the usual handles. Another variant is represented by Find 217, a collarless jar with an upward flanging lip and horizontally placed loop handles which extend upward almost vertically.

(*b*) *Flare collar jars.*—Based on differences in lip shape, collar surface

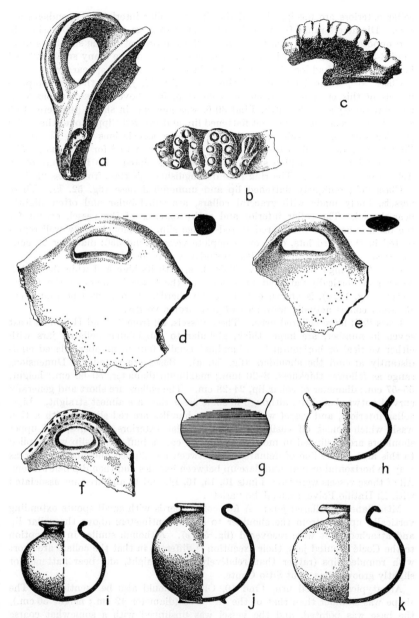

FIGURE 52.—Red-buff ware vessel shapes. *a–f*, Mound III; *g*, slipped; *i*, class "a"; *j*, class "b," Find 30-6; *k*, class "c," Find 356.

treatment and type of base, there appear to be at least four relatively distinct types of flare collared jars present in the collection.

Class "a"; unmodified lip and round base (fig. 52, *i*). Generally the body shape is slightly subglobular, the slip covers the entire exterior (occasionally collar exteriors are unslipped) and the lip and collar interior. Appendages are rare. Diameters range from small (10–14 cm.) to large (28 cm.). Occasionally two opposed horizontally placed loop handles are present on the shoulders as in Find 8-5, Find 346-7, and in a few other cases. One of the many small collared jars of Find 377 had loop handles modeled to give a ropelike appearance.

Class "b"; unmodified lip and ring base (fig. 52, *j*). Of the six complete vessels of this class noted from the collection, four have no associations with polychrome styles. The fifth, Find 30-6, was globular in shape (diameter 19.5 cm.), had a broad and somewhat flattened lip, and was red-slipped over the entire exterior surface. In this case, the polychrome associations were El Hatillo Polychrome, El Hatillo variety. No appendages are noted for this class. The sixth, Find 1-*a*, had a high shoulder and was associated with fragments of an Achote variety vessel. The ring base distinguishes this class from class "a."

Class "c"; obliquely flattened lip and unmodified base (fig. 52, *k*). These vessels, finely made with graceful collars, are subglobular and often slightly pear shaped. The collar interior and entire exterior of the vessel, except for the base, is covered with a red to red-orange slip. Although fairly well represented in the sherd lots, only one complete vessel (Find 356; diameter 22 cm.) was recovered. No examples with appendages were found.

Class "d"; high flaring collar. This class, with its high and wide flared tall collar and vertically flattened lip similar to the "atlas" collars of the Ortiga variety (fig. 17, *e*), is known only by collar sherds. It may well be that these Red-buff collars actually were part of polychrome vessels.

Class "e"; large collared urns. These vessels, all from Mound II and at least seven in number, are large, thick, globular to subglobular collared jars with either vertical or horizontal loop handles, usually four in number, placed equidistantly around the shoulders (fig. 53, *a*). Bases are rounded. Dimensions range as follows: thickness, 8–20 mm.; maximum diameter, 50–60 cm.; height, 55–57 cm.; diameter of collar lip, 24–28 cm. The collars are short and generally curved outward slightly, although in some cases they are almost straight. Lips, collar interiors, and vessel walls below the handles are red slipped with a thin wash which comes off easily in water. Collar exteriors, handles, and upper shoulders are unslipped in most cases; in one case a buff-cream slip was applied to this area. The line of demarcation between red-slipped and unslipped areas may be horizontal or may undulate up between handles and then dip below them. All of these vessels were from Finds 10, 15, 16, 14, and 18 and are thus associated with El Hatillo Polychrome, Jobo variety.

Miscellaneous collared jars: A few collar sherds with small spouts extending vertically upward from the shoulder to a few centimeters above the collar lip and attached to it were recovered (fig. 53, *e*). Although similar in conception to the Coclé spouted jars, their execution is different in that the collars are short with rounded lips (rather than relatively tall), straight, and bear flattened or slightly grooved lips as at Sitio Conte.

An atypical collared urn, Find 10, Olla 4, should also be mentioned. The shape was slimmer than that of the "e" urns (diameter 42 cm.; height 56 cm.), the base was pointed, and the vessel was unslipped with a somewhat coarse finish. Four double loop handles (fig. 53, *c*) were placed vertically and equidistantly around the shoulders.

(*c*) *Reverse flare and median flange collar.*—A few collar sherds and one complete vessel (Find 379-1), in which the collar is turned in similar to some of the face collars of the Ortiga variety, were recovered (fig. 27, *a*, *b*). Find 379-1, a miniature vessel 6.2 cm. in diameter, was decorated on the rim with incised and punctated nodes, presumably representing the eyes and beak of a bird, and

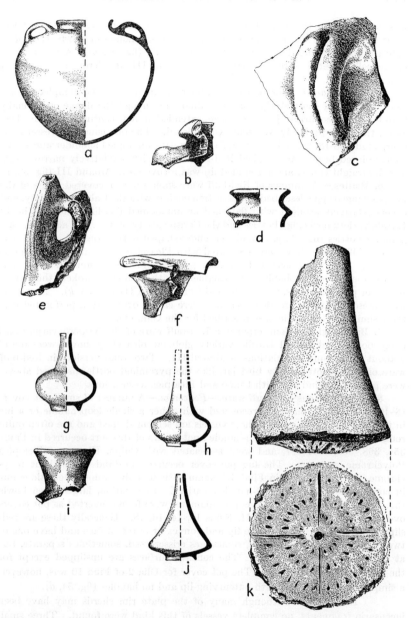

FIGURE 53.—Red-buff ware vessel shapes. *a*, Find 10, class "e" collared jar; *b*, *e*, *f*, *i*, Mound III; *c*, Trench 2, Level 1 (used for shape only), Find 10, olla 4; *d*, P-28 (used for shape only; polychrome collar, black band on cream red lip); *g*, Find 369-4; *h*, P-32; *j*, Find 369-6; *k*, Mound III "rattle."

was associated in the Find Unit with a Pica-pica variety vessel. One of the reverse flare collar sherds from Mound III retained enough of the body wall to indicate broad modeled bulges similar to a squash (fig. 53, *b*). A few median flange collar sherds were recovered from Mound III and Trench 2, Level 1 (fig. 53, *d*, *f*).

(*d*) *Straight collar jars.*—A number of sherds and one complete vessel were found with short straight collars, almost as though the flange occasionally found on the collarless jars had been extended a few centimeters. In these cases, the body probably was round-shouldered. The one complete vessel however, Find 368-18, is a miniature collared jar with an angled shoulder and somewhat pointed base. An atypical Red-buff collar with a relatively narrow neck, a high straight collar, and a rounded lip was recovered in Mound III (fig. 53, *i*).

6. Bottles.—A number of Red-buff ware spouts were recovered, some of the inward flanged type described in the section dealing with the Calabaza variety, and others relatively straight with flattened or unmodified lips like those of the El Hatillo variety bird effigy bottles and the Ceritó variety bottles. In addition, subglobular bottles (fig. 53, *g*, *h*) and pyramidal-shaped bottles (fig. 53, *j*) were part of Find 369 where they were associated with Pica-pica and Cuipo variety polychromes. They also occurred without polychrome associations in Find 377. Two funnel-shaped probable rattle fragments with both ends broken, thus either spouts or pedestal bases, were recovered from Mound III (fig. 53, *k*). No pellets were present but the broader apertures were closed over with a perforated clay layer similar to the rattle base described for the Cuipo variety.

7. Bird effigies.—Counterparts in Red-buff ware of the Níspero variety bird effigy bowls, and the El Hatillo variety globular bird effigy bowls were found without polychrome associations in Mound III. Two squat versions in Red-buff ware of the Achote variety bird jar, like the pyramidal bottle discussed above, were present in Find 369 with Cuipo and Pica-pica associations.

8. Miscellaneous Red-buff ware.—*Pot covers.*—A number of small pot covers (8–10 cm. in diameter) were recovered with either a single loop handle or a lug in the center (fig. 54, *a*, *c*). These vessels are seldom slipped and are often quite rough in surface texture. Loop-handled pot covers of this sort occurred in Finds 354, 368, 369, and 377, and were associated with Cuipo, Higo, and Pica-pica Polychrome varieties. The lug pot cover occurred in Find 366 without polychrome associations and in Find 377 again without polychrome associations but in conjunction with the loop-handled variety. In addition, larger open bowls (fig. 54, *b*) averaging about 30 cm. in diameter were found inverted as pot covers over the large urns of Mound II, Finds 10, 14, 16, 18. Generally these are red-slipped with a thin wash on the lip and convex or outer surface and have one or two loop handles in the center, sometimes crisscrossed, sometimes separate, but at right angles to each other. The concave surfaces are unslipped except for the area adjacent to the lip. The pot cover for Olla 2 of Find 10 was, however, a simple ring-based bowl with outcurving lip and no handles (fig. 54, *d*).

Incensarios.—Although many of the plate rim sherds may have been incensario fragments, no complete vessels of this kind were found. Three small flat handles similar to that illustrated by Lothrop (Lothrop, 1942, fig. 353, *d*) were found in Level 2 of Trench 8, but two of these, instead of being rectangular, had a slight fishtail shape (fig. 54, *e*). One of the latter, apparently broken near the point of juncture with the dish, measured 7 cm. long by 3 cm. wide by 1.2 cm. thick. None of the round type found at Sitio Conte were present in the Peabody collection.

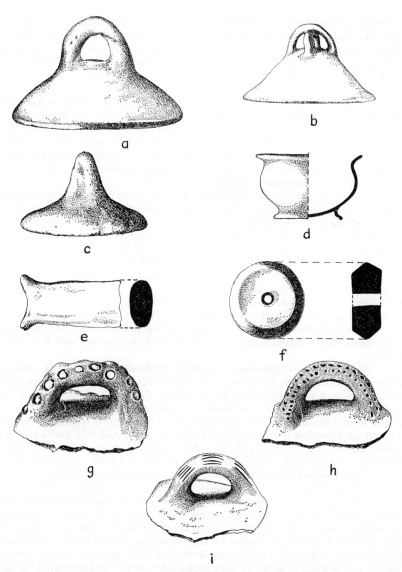

FIGURE 54.—Red-buff ware and Buff ware vessel shapes. *f*, Buff ware, mixture
Trench 11 and Trench 8; *a–e*, *g–i*, Red-buff ware; *a*, Find 369-13; *b*, 14-10;
c, Find 360; *e*, olla 2, Find 10-21; *e*, Trench 8, Level 2; *g–i*, Mound III.

Spindle whorls.—One probable spindle whorl, unslipped, buff, diameter
4 cm. and 1.6 cm. thick with a perforation 5 mm. in diameter was found (fig.
54, *f*).

Plastic treatment.—Gadrooning. The one definite example of gadrooning is a fragment of a Red-buff round-based globular vessel (estimated diameter
18.5 cm.) with unknown collar or rim characteristics. This vessel, Find 382-2,
was associated in the find unit with Pica-pica variety polychrome.

Incision and punctation.   Instances of incision and punctation are almost always limited to handles or applique figures on handles and rims.   Thus, reed punctation, jabbing, and dashing (fig. 54, g–i) occurred fairly frequently on loop and angular handles, both on collarless jar shoulders and on the incurved rim open bowls. Reed punctation was present also on the lizard handles of the Red and White ware discussed earlier.

In addition, a group of rough, often blackened, buff strap handles or legs with upturned edges for rims and line incision, reed punctation, and simple punctation were recovered from Mound III (fig. 55).   Unfortunately, none of these had sufficient body wall section attached to indicate vessel shape or finish.   Handle width ranges from 3–8 cm. with two groupings apparent: one around 3 cm., the other 5–7 cm.   One was decorated with a crude angular scroll pattern (fig. 55, d) reminiscent of the Pica-pica rectangular scroll motif.

Supports.—A number of unslipped pedestal bases decorated with vertical lines or zones of jabbing punctation were recovered in Mound III (fig. 55, f, g). In at least one case, enough of the vessel body was attached to indicate a red slipped exterior; otherwise, total vessel shape and finish are unknown.   Lothrop, however, illustrates two vessels with pedestal bases of this sort, both open bowls with vertical or slightly incurved sides.   One, a buff ware vessel with two small modeled heads and wings attached to the rim, is from the mouth of the Rio Grande, Coclé (Lothrop, 1942, fig. 438).   The other, again with effigy adornos on the rim, is from Soná, Veraguas (Lothrop, 1950, fig. 49, c).

Other supports in Red-buff ware included one hollow closed tube (leg?, handle?), a few lugs with flattened bases, and a broad flaring pedestal base with four oval perforations spaced equidistantly around the point of juncture with the vessel body.

Appendages.—Appendages include: applique "worms" and slashed nodes on incurving open bowl rims and occasionally around handle bases (figs. 52, b, c; 56, a, b); "monkeys" on jar shoulders (fig. 56, e); "dragon heads" of various kinds, some of which occurred on collarless jar shoulders (fig. 56, c, d); a "deer head," location unknown (fig. 56, f); "toad monsters" of typically Veraguas type on jar shoulders and loop handles (fig. 56, g, h); and frog handles of the Ortiga variety, but in plain red slip.   As mentioned earlier, lizards are often modeled on large loop handles of the cream or Red and White ware (fig. 51, a).

Unclassified Red-buff ware.—Two vessels from Mound II, Find 15–2 and Find 17–2 are treated here as unclassified largely because of the nature of the paste which, though fired the usual brick red, was much more friable than that of the general Red-buff wares and averaged only about 5 mm. thick.   The collars are rather straight with a flaring lip, bases are ring and about 16 cm. in diameter. The vessels were too badly crushed for full restoration, so that the degree of body globularity is unknown.   Both were decorated with modeled circular bosses (fig. 56, i, j) 6–8 cm. in diameter with appliqued "worms" and punctated "eyes." I know of no other vessels like them, although the general style of plastic decoration is reminiscent of Veraguas.   Their chronological position is not clear, since the only polychrome association, an Achote vessel in Find 17, is questionable.

Coclé Red Ware

Sample.—171 sherds.

Paste.—The temper is crushed rock and the light gray color to which the paste is fired was considered as diagnostic of the ware in this study (Munsell 10YR, 8/1 to 7/1–2).

Shapes.—Forms noted at the El Hatillo site were open bowls with

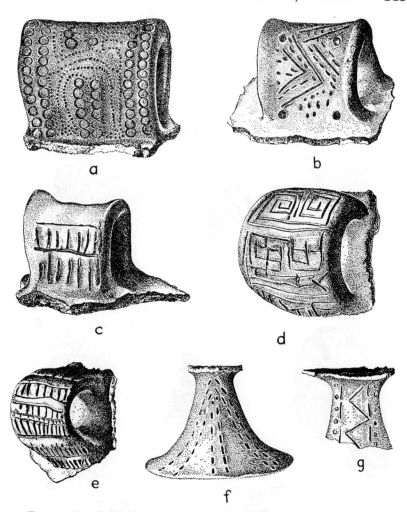

FIGURE 55.—Red-buff and Buff ware vessel shapes from Mound III.

gutter or modified-gutter rims, plates or shallow bowls with drooping lip, collared jars, incurving bowl or jar rims with rounded lips (probably the shape illustrated in Lothrop, 1942, fig. 267, *d*), ring bases, and one pedestal base.

Geographic range.—Probably similar to Coclé Polychrome; definitely known at Sitio Conte, Coclé, Venado Beach, Canal Zone, and the Parita Region, sites He-4 and He-2.

Chronological position.—Both Early and Late Red ware lip types were encountered, but sample sizes were too small in any given level for meaningful statistical analysis.

Relationships of type.—Coclé Red ware is related in shape and paste

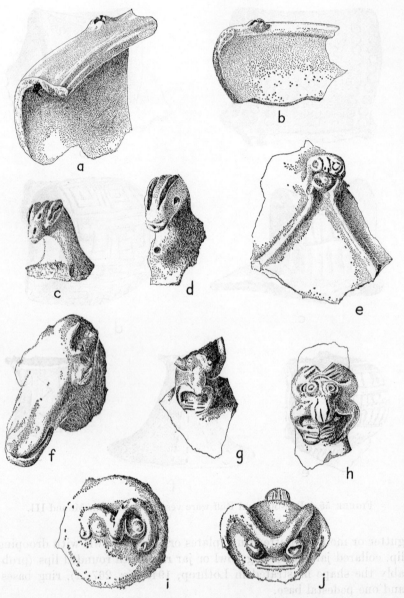

FIGURE 56.—Red-buff ware vessel shapes.   a–h, Mound III; i, Find 15; j, Find 17.

to the Coclé polychromes and also to some Smoked ware forms recovered at Sitio Conte, He-1, and He-2, e.g., the gutter and modified-gutter lip.

Bibliography.—Lothrop, 1942, pp. 135–142.

SMOKED WARE

Sample.—123 sherds; 9 complete vessels.

Paste.—Fired to a gray or gray-brown; temper is black (blackened through firing) crushed rock.

Surface.—Polished black or chocolate-brown hue. Complete vessels included the following shapes: a plain-based unmodified rim plate 19 cm. in diameter (Find 129); three miniature tripod bowls 4–5 cm. in diameter with bulbous legs and flattened or gutter rims (Finds 369-19, 372-16, 375-7) (fig. 57, *a*); a plain-based plate with two opposed loop handles on the rim, each handle flanked by two nodes (Find 372-28); ring-based open bowls with gutter rims and high interior flanged lips, similar in rim form (but not bases) to the Smoked ware, Sangre variety at He-1 (Find 378-3, 378-4, fig. 57, *b*); and two open pedestal bowls with modified gutter lips and diameters of roughly 20 cm. Sherd rims for the most part were of open bowls, often with modified gutter rim (fig. 57, *c, d*), a rim type shared by the Platanillo variety, or with an interior flange extending upward (fig. 57, *e*) like the Sangre variety and similar to that illustrated by Lothrop (1942, fig. 320, *b*) for Early Smoked ware. In addition, a few sherds with sharp medial bevel and slightly incurved upper walls, another Early shape at Sitio Conte (Lothrop, 1942, fig. 321) and similar to the Red ware median flange (fig. 51, *f*) were recovered, as well as a few cone-shaped and rounded lugs (fig. 57, *i, j*). Rims were often decorated with reed punctation and short parallel line incision (fig. 57, *g, h*). Occasionally, lobes extended horizontally out from the rim exterior.

Two additional Smoked ware vessels which remained in Panama, Finds 369-16 and 369-17, have been described as black polished pedestal bowls or plates. Find 369-16 had a flat lip with an interior bevel and two exterior rim projections, one of which was rectangular and the other a semicircular form with punched node eyes. Find 369-17 had a deep lip channel with an interior flange, and thus is somewhat similar to the Sangre variety.

Geographic range.—Sitio Conte, Venado Beach, Parita Region (He-4, He-1, He-2).

Chronological position.—Most of the rim types at the El Hatillo site were similar to Early Coclé Smoked ware at Sitio Conte. The Platanillo variety (with ring base, not tripod) had Early associations at He-1 and He-2 and the Sangre variety with pedestal base had both Early and Late associations at He-1.

Relationships of type.—The ware is often similar to Coclé Red in rim, lip, and other characteristics of form.

Bibliography.—Lothrop, 1942, pp. 158–163.

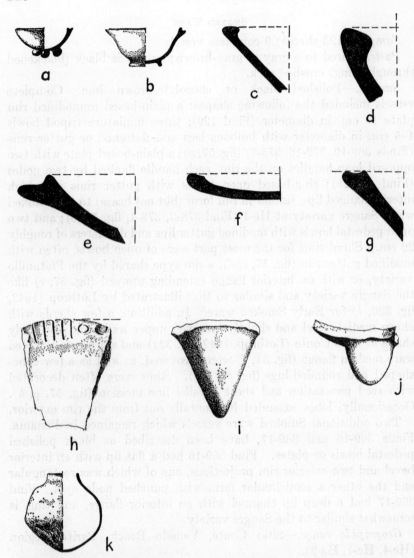

FIGURE 57.—Smoked ware and Buff ware vessel shapes. *a*, Find 372-16 Smoked ware; *b*, Find 378-3 Smoked ware; *c*, Trench 7, Level 3 Smoked ware (?); *d*, Trench 7, Level 4.1–5.4; *e*, Trench 7, Level 3, Smoked ware; *f*, Find 5-*c*, Smoked ware; *g–h*, single Trench 2, Level 1 sherd; *i–j*, Mound III Smoked ware; *k*, Find 10, Sandy buff.

RED DAUBED BUFF WARE

As noted earlier, this category was established to account for those buff sherds without red paint which probably belonged in the Red Daubed variety on the basis of paste and surface characteristics. As such, the comments for the Red Daubed variety apply here.

SMOKED BUFF WARE

Sample.—4 complete vessels (Finds 5-*c*, 6-*a*, 8-2, 9-4).

Paste.—Fired a brown to red-brown color; crushed rock temper both white and black.

Form.—All three vessels were plain-based plates ranging from 17.5–20 cm. in diameter and relatively thick, about 0.8–1 cm. The vessels have a dull polish and are covered with a light gray-brown slip. One example (Find 6-*a*), more buff than smoked, has a rounded lip. On the other three (Finds 5-*c*, 8-2, 9-4), one of which is gray and two of which are brown, the upper surface of the lip is flattened and the entire lip thickened (fig. 57, *f*). It is quite possible that these three should be classified as Smoked ware.

SANDY-BUFF WARE

Sample.—7 complete vessels (Finds 10-19, 10-20, 10-22 through 10-26).

Paste.—Gritty paste with crushed rock temper fired to a gray and brown color.

Form.—All the vessels are miniatures, either collared jars with round bases, class "a," or globular jars with small orifices and short straight collars, round bases; almost a bottle shape with short spouts (fig. 57, *k*). Vessel walls are unevenly modeled and thin; 3 mm.

Surface.—The surfaces are rough, gritty, unslipped, and a sandy buff color.

Geographic range.—Unknown.

Chronological position.—Vessels were associated in Find Unit 10 with El Hatillo Polychrome, Jobo variety, bird jars and bottles.

Relationships of type.—The nearest parallel for the collared shape that I know of is the Early Coclé polychrome bottle shape (Lothrop, 1942, fig. 119) and the Pica-pica straight-collared jars or bottles with constricted orifices. The class "a" collared jar is roughly similar to others in its class although the orifice is larger than usual in proportion to the body diameter.

Bibliography.—None.

STONE ARTIFACTS

The worked-stone inventory for all the sites is meager, especially at He-4 where the ceramic crafts are so elaborate and profuse. Celts, polishers or rubbing stones, a point, a few possible scrapers, chisels, and miscellaneous chips comprise the list. Materials are varied. Basalt altering to serpentine, thus relatively easy to polish, was preferred for celts. Jasper and chert served for the flakes and point. Various river pebbles, either of igneous or sedimentary rock, make up the category of polishers or rubbing stones. The single metate fragment is of a hard sedimentary rock.   Miscellaneous round stones, of indeterminate functions, appear to be river pebbles.

Metates.—One fragment of what appears to be a table type metate was recovered in Trench 11, Level A–2.   One surface is flattened, the other slightly convex.

Manos.—Two granite fragments of probable manos with oval cross section and well-polished surfaces were recovered, one from the fourth level of Trench 1, and one from a mixed lot from Trench 8 and Trench 7.   An oval and flattened stone of sedimentary rock 10×8×4.5 cms. with well-smoothed surfaces is included here as a possible mano.

Celts.—A number of celts were recovered at the site, most of them in the refuse of various trenches, but a few in association with definite ceramic types.   The celts may be divided into three categories: a beveled edge group; a chipped poll group with broad blade and narrowing poll; and an ovoid group with a tendency toward overall polishing.

The first group (pl. 18, *a*, *b*) is represented by the following: a few examples (fragments only) in Mound III; one large fragment from Trench 10, Level 5; a complete example, Find 219, from a 20-cm. depth in Trench 6; and a miniature celt with Find 368.   All are made of basalt largely altered to serpentine and all are finely polished with the exception of a chipped poll from Find 219.   They tend to be long and narrow with sides which extend straight back from the cutting edge and maintain a consistent width until they narrow fairly abruptly at the poll.   The cutting edge is slightly curved.   Each lateral edge is flattened on three planes for the length of the celt; one plane is perpendicular to the cutting edge of the celt with one oblique plane on either side.   Most of the examples suggest a relatively large tool ranging from 5–6 cms. wide, 3–4 cms. thick, and, in the case of the one complete example, 25.5 cms. long.   Pottery associations with the single miniature example (2.6 cms. long) in Find 368 are with the Macaracas type.

Most of the celts or celt fragments recovered at He-4 belong in the second group or chipped poll category, an apparently ubiquitous one in Panama, well represented both in Veraguas and at Sitio Conte (Lothrop, 1937; 1950).   These have a relatively broad blade, generally slightly curved, and a body which narrows down to the chipped poll (pl. 18, *c*, *d*).   Polishing occurs at the blade end and continues, to some extent, along the body of the tool, except for depressions in the stone.   Measurements for the larger examples approximate 9×5×2 cms.   Unlike those recovered at the Girón site, these have an oval rather than a thickened cross section.   Two miniature examples (length about 3 cms.) and one small specimen (length 6 cms.) were associated with Macaracas pottery in Find 372, one full size example was recovered from the third level of Trench 1, and a small one of schist from Trench 7, Level 2.   The remainder came from unstratified circumstances in Mound III.

Two examples of the ovoid category (pl. 18, *e*) were recovered, both with pottery associations.   The first, associated in Find 370 with Red-buff collarless jars, was polished overall and measured 13×4.8×1.8 cms.   The second, associated in Find 384 with Macaracas pottery, measured 6.5×2.5×1.5 cms.   The poll showed signs of battering and chipping which may have been the result of use after manufacture. As noted below, and a common feature of the He-1 site, stones which had apparently been prepared originally as celts often showed signs of subsequent battering on both poll and cutting surfaces.

Hammers.—A few stones, presumably originally celts, were found which showed signs of battering or pecking on both ends and, occasionally, along the edges.   Body surfaces were often polished.   One Mound III example (pl. 18, *f*) with battered ends exhibited signs of pecking on the beveled edges and had two very light grooves running diagonally across both faces and around the edges.   Another, apparently a well-smoothed river pebble roughly 10 cms. long, was flattened and pecked at both ends.

Points.—One red jasper point or drill 5 cms. long by 1 cm. wide was recovered from Level 7 of Trench 10.   Roughly chipped with triangular cross section (pl. 18, *i*), it resembles those illustrated by Lothrop for Veraguas (Lothrop, 1950, fig. 25, *c–e*).

Scrapers and chisels.—A chert chip which may have been utilized as a scraper (pl. 18, *h*) and a fragment of a stone chisel (pl. 18, *g*) with a roughly diamond-shaped cross section were found without pottery associations.

Rubbing stones.—A number of smoothed elongated stones with generally oval cross section and often made of a relatively soft stone (pl. 18, *j–n*) were scattered through the refuse.   Some showed definite signs of rubbing or polishing on one or more surfaces.   These ranged from 4–10 cms. in length and 2–3 cms. in thickness.   A few smoothed round stones of granite about 5 cms. in diameter, which may have been simply river worn, were recovered.

Jewelry.—The only stone jewelry consisted of jade or jadeite beads with straight circular shafts.   Four of these recovered with Macaracas pottery in Find 368 were tubular and ranged from 6–8 mm. in length, from 3–3.8 mm. in diameter, and from 1.5–1.8 mm. in shaft diameter. Four other jade beads with flat surfaces, trapezoidal shape, and lateral perforations were recovered at the site.   A typical bead measures 8×6×3 mm. and is 2 mm. thick.

WORKED BONE AND SHELL

Although limited in quantity, worked bone and shell at He-4 exhibited extremely fine carving and occurred in a variety of objects including necklace pieces, ceremonial batons and tubes, and earplugs or labrets. Bone tools recovered at He-4 were restricted to a gouge from Mound III (pl. 19, d) and a simple point or awl (pl. 19, i) without provenience within the site.

The earplugs or labrets (pl. 19, j–l) were all made from fish vertebrae and are generally uncarved although they may be polished. Angular geometric and swastika designs, similar to those on El Hatillo Polychrome pottery, are sometimes carved into the sides. Diameters range from 1.5–4 cms. Aside from one undecorated example from Find 10, and another from the fourth level of Trench 1, all of these were recovered under unstratified conditions in Mound III.

Also recovered from Mound III were three bone tubes (pl. 19, e, f, m); two are undecorated and the third exhibits a deep groove circumventing the tube near one end.

The most spectacular examples of excellent bone carving, the manatee bone batons of Find 10 (pl. 1, a, b, c), were associated with El Hatillo type, Jobo variety, pottery. Although most of these examples were found broken, one measured 49 cms. when restored to almost its full length. The carvings depict alligators and frogs and are done with amazing precision and delicacy. For example, the undamaged frog of plate 1, c, is only 2.3 cms. long. The grooves across its back are about 0.5 mm. in width, and appear, under magnification, to be entirely even and parallel. It is difficult to conceive of these objects being carved with aboriginal tools, but at present there is no evidence of European contact during the Herrera Phase.

Another bone baton, shaped like a ceremonial ax and intricately carved, was recovered with Find 376 (two gold disks), but unfortunately is so encrusted with calcified mud that the carving cannot be discerned.

Mention should be made here of the human tooth necklaces found with Finds 10, 14, and 347. The Find 10 necklace, which consists mainly of incisors perforated at the root, contains 737 teeth and is by far the largest of the group.

A few objects of worked shell were found at He-4 including a polisher or worn scraper and a number of elongated and perforated beads. The former (pl. 19, g), from Mound III and made from the shell of *Anadara grandis*, was worn smooth on one side and all edges, and had five V-shaped grooves worked into one of the upper edges. Roughly circular, the object has a diameter of 5.5 cms. and is 2 cms. thick.

The beads, encountered in Finds 361 and 381, were carved from

Spondylus shell, are perforated at one end, and range in length from 2.5–6 cms. (pl. 19, *n–v*).   In Find 381, this kind of shell bead necklace is associated with Macaracas type pottery.

SUMMARY

He-4 appears to be a ceremonial or cemetery site, probably with areas of occupation in the immediate vicinity as evidenced by the middenlike deposit excavated by Trench 10 on the North Ridge. Despite the fact that Mound IV and possibly Mound VI appeared to be occupational refuse, all the other mounds were apparently built of intentional fill.

The time span represented by the pottery at the site overlaps that of the Late Coclé Phase at Sitio Conte and extends into the Herrera Phase.   Although there is as yet no evidence of European contact, a carbon-14 date of 415±90 B.P., obtained by Philip L. Dade from a deep grave at the site, suggests an extremely late terminal date (Isotopes Inc. No. I-367, personal communication from Dr. Matthew W. Stirling).   The chronological interpretation presented here is based on: the scarcity of Early Coclé Phase pottery; the high frequency of Macaracas type pottery which also occurs in Late Coclé Phase graves at Sitio Conte; and the high frequency of Parita and El Hatillo type sherds and vessels which, on the basis of a combination of admittedly scanty stratigraphy and absence of grave or cache associations with the Macaracas type, are postulated as perhaps developing in the Late Coclé Phase but more definitely continuing after the Late Coclé Phase, at least at this site.   With regard to Early Coclé Phase ceramics, it will be recalled that only 49 Aristide group sherds were recovered and they were all of the Girón type (Interior Banded variety) which, while beginning in the Santa Maria Phase, extends into the subsequent Early Coclé Phase.   Of the 108 Coclé polychrome sherds recovered at He-4, although most are indeterminant, only a few are clearly Early and more are definitely Late. The indications are not as definite within the Smoked ware type, for a number of modified gutter rims (Platanillo variety, considered Early at He-1 and He-2) were found.   However, Sangre variety rims (Early and Late at He-1 and He-2) were also common and thus not at variance with a Late Coclé Phase interpretation.

Evidence of subsistence patterns is rare, but the shallow irregular metate stones of Mound I, the legs from ceremonial metates (Mound III), and the manos of Trench 9 and Mound III indicate a dependence on agriculture which could be reasonably postulated on the geographical affinities, high technical skill in ceramics, and Late time period. Although a small amount of unworked shell was present in Trench 10 (see Appendix 5, p. 268), shell was rarely found in the excavations, possibly because of the apparent ceremonial rather than occupational nature of the site. Both deer and bird bones, among others, were found, but only one projectile point, again from the Trench 10 midden, was recovered. A fairly large number of stone celts were excavated, but their probable functional range is so broad that their presence adds little information to our knowledge of their users' way of life. One probable spindle whorl, suggesting textile manufacture, was found.

Some of the mounds (Mound I; possibly Mounds VI and VII) seemingly were constructed in a number of stages. Others (Mounds II, III, and V) appear to have been built up in a single stage. Evidences of structures within the mounds are rare; fragments of burned floors were found in Mounds I and VII and a layer or "floor" of waterworn pebbles was encountered in Mound I. The latter was faced at one end with boulders. No postholes or wall remains were found and, in view of the apparent use of fire in connection with some of the burials, it is probable that the "burned floors" were related to burial ceremonies rather than to habitations or "temples."

Burial practices indicated at He-4 include the use of fire at some stage in the burial ceremony, cremation proper, and secondary urn burial. Spanish accounts attest to the practice of smoking or drying the bodies of high ranking individuals.[13] It is possible that the fragments of burned floor mentioned above, as well as the ash found with some caches and burials (Find 10-olla 2, Find 357, Find 382) and the interior fire blackening of some vessels (Finds 5-d, 6-b, 9-3, and 10-olla 2), may be related to this custom.

Examples of cremation definitely were present in Finds 347, 361, and 377, but unfortunately the furniture associations do not provide us with definite connections to polychrome styles. Find 347, four partially cremated individuals including at least one adult and one child, was accompanied by 51 pottery vessels of ubiquitous Red-buff shapes; class "a" collared jars, ring-based plates, and one low pedestal plate. Find 361 consisted of cremated human bone, several pieces of copper, and an elongated shell bead. Although the bead is probably the same as the shell beads of Find 381, the contents of the latter are not particularly helpful, consisting as they do of two small Red-buff collared jars (class "a"), fragments of gold-plated copper and some perforated gold disks. Find 377, although containing many vessels, is comprised largely of Red-buff ubiquitous shapes. The exception is a pyramid-shaped bottle with affinities to Ceritó and El Hatillo

---

[13] Lothrop (1937, pp. 43–48) notes that fire was used to desiccate the body of a deceased chief before placing in the house of the dead. Adrian de Santo Thomas, a Spanish priest who worked in the Tabasará River area of western Veraguas between 1622 and 1637, also reports the use of fire for "smoking" the bodies of high ranking personages before interment (Lothrop, 1950, p. 101). In neither instance are mounds mentioned.

shapes; thus probably post Late Coclé. The same Red-buff bottle shape, however, was found associated with Cuipo and Pica-pica varieties in Find 369. Fragments of a carved bone baton present in Find 377 are reminiscent of Find 10 with its Jobo variety ceramics.

Secondary urn burials (Finds 10, 14, 16, and 346) are associated with Pica-pica variety polychrome in one case, and in others with varieties of the El Hatillo type. Other secondary burials (not cremations) were represented by Finds 359, 368, 370, 372, 374, and 381, three of which contained Macaracus type polychromes.

Many of the burials were multiple, sometimes combining adults and children, a practice found both with urn burials and cremation. Find 10 contained the bodies of 15 individuals, at least 2 of whom were infants, Find 377 had 4 cremated bodies among which 1 adult and 1 child were recognizable, and Finds 372 and 370 each consisted of 2 adult skulls. This custom of partial burial was also indicated by Find 374 which contained the long bones of an adult, but no skull. Ollas 2 and 3 of Find 10 were crammed with bones but contained mandibles without calvaria.

Other noteworthy burial associations include the human tooth necklaces of Find 10 (Jobo Polychrome variety), Finds 14 and 347, and the carved bone batons of Finds 10, 348, and 377 (pl. 1, a–c). In addition, the practice of placing vessels in the ground in an inverted position was present in Finds 10 and 15–17. Vessels were found inside each other in Finds 5, 6, 8, and 9, and pottery covers were found in place in Find 10 and possibly Find 14.

Thus, the material remains at He-4 represent a culture or cultures in existence during the Late Coclé Phase at Sitio Conte and probably later. The inhabitants practiced agriculture, possessed highly-developed skills in ceramics, stone and bone jewelry, and metal work, practiced cremation, and erected burial mounds in which they placed their dead in urns or in other secondary burial forms.

GIRÓN (Co-2) SITE

SITE DESCRIPTION

The Girón site lies on the north bank of the Santa Maria River some 25 air kilometers north of the El Hatillo site and roughly midway between the latter and Sitio Conte. Excavations were made in April 1952, by Dr. Gordon R. Willey, Dr. Charles R. McGimsey,

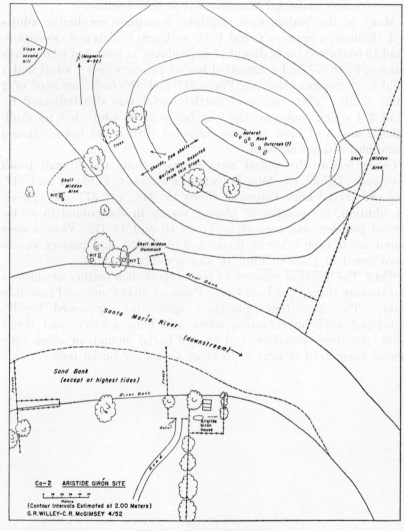

Map 2.—Girón (Co-2) site.

and Mr. James N. East, on the slopes and around the base of a low hill arising out of the broad alluvial plain, thus close to fertile agricultural areas. As it is only 7 air miles from the delta, the inhabitants also had nearby extensive resources of marine shellfish.

Physically, the site consists of three refuse piles around the base of the hill, one of which has been cut through by the river. Quoting from Willey and Stoddard (1954, p. 333):

In extent, this particular refuse hummock appears to be the smallest of the three, measuring not much more than 10 by 20 meters; but a full depth of 1.80 meters is shown in the riverbank. As there is a tremendous quantity of broken pottery in the mud and under the water at the foot of the bank, it is obvious that the deposit once extended farther out into what is now the river but has been carved away by the action of the stream. Viewed from the surface the refuse mound shows only as a slight eminence a few centimeters higher than the surrounding ground level; but the river-edge profile makes it evident that alluvial clays have been built up surrounding the shell and pottery heap until they almost, but not quite, cover it. Twenty meters west (upstream) or east (downstream) from this debris pile there is only a thin zone of shell midden, 30 centimeters thick, which is buried at a depth of 1.80 meters beneath the flood-carried clays. Apparently this represents the original ground level at the time of first occupation. The refuse pile must have been begun on this older level.

The other two refuse concentrations at Girón are larger in extent than the first. One lies off the northwest corner of the hill, 70 meters northwest of the first pile. The extent of this dump is at least 50 by 60 meters, and the one small test which we made in it showed 1.30 meters of refuse depth. The last midden area is over 200 meters northeast of the riverbank midden pile, and it extends over a diameter of more than 100 meters on the east slope and at the east foot of the hill. No tests were made in this section, but the surface mounding of shell suggests that it is at least 1.00 meter deep.

Turning to the excavations, three test pits were dug: Pit 1 in the riverbank refuse pile, the first midden described above; Pit 2 located 40 meters west of Pit 1 and 5 meters from the riverbank; and Pit 3 placed in the refuse pile at the northwest corner of the hill and about 100 meters northwest of Pit 2. Pit 1, a 3×3 meters cut excavated in 10 cm. levels, was carried down to a depth of 2.2 meters and proved to be the most rewarding of the three tests. The physical stratigraphy reflected by the profile chart consisted of four layers: an upper layer of gray humus with crushed shell extending to a depth of approximately 50 cms.; a second layer of brown sandy soil and shell extending from 50–90 cms.; a third strata of compact shell and brown clay extending from 90–165 cms.; and a fourth and final strata of dark red-brown alluvial clay. The top three layers contained considerable amounts of sherds. In fact, the three highest or peak frequencies of sherds recorded for the pit correspond roughly to the midpoint of each layer, but the final layer of red-brown clay contained negligible amounts of cultural refuse, and these in the upper 20 cms. only. Willey and

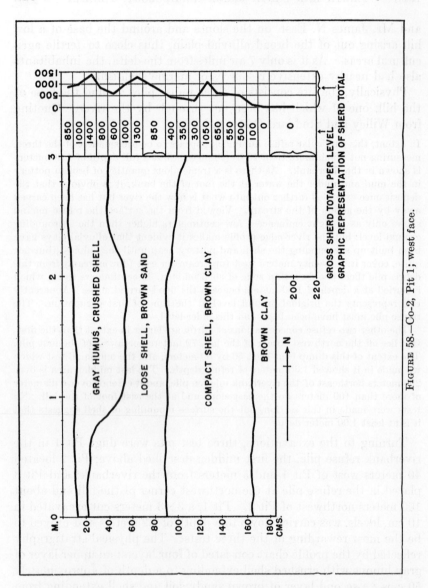

FIGURE 58.—Co-2, Pit 1; west face.

Stoddard (1954) note that the lower portion of the midden had obviously been infiltrated by river floods.

Referring to charts 8–11, it is evident that of the three main ceramic groups represented at the site, Azuero, Coclé, and Aristide, the latter was by far the most popular, particularly in the two middle strata. Coclé Polychrome is barely represented below the uppermost strata and even there comprises only 0.64 percent of the total. The Azuero

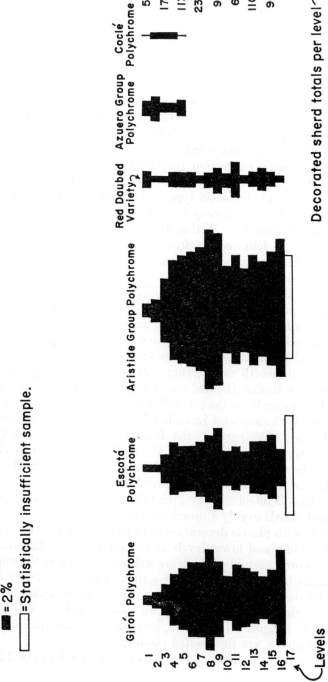

CHART 8.—Co-2, Pit 1; major decorated ceramic types and varieties.

group (represented almost entirely by Macaracas type sherds) is restricted to this strata but represents 3.19 percent of the total. The Aristide group, while maintaining a percentage of around 15 percent in the lower portion of the upper strata, is most heavily represented (22.37 percent) in the second or brown sandy layer. In the third layer it ranges from about 16–19 percent in the two lowest significant (in terms of total sherd numbers) levels, at 150–170 cms. Within the Aristide group, the frequencies of the two types, Girón and Escotá, parallel each other in gross distribution from top to bottom of the pit, especially if one ignores levels below 170 cms. where total sherd counts fall below 100. More Girón sherds (846) were found than Escotá (658).

There is some suggestion (chart 9) that the Banded Lip variety was relatively more popular in the upper levels than was the Interior Banded (both of the Girón type). In total number of sherds for the pit, the Banded Lip variety is represented by 590 as against 256 for the Interior Banded. Within the Escotá type, Black-on-buff with 313 sherds is followed in frequency by Black Crosshatched (192 sherds), Black-on-red (141 sherds), and by a negligible amount (12 sherds) of the Black Chevron variety. With regard to the temporal pattern of these varieties, it is difficult to draw specific conclusions except to point out that the Black-on-buff variety maintains relatively high frequencies in all three main strata, whereas Black Crosshatched and Black-on-red both have their highest proportions in the second and third strata below the surface.

It may be worth noting that within the Girón type Banded Lip variety, the Radial Banded subvariety was the most heavily represented (173 sherds for the pit) followed by Black Banded (114 sherds). Scalloped (112 sherds), Circumbanded (91 sherds) and Crosshatched (82 sherds). Temporally, the Radial Banded and Black Banded were relatively more popular in the middle and upper levels, Crosshatched in the upper levels, Scalloped in the lower levels, and Circumbanded in the middle and lower levels.

The Red Daubed variety maintained between 2 and 3 percent of the total sherds evenly throughout the pit.

Sherds with plastic decoration tend to be more heavily represented in the middle and lower levels of the pit with the exception of the Rough Scored examples which are well represented in the upper levels and attain higher frequencies there than in the lower levels (see chart 10). Of the five kinds of decoration separately recorded, Reed Punctation is clearly in the minority and occurs only in the uppermost 50 cms. of the pit. The others, with the exception of rough scoring as noted above, are distributed randomly.

Pit 2, another 3-meter square pit carried to a depth of 2.20 meters

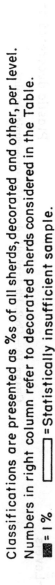

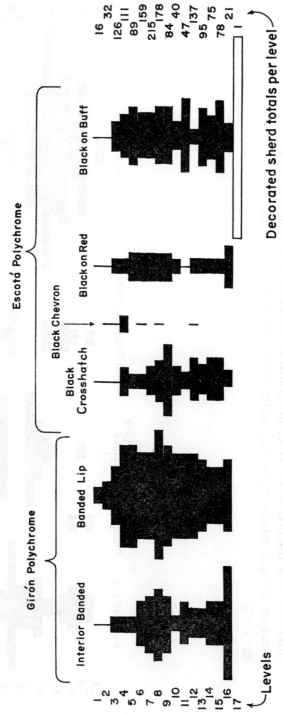

CHART 9.—Co-2, Pit 1; varieties of Aristide group polychromes.

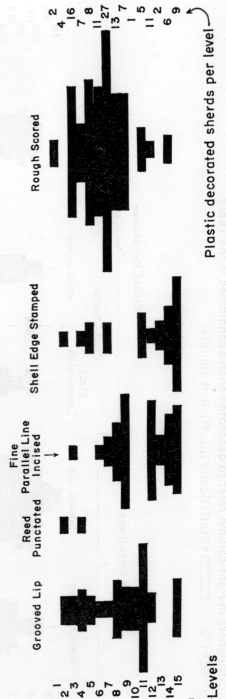

Classifications are presented as %s of all sherds, decorated and other, per level.
Numbers in right column refer to plastic decorated sherds per level.

■ = 0.1%

CHART 10.—Co-2, Pit 1; plastic decoration on ceramic remains.

yielded nothing of apparent stratigraphic significance. The top 80 cms. consisted of sterile red-brown river clay. Although the remaining 140 cms. contained sherds, these were badly eroded and probably deposited by the river, rather than as midden refuse. In any case, the total number of distinguishable typed painted sherds for the pit was only 62, far too few to allow any sort of significant comparison by level. Five plastic decorated sherds were recovered.

Pit 3, on the other hand, yielded some support for the general findings of Pit 1. This excavation, a 1-meter square test in the midden heap at the edge of the hill, was dug to a depth of 1.60 meters. The refuse composition has been described as much like that of Pit 1 with numerous shells and sherds down to 1.10 meters, fewer from 1.10–1.35 meters and nonexistent from 1.35–1.60 meters (sterile red-brown clay). The support for the stratigraphic evidence of Pit 1 lies in the fact that Azuero group or Coclé polychrome sherds were not found, but Red Daubed and both types of the Aristide group were. Apparently this pit corresponds to the middle and lower levels of Pit 1.

Reviewing the pit by type and variety, 87 sherds of the Escotá type were recorded (as against 69 for the Girón) with the following breakdown by variety: Black Crosshatch, 34 sherds; Black-on-buff, 30 sherds; Black-on-red, 23 sherds; and Black Chevron, no sherds. The Girón type is represented by 46 sherds of the Banded Lip variety and 23 of the Interior Banded variety. As may be seen from chart 11, there does not appear to be a meaningful pattern of frequency distribution. The Red Daubed variety was represented by 51 sherds randomly distributed.

Shells from Pit 1 (see Appendix 5, p. 268) were mainly oyster or clam. Although a formal count was not made, it was the excavators' impression that oysters were found in numerically greater proportions above the depth of 1 meter in Pit 1; i.e., in the upper two strata. The presence of mano and/or metate fragments indicates a shared dependence on corn as well as shellfish.

CERAMIC REMAINS

In preparing Willey and Stoddard's 1953 typological and statistical analysis for publication in the 1960's, two difficulties were encountered. First, the use of the name "Santa Maria," already fixed as a Phase title in the Panamanian archeological sequence for a pottery type, tends to confuse the temporally limited Phase with the particular class of pottery which may extend beyond the Phase limits. Secondly, on reexamination of the sample type collections in the light of similar pottery recovered at He-1 and He-2, it was apparent that instead of including all Santa Maria Polychrome under one classification, a more appropriate method would be to break it down into two

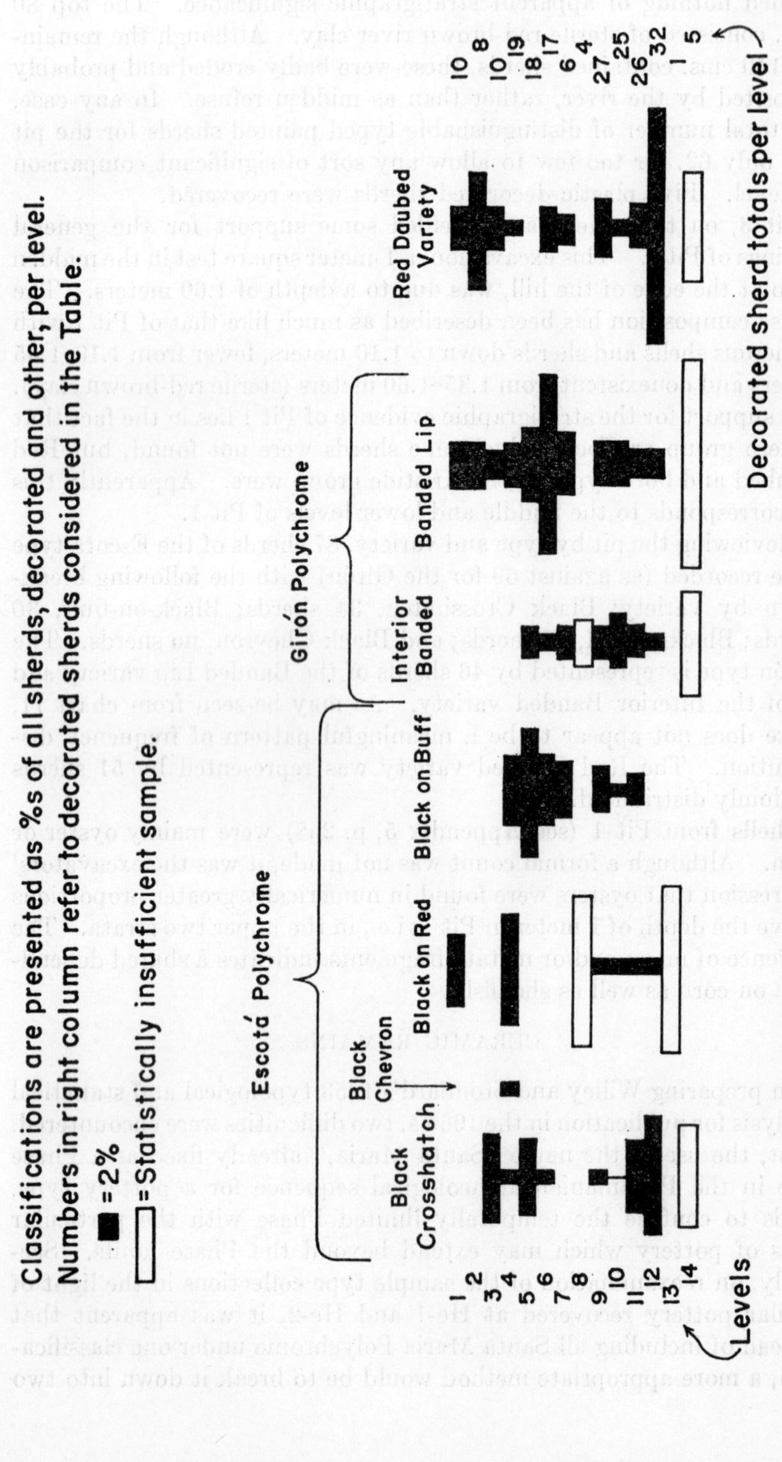
Classifications are presented as %s of all sherds, decorated and other, per level.
Numbers in right column refer to decorated sherds considered in the Table.
■ = 2%
□ = Statistically insufficient sample.
Escotá Polychrome
Girón Polychrome
Black Crosshatch
Black Chevron
Black on Red
Black on Buff
Interior Banded
Banded Lip
Red Daubed Variety
Levels
1 2 3 4 5 6 7 8 9 10 11 12 13 14
Decorated sherd totals per level
10 8 10 19 18 17 6 4 27 25 26 1 32 5

CHART 11.—Co-2, Pit 3, major decorated ceramic types and varieties.

types within a group, since one of these divisions or types was found without appreciable amounts of the other at the two Herrera sites. In view of these considerations the polychromes and associated red and plain pottery included under the Santa Maria label in 1954 (Willey and Stoddard) and in 1957 (Ladd) were reclassified into the two types, Girón Polychrome and Escotá Polychrome, as set forth below. In order to emphasize the essential similarity between these two types in terms of paste, general size, surface treatment, and decorative motifs, the concept of the pottery group was employed (Gifford, personal communication) and they were classed within an Aristide pottery group.

GIRÓN POLYCHROME; BANDED LIP VARIETY

CROSSHATCHED SUBVARIETY

Sample.—85 sherds.

Paste.—Paste is homogeneous with fine-grained temper of white, reddish, and dark particles. Pores are finer than the smallest particles. Fractures usually reveal negative impressions of particles. Structuring is rarely apparent, although it tends to be lamellar (parallel to the vessel surface) when present. Occasional larger particles of red hematite are found. Color of the paste is most commonly orange-yellow (Maerz and Paul, 1930, "cork," 12–B–7). Occasional dark fired zones occur on the interior, exterior, or both, and are usually brown (Maerz and Paul, "beaver," 15–A–6). These zones rarely approach blackness. Hardness ranges from 2.5–3 on Mohs' scale. Thickness ranges from 6–12 mm. with the average at about 8 mm.

Firing is generally uniform. Occasional sherds show thin surface layers darker than the rest. In a few sherds the dark fired zones may make up three-quarters of the sherd's thickness. Firing clouds appear frequently on the outside surface.

Shapes.—Open bowls, medium to deep. The largest vessel measured 43 cms. in diameter taken at the inside of the orifice. Lips are flat and wide (1–3.5 cms.) and are generally flanged either to the exterior or to both interior and exterior of the vessel. The upper surfaces are slightly rounded or flattened, generally on a more or less horizontal plane, or slanting slightly outward (fig. 59, *a–g*). Bases are unknown for this subvariety, but they are probably rounded.

Surface.—Decoration consists of black painted designs confined to the upper surface of the lip, except for an occasional slight extension over the inside of the lip (pl. 13, *f, g*). The design crosshachure is arranged within a subtriangular zone in which the truncated apex is pointed outward. The base of the triangle consists of a black band or line running along the interior edge of the lip. The crosshachure is limited laterally by the solid black borders of the enclosing triangle design. Lips and interiors of the vessel are usually red slipped, although occasional buff or possibly white slip ground colors occur on the lip. Exteriors of the vessels are buff, often with smearing and dribbles of the interior red slip extending down from the lip.

The design units were probably spaced equidistantly around the lip and arranged four to a vessel.

RADIAL BANDED SUBVARIETY

Sample: 189 sherds.

Paste.—Paste is somewhat more variable than the crosshatched subvariety, although most sherds fall within its range. There are a few, however, which

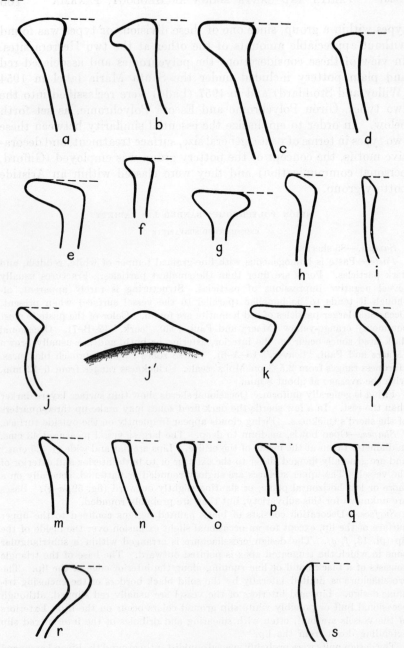

FIGURE 59.—Girón type, Banded Lip variety, vessel shapes. *a–g*, Crosshatched
subvariety; *a–j*, Radial Banded subvariety (*a–g*, both; *h–j'*, Radial Banded
alone); *c, e*, Circumbanded (rarely, *k–m*); *a–j'*, Black-Banded; *n–s*, Scalloped
(rarely, *j–j'*). All based on Willey Co-2 drawings.

have perceptible quantities of limestone or shell temper, and a few have large grains of hematite, as much as 2-3 mm. in diameter.

The color falls within the Crosshatched subvariety range except for a small group of sherds which have a lighter or darker salmon color (Maerz and Paul: "musk melon," 11–A–8; "persimmon," 6–E–12). The darker pastes are most frequently associated with unslipped, buff-colored sherds.

Hardness ranges from 3-4 on Mohs' scale with the average about 3.5. Thickness ranges from 5-13 mm. with modes at 6 and 8 mm. Firing is generally uniform but dark cores or darkened edges occur.

Shapes.—Medium deep to medium shallow open bowls ranging in interior orifice diameter from 12-40 cms. Lips are often flanged on the exterior. Some have a slight interior flange (fig. 59, *h–j*), but otherwise fall within the rim form range of the Crosshatched subvariety. Occasionally they exhibit "ears" or painted exterior flanging (fig. 59, *j, j'*).

Surface.—All interior surfaces are smooth with a burnished appearance. Exterior surfaces are usually smooth, but less careful work has often left granular areas. Virtually all interiors are covered with a red slip, often light enough to be termed a wash (Maerz and Paul: "nasturtium," 4–I–12; "Spanish cedar," 6–J–10). On a few salmon-colored sherds (Maerz and Paul, 12–D–8), the red paint occupies a circumferential zone of variable width below the lip exterior. Exterior surfaces are more variable; a few are slipped, but mere streaks or daubed areas are the rule. Smoke clouds appear frequently on the exteriors, rarely on the interiors.

Design units are subtriangular zones, probably four to a vessel, in which the truncated apex generally points out. In those cases where the apex points in, the ground is always buff rather than red. These subtriangular zones are bordered by solid black triangles which are connected by a continuous black line along the interior edge of the lip. The designs within the subtriangular zones consist of parallel black lines arranged parallel to the radius of the vessel, or transversely across the lip. The black decoration occasionally extends over the lip edges and the lines are rather unevenly drawn (see pl. 13, *a, b, e*).

CIRCUMBANDED SUBVARIETY

Sample.—93 sherds.

Paste.—Falls within the range of the two previous subvarieties except that it is somewhat harder, ranging 3.5-4 on Mohs' scale.

Shapes.—Deep and shallow bowls, primarily with rim forms "*c*" and "*e*" of figure 59. Three additional rare rim shapes, including a collar rim, are illustrated in figure 59, *k–m*.

Surface.—Surfaces are generally the same as in the two previous subvarieties with respect to color and type of finish. The decoration in this subvariety, however, consists of two to five parallel black lines arranged circumferentially around the lip (pl. 13, *c*). The latter may be either buff or red slipped. Eight sherds are treated with shell edge stamping on the outside edge of the lip.

BLACK BANDED SUBVARIETY

Sample.—117 sherds.

Paste.—Same as previous subvarieties.

Shapes.—Same as previous subvarieties.

Surface.—A single black line along the inner edge of the lip and/or part of a black triangle pattern. Since both of these elements occur in the Radial Banded and Crosshatched subvarieties, this group will be treated as a residual category.

Sample.—133 sherds

Paste.—Same as previous subvarieties.

Shapes.—Moderately deep bowls almost always with an unthickened or slightly thickened rim and a horizontally flattened lip (fig. 59, *n*). Various types of flange (fig. 59, *o–r*) occur rarely as do occasional "ski-tip" lips (fig. 59, *s*). One example with a horizontal pointed projection (fig. 59, *j, j*) was found.

Surface.—The surface treatment is the same as the previous subvarieties except that the painted decoration is in the form of a black band on the inner edge of the lip with lobes extending outward giving a scalloped effect   (pl. 13, *d*).

Sample.—3 sherds.

Paste.—Same as the previous subvarieties.

Shapes.—Deep bowls with everted lips.

Surface.—Same as the previous subvarieties except for the decoration which consists of shallow, three or four line chevrons with the apex pointing outward, as in figure 60, *d*.

Geographical Range.—Sherds of this variety have been recovered in the Parita area (He-1, He-2, He-4) and at Sitio Conte (Lothrop, 1942, figs. 234, 239, *a*; Ladd, 1957) as well as at Venado Beach on large bowls with everted lips (Peabody Mus. cat. No. 15–25–20/20–29–6 and other vessels). It is probable that a more detailed study of both varieties of the Girón type would allow a clearer and more stable division of the varieties with a resultant clarification of their temporal and geographical distribution. At the present time, however, one can make the broad statement that open bowls with black geometric designs over a red, buff, or buff-white slip on the flattened lip occur from the Panama Canal Zone to the base of the Azuero Peninsula and possibly over a considerable span of time. I know of no examples in Veraguas or further west and north.

Chronological position.—As indicated above, the chronological position is still vague. Vessels which could be assigned to this variety occurred in both Late Period (Grave 26) and Early Period (Grave 2) graves at Sitio Conte (Lothrop, 1942, fig. 234). Aristide group sherds, including those of the present variety, underlay and, to some extent, overlapped Coclé polychrome in Trench 11 at the same site (Ladd, 1957). At He-1 and He-2, sherds of both Girón type varieties were recovered, but the stratigraphic relationship to Coclé and Azuero types is confusing. Within the type, however, the relationship between the two varieties at He-1 was consistent. In all three relevant excavation units the Banded Lip variety dropped in frequency from the lower to the upper levels and the Interior Banded variety increased in relative popularity from lower to upper. This relationship is the reverse of that holding at the Girón site, although the indications at the latter are not as definite as at He-1.

Stratigraphic conditions at He-2 did not warrant analysis. How-

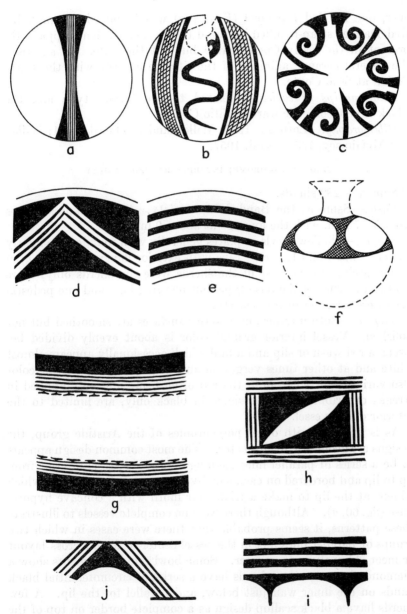

FIGURE 60.—Girón and Escotá type design elements. *a,* Girón Interior banded, design inferred from Co-2 sherds; *b,* Girón Interior banded, serpent design, Find 8 from He-2; *c,* Girón Interior banded, scroll design, Find 5-*a* from He-2; *d,* Girón Banded lip, chevron design; *e,* Girón Interior banded, circumferential banding; *f,* Escotá Crosshatched, hourglass design reconstructed from Co-2 sherds; *g–j,* Escotá Black on red elements, from Co-2 sherds 1–4.

ever, one Banded Lip bowl (Find 1–*a*) was found with a probable Red Daubed strap-handled jar (Find 1–*b*), a shape which is apparently present in the Early Coclé Period but not the Late. In addition, the general ceramic affinities of the site are entirely with the Early Period at Sitio Conte.

Relationships of variety.—Related to the Escotá type and the Black Line Geometric ware at Sitio Conte.

Bibliography.—Lothrop, 1942; Willey and Stoddard, 1954; Willey and McGimsey, 1954; Ladd, 1957.

GIRÓN POLYCHROME; INTERIOR BANDED VARIETY

Sample.—282 sherds.

Paste.—Same as the Banded Lip variety. Rim thickness ranges from 5–17 mm. with the average at about 9 mm.

Shapes.—Shallow bowls or plates generally with rounded or slightly flattened lips (fig. 61, *a–c*). Lips with exterior flanging (fig. 61, *d, e*) occur rarely. Since most of the sherds were rim sherds only, there is little evidence of the base type, but one ring base and one pedestal base were assigned to this variety.

Surface.—Both interior and exterior surfaces are smoothed but not polished. Vessel interior ground color is about evenly divided between a red wash or slip and a buff which occasionally appears almost white and at other times verges on an orange shade. Exterior color also varies from red to buff, the red often being unevenly applied in streaks or dribbles. The designs, in black only, are limited to the interior of the vessel.

As is the case with other polychromes of the Aristide group, the designs are geometric in character. The most common design appears to be a series of parallel lines running across the vessel interior from lip to lip and bordered on each side by a somewhat broader line which widens at the lip to make a triangular motif with a concave hypotenuse (fig. 60, *a*). Although there were no complete vessels to illustrate these patterns, it seems probable that there were cases in which two groups of parallel lines met in the vessel center to form a cross layout or meet obliquely in the center. Some bowl center fragments show a diamond element, other sherds have a series of circumferential black bands on the inner wall just below, and parallel to, the lip. A few sherds have a black scallop design as a complete border on top of the lip, but this is an uncommon motif. Examples of Interior Banded vessels from other sites are illustrated in plate 10, *a, b*.

Geographical range.—This variety is not illustrated for Sitio Conte, but it may have been present in the sherd lots. It is present at Venado Beach (Peabody Mus. cat. Nos. 51–25–20/20342, 20717, 20840, and possibly others) although the specific associations of these sherds and

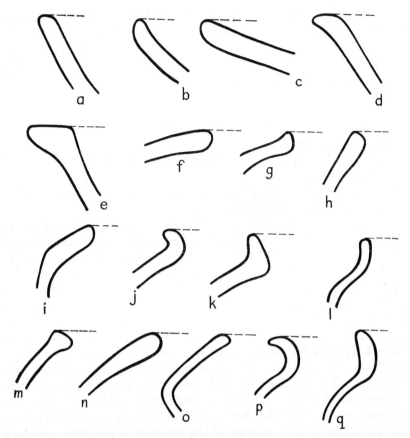

FIGURE 61.—Girón polychrome vessel shapes from Co-2.   a–e, Interior banded
variety (d–e are rare); f–l, Girón plain; m–q, Girón red.

vessels await publication of the report on that site.   It was, moreover,
the dominant variety within the Girón type at both He-1 and He-2
and was represented at the latter site by two complete vessels (Finds
5–a and 8) as well as by sherds.   No instances that I know of have
been reported from Veraguas or Chiriquí, but Linné (1929, fig. 24) and
Cruxent (1958, pl. 13) illustrate examples from the Pearl Islands and
the Gulf of San Miguel respectively.   Thus, the variety as known at
the present time has a southerly and easterly distribution.

Chronological position.—As is the case with the Banded Lip variety,
the Interior Banded variety also apparently was popular both before
the Early Period at Sitio Conte and during it, a conclusion based on its
relative position at the Girón site and at He-1 and He-2.   There is a
clear indication at He-1 that the Interior Banded variety reached its
peak of popularity after the Banded Lip had begun to decline, but
the stratigraphic situation at the Girón site suggests the opposite.

Relationships of variety.—Besides its obvious relationships to the Escotá type and Lothrop's Black Line Geometric ware, the general technique of simple black geometric designs on red-slipped bowl interiors is also present in the Black-on-red ware bowl illustrated by Lothrop (Lothrop, 1942, fig. 277, *b*) for Sitio Conte.

Bibliography.—See the Banded Lip variety.

GIRÓN TYPE; PLAIN VARIETY

Sample.—175 sherds.

Paste.—This variety is a residual category for buff, reddish, and grayish unslipped ware.

Shapes.—Globular or subglobular jars with constricted orifices and little or no rim modification (fig. 61, *f–l*).

Appendages and construction.—Ring bases, probably for plates or shallow bowls. Pedestal bases of varying heights from a minimum of 2.2 cm; at least one had a flanged foot or rim. Adornos affixed to the vessel wall included a free-standing human or monkey figure with head missing, and three small buttonlike nodes with incised and modeled faces. Lugs were of both the flattened flange type (occurring just below the rim and roughly triangular in shape when viewed from above) and the node type. The latter range in length from 1.2–4 cms. Loop handles are the most common in this plain ware, strap handles are much rarer, and a few ropelike loop handles were also recovered. Vessel shapes to which these were attached are unknown.

Geographical range.—Like many other presumably utilitarian undecorated wares, both the Red and Plain varieties of the Girón type are difficult to identify because of the ubiquity of the forms and lack of distinctive features. For instance, the two Plain Buff ware collared jars illustrated by Lothrop (Lothrop, 1942, fig. 336, *a*, *b*) might or might not be classified as Girón Plain although they come from a Late Period grave. At He-4 practically all the plain ware was so eroded that it is impossible to say whether the vessels originally had a red slip or no slip at all. However, ropelike loop handles were found there, but always in red slipped ware and in some cases clearly as part of the Delgado Red collarless jar assemblage. Major categories of plain ware did not emerge at either of the He-1 or He-2 sites. At the present time one can only say that Girón Plain cannot be definitely identified beyond the Girón site.

Chronological position.—At the Girón site, this variety showed a definite increase in the upper levels, and thus would be equated with the appearance of Coclé and Azuero polychromes.

Relationships of variety.—The collarless constricted orifice jars of this variety are similar in shape to those of the Delgado Red type.

Bibliography.—See the Banded Lip variety.

GIRÓN TYPE; RED VARIETY

Sample.—285 sherds.

Paste.—Same as that of the other Girón varieties except somewhat harder, rating at 5–6 on Mohs' scale. Thickness ranges from 4–9 mm. with the average at about 6 mm. The firing is generally uniform although a few sherds have dark cores.

Shapes.—The predominant shape is a constricted orifice jar with or without small out-curving collars. Rims are illustrated in figure 61, *m–q*. Large jars are rare; small and medium sizes are more characteristic. Occasionally loop handles, horizontally placed, are present. Strap handles are rare.

Other, unknown, shapes are suggested by the presence of small conical feet or legs and fragments of pedestal bases. A red slipped spout was also classified with this variety.

Surface.—Interiors are smoothed and are often fire clouded. Exteriors are smoothed, burnished, and are covered with a red slip which usually reaches the lip, but does not extend over into the interior. There is no decoration.

Geographical range.—The comments made in connection with the Girón Plain variety pertain here with the addition that this variety is so similar to the Delgado Red type in shape and exterior decoration that the two cannot be distinguished on the basis of photographs alone.

Chronological position.—This variety, like the Plain variety, also appeared in definitely higher frequencies in the uppermost levels of Pit 1 at the Girón site, along with the Coclé and Azuero polychromes.

Relationships of variety.—The variety shares collared jars and collarless constricted orifice jars with horizontal loop handles with the Delgado Red type, thus demonstrating affinities with the Azuero group.

Bibliography.—Same as that for the Girón type, Banded Lip variety.

ESCOTÁ POLYCHROME; BLACK-ON-RED VARIETY

Sample.—170 sherds.

Paste.—Temper consists of fine white particles of crushed quartz with occasional larger hematite particles. The paste is generally fired a brown color, although gray cores occur, and has a slightly contorted appearance. Hardness ranges between 3 and 4 on Mohs' scale, and the thickness ranges from 6–12 mm.

Shapes.—Three main shapes are noted for this variety. Large collared jars are the most common form. These have angled shoulders and tall, straight, flaring collars with lips which are rounded or slightly flanged (fig. 62, *a*). Dimensions on the larger examples of this form

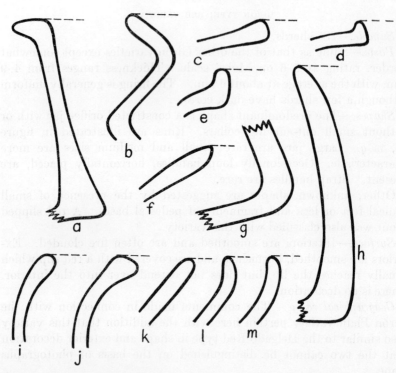

FIGURE 62.—Escotá type vessel shapes from Co-2. *a–e*, Black on red; *f–h*, Crosshatched; *a, h, i, j*, Black on buff; *k–m*, Chevron. All based on Willey Co-2 drawings.

reach a shoulder diameter of 40 cm., a collar height of 14.5 cm., and an orifice diameter of 11 cm. The body below the shoulder angle appears to be rounded, although no actual bases were identified. Globular or subglobular bowls with unmodified or slightly folded rims also occur (fig. 62, *c–e*) as do wide-mouthed bowls with angled shoulders and sharply out-flared rims (fig. 62, *b*). One pedestal base was classified with this variety.

Surface.—The vessel exterior is usually red (either a slip or wash), while the untreated interior retains the buff to buff-brown color of the paste. Decoration, limited generally to the upper exterior portion of the vessel, is done in black paint.

Four design arrangements are noted.

The first arrangement is composed of parallel lines which encircle the shoulder just below the juncture of collar and body (fig. 60, *g*). These are bordered at the top by a broad black band, 1 cm. or a little more in width. Three to five of these lines may be grouped together, the bottom line bordered with small black triangles, then a vacant space followed by another group of parallel encircling lines, the uppermost of which is also bordered with the small triangles. Variations on this theme include broken or dashed horizontal lines. On a few sherds, the horizontal groups of lines are carried up onto the collar.

Groups of horizontal lines, beginning below the collar and separated by a field of vertical lines, comprise the second arrangement. Leaf-shaped elements often are expressed negatively in the rectangular fields of black appearing between the vertical lines (fig. 60, *h*). This leaf-shaped element within a black rectangular field is especially common at the Venado Beach site. Occasionally the bottom horizontal line will be decorated with triangular appendages.

Another arrangement consists of trianguloid elements pendent from broad black bands at the collar base (fig. 60, *i*).

Still another motif is a chevron panel composed of nested triangles of black lines (fig. 60, *j*).

Geographical range.—The exterior-decorated bowls and jars of all varieties of the Escotá type appear at the present time to be limited to the Coclé, Santa Maria River, and Canal Zone areas of Panama. A few Escotá type sherds were recovered at He-1, none at He-2, and I know of none from farther west or north. The Black-on-red variety and/or the Black-on-buff variety is illustrated for Sitio Conte, however (Lothrop, 1942, fig. 236), and some of the designs, especially the leaf-shaped element as mentioned above, are very common at the Venado Beach site, e.g., on the shoulders of two jars with tall collars (Peabody Mus. cat Nos. 51–25–20/20373 and 51–25–20/10370) among others.

Chronological position.—Although two of the fragments illustrated by Lothrop came from an unstratified cache at Sitio Conte, the third (fig. 236, *b*), which is a clear example of the leaf-shaped motif mentioned above, came from the Late Period Grave 26. On the other hand, the situation at both the Girón site and Trench 11 of Sitio Conte suggests an earlier chronological position, before the development of Coclé Polychrome, and only possibly during its earlier stages. In addition, at both the He-1 and He-2 sites, where the Girón type was the dominant polychrome in the sherd lots, the Escotá type was either barely present or missing. This may be due either to contemporary differences in regional preference, or to the fact that the Escotá type had largely dropped out of use by the time of the He-1, He-2 occupations, while the closely related Girón type continued on in popularity.

Relationships of variety.—In form, that is collared globular or sub-globular jars, occasionally with angled shoulders, and bowls with incurved rims, the decorated varieties of the Escotá type bear similarities to the later Azuero group as well as to the Late Period Coclé jars.

Bibliography.—See Girón type, Banded Lip variety.

ESCOTÁ POLYCHROME; CROSSHATCHED VARIETY

Sample.—266 sherds.

Paste.—Same as the Black-on-red variety.

Shapes.—Like the Black-on-red variety, the most common shape is that of the large collared jar with angled shoulder and a tall, straight, flaring collar. Another form is the simple collarless jar (or bowl; the orifice is very wide) with an incurved rim and unmodified lip. One sherd with an apparently recurved collar (the lip or upper portion was missing) was found (fig. 62, *f–h*).

Surface.—The surface has a chalky feel and is well smoothed on the exterior to a dull rather than a polished finish. The interior often shows prominent scrapings or striations. Shoulders are generally buff in ground color; collar exteriors and interiors, and the body below the shoulder, are covered with a thin red wash or slip. This red wash may stop about three-quarters of the way down the interior of the collar. The most common buff shade corresponds to plate 13, 7–D, "oak-buff," with a range B to H and 8 to 6 in the Maerz and Paul color chart. The red slip of the collar and vessel base corresponds to Maerz and Paul's "Korean red," plate 5, J–11 and "Moroccan red," plate 5, K–11.

The decoration is limited to the upper half of the vessel body and consists of black crosshachure in hourglass-shaped elements. Generally a black line encircles the vessel at the juncture of neck and body forming a border between the red wash of the collar and the buff of the upper body. Another similar black line or band encircles the body at the shoulder angle, forming a border between the buff and the red of the lower body. The hourglass-shaped elements (probably two, although possibly four) occur between these two borders and are connected to them with the vertical axis of the hourglass running parallel to the vertical axis of the vessel (fig. 60, *f*).

Geographical range.—In general, the comments made about the Black-on-red variety hold for the present one with the exception of the Venado Beach site where this variety does not appear to be as common as the former. An example of this variety at Sitio Conte is illustrated in Lothrop, 1942, figure 237.

Chronological position.—It is probably the same as that for the Black-on-red variety. The Crosshatched variety vessel illustrated by Lothrop for Sitio Conte (Lothrop, 1942, fig. 237) came from Cache 7, an undated cache, the illustrated vessels of which are Escotá, Girón (ibid., fig. 239, *a*), or plastic decorated ware (ibid., fig. 345, *g*).

Relationships of variety.—See the Black-on-red variety.

Bibliography.—See the Girón type, Banded Lip variety.

ESCOTÁ POLYCHROME; BLACK-ON-BUFF VARIETY

Sample.—343 sherds.

Paste.—Same as Black-on-red variety.

Shapes.—Two shapes occur in this variety: (*a*) large collared jars with straight flaring high collars and angled shoulders (fig. 62, *a*, *h*) though not as sharply angled as those of the Crosshatched variety and (*b*) smaller bowls with incurved rims and generally unmodified lips (fig. 62, *i*, *j*).

Surface.—The ground color of the shoulder or upper portion of the vessel body is of a buff which sometimes approaches a white shade. The body below the shoulder may be buff, but is more often covered with a red wash. A black line often encircles the vessel, forming a border between the buff and the red. Designs on this buff ground are in black line and sometimes red and include:

1. A broad red horizontal band at the top of the design zone under which is arranged a series of two to four narrow black horizontal lines with black triangles pendent from the lowest line. These black lines may be arranged in vertical or diagonal groups below the collar, or in such a way as to form a chevronlike zone. Occasionally, a black line from the apex of the triangle will be extended down to join the shoulder border.

2. A row of small black squares may be interspersed between the parallel horizontal black lines.

3. Negatively expressed leaf-shaped elements framed in black occur.

4. Vertical lines occur rarely on the collar exterior.

5. Rows of parallel horizontal black lines may occur below the rim, generally accompanied by a black line on the lip.

6. Other miscellaneous elements which occur are black double spirals, a series of black and white diamonds, and spear point elements.

Geographical range.—See comments for Black-on-red variety.

Chronological position.—Probably the same as the Black-on-red variety.

Relationships of variety.—See comments for the Black-on-red variety. Actually, these two are so close in design and form that they might well be classed as one variety.

Bibliography.—Same as that for the Black-on-red variety.

ESCOTÁ POLYCHROME; CHEVRON VARIETY

Sample.—13 sherds.

Paste.—Same as Black-on-red variety.

Shapes.—Bowls or jars with incurving rims and unmodified to slightly pointed lips (fig. 62, *k–m*).

Surface.—Design area surfaces are well smoothed and have a low polish. The vessel exteriors are red slipped (or wash) except for the design area which remains a buff. Lips are covered with the same red wash which sometimes extends well down into the vessel interior. Red hues vary from a light red (Maerz and Paul, "nasturtium," plate 4, I–12) to deeper colors (Maerz and Paul, "Korean" or "Moroccan," plate 5, J–11, K–11). Below the red lip band a broad (4–6 cms.) black band encircles the vessel. Within this black band are long (6–11 cms. in horizontal length) buff chevron designs that take up most of the width of the band.

Geographical range.—Lothrop does not illustrate any vessels with the chevron design of this variety although there may have been some sherds present at Sitio Conte, and it apparently was not present at the Venado Beach site. It appears that this variety, also missing at He-1 and He-2 and with minimal occurrence at the Girón site, was neither widespread nor long lasting. I do not know of any reports of its presence to the west or north.

Chronological position.—In the light of the evidence of Pit 1 at the Girón site, the variety's existence was probably short and relatively late in the Escotá time span (see chart 9).

Relationships of variety.—Although the chevron motif is a common one in most complexes of pottery characterized by geometrical designs, there do not appear to be any significant relationships outside of the Escotá type.

Bibliography.—Same as that for the Black-on-red variety.

ESCOTÁ TYPE; RED VARIETY

Sample.—1,044 sherds.

Paste.—Temper and general characteristics are the same as that for the polychrome except that the Red variety rates as somewhat harder, between 4 and 5 on Mohs' scale.

Shapes.—The shapes include: deep bowls with everted lips (fig. 63, *a–c*); high collared jars (fig. 63, *i*); short, everted collared jars (fig. 63, *d, h*); open bowls or plates with unmodified lips (fig. 63, *j–l*); open bowls or plates with flanged lips (fig. 63, *e–g*); and various minor rim and lip forms as illustrated in figure 63, *m, n*.

Surface.—Both interior and exterior surfaces are usually smoothed and plate and collar interiors have a burnished appearance. The red slip used on both interior and exterior surfaces is very thin, almost a wash, and was applied unevenly so that the basic paste color shows through in streaks.

Often the red slip is applied selectively, only as far as lip edges or only on the interior or exterior rather than both surfaces. Occasionally it is limited to the lip, or a band extending just below the lip.

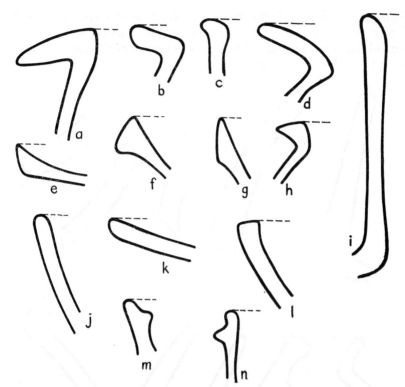

FIGURE 63.—Escotá red type vessel shapes from Co-2.   *a–c*, type 1; *i*, type 2; *d, h*, type 3; *j–l*, type 4; *e–g*, type 5; *m–n*, type 6.   All based on Willey Co-2 drawings.

Geographical range.—Because of the general lack of distinguishing features (rims only are distinctive, and even they, as in the case of the unmodified lip, may blend into many other utilitarian wares), both this variety and the Escotá Plain are difficult to place geographically. There are no clear examples illustrated in Lothrop for Sitio Conte, nor do I know of any from any site other than the Girón.

Chronological position.—Presumably the same as the decorated Escotá varieties.

Relationships of variety.—None in particular outside of the Aristide group, with the exception of one "Late" rim form (fig. 63, *g*) which could be a prototype for the "drooping lip" of the Coclé Red ware.

Bibliography.—Same as for the decorated varieties of the type.

ESCOTÁ TYPE; PLAIN VARIETY

Sample.—476 sherds.

Paste.—In general characteristics such as temper, hardness, and color, the paste is the same as that for the other Escotá varieties.

Thickness varies with the vessel size from over 1 cm. thick in the larger vessels to as thin as 5 mm. in the smaller ones. Surface smoothing is not as noticeable, except for some of the smaller vessels, as in the polychrome varieties.

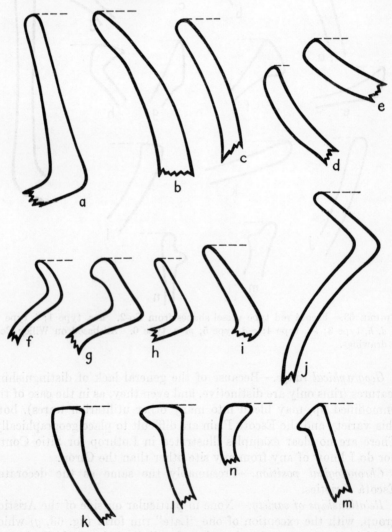

FIGURE 64.—Escotá plain type vessel shapes from Co-2. *a–c*, Type 1; *f–j*, type 2; *d–e*, type 3; *k–n*, type 4. All based on Willey Co-2 drawings.

Shapes.—Characteristic shapes include:

Large globular jars with tall out-flared collars (fig. 64, *a–c*). Orifices on these vessels run 20–25 cms., and diameters must be at least 40 cms. Average collar height is 10 cms.

Small globular or subglobular vessels with short, everted collars (fig. 64, *f–j*) and orifices which run about 10 cms. in diameter, sometimes up to 20 cms.;

Shallow bowls or plates, usually with unmodified rims (fig. 64, *d, e*); and

Medium to deep steep-sided bowls with thickened or flanged lips (fig. 64, *k–n*).

Appendages.—Two lugs about 6 cms. long by 2.5 cms. in diameter, one with deep incisions along one side, were assigned to this variety but their position on the vessel is not known.

Geographical range and chronological position.—See comments for the Escotá Red variety.

Relationships of variety.—None outside of the Aristide group.

Bibliography.—Same as for the decorated varieties of the type.

Plastic decoration.—In addition to the polychrome, red, and plain or buff pottery already discussed, a number of plastic decorative techniques were utilized on Girón site wares similar to the Escotá type.

1. Lip grooving. 27 sherds with this type of decoration were recovered. The decoration occurs on the upper surface of the everted lips of bowls or jars and consists of three or four deep (1–2 mm.) and wide (2–3 mm.) parallel grooves encircling the orifice. In rare instances the grooves are radially placed about the lip. They are usually smoothly executed, although on occasion the clay is piled up along the edges. Often the lips are grooved only, in other cases the following additional plastic techniques were combined with the grooving (pl. 14, *g, p*): reed punctation, that is, incised circles about 1 cm. in diameter and deeply impressed; deep angular punctations; a combination of "b" and buttonlike applique pellets with a central punctation placed between the grooves; the punctated buttonlike pellets alone; and a combination of "a" and "b."

2. Broad line incision. The two sherds found with this type of decoration were apparently from subglobular bowls or jars with incurved rims. The grooves, 2–3 mm. wide and 1–2 mm. deep, are 3–7 mm. apart placed vertically on the vessel below a red rim band. They are apparently part of a pattern, since they do not continue around the entire vessel (pl. 14, *j*).

3. Fine parallel line incision. 26 sherds with this type of decoration were recovered, all from small collared jars with short outcurving collars. The lines are rather unevenly done and irregularly spaced, from 2–13 mm. apart. In most cases they are arranged vertically beginning shortly below the rim and extending down beyond the collar. One case of zoning was found in which a panel of diagonal lines was bordered by two panels, one with vertical lines and one vacant. Red paint occurred on two of the sherds in bands, and one sherd combined two horizontal lines with the usual vertical arrangement (pl. 14, *f*).

4. Lip engraving. The few sherds decorated in this manner were all of well-smoothed and polished buff ware with a horizontally flattened lip, flanged to the outside and probably belonging to a large bowl. The engraved lines are arranged radially on the upper surface of the lip in groups of seven or eight and are irregularly spaced and unevenly executed (pl. 14, *d*).

5. Rough scoring. Three shapes were represented among the 67 sherds found with rough scoring: large jars with tall outflaring collars; shallow bowls or plates; and bowls with incurving sides. The scoring appears on the interiors and on collar

exteriors and appears to have been made with some sort of fiber or grass brush. It is fine to coarse and generally applied in a horizontal direction, although occasional diagonal brushings are found. Scoring or brushing of this sort has been noted for the Red Line type, especially the Red Daubed variety as represented at He-1 and He-2, and was often associated on individual sherds with red smeared paint similar in appearance to that of the Red Daubed variety (pl. 14, *i*).

6. Punctation. The few sherds with plain punctation include only one rim sherd, probably from a collared jar, thus little can be said about vessel forms associated with this decoration. The punctations occur on buff-colored sherds, are very deep, in some cases extending through the body wall; and are dotlike in shape with diameters of 2–3 mm. They are arranged in vertical rows about 2 cms. apart (pl. 14, *c*).

7. Reed punctation. In addition to occurring on the lips of bowls and jars in combination with lip grooving, reed punctation also occurs on the exterior of collared jar sherds. In these cases the punctations are arranged in a field or zone below deep groove incision. Rim sherds in this instance often have red bands on the lips (pl. 14, *g*, *m*).

8. Fingernail punctation. The one sherd with this type of decoration is part of the rim of a bowl or jar with incurving sides. The sherd is red slipped. About 2 cms. below the lip on the vessel exterior are two parallel rows, horizontally placed, of what appear to be fingernail punctations (pl. 14, *e*).

9. Slash punctation. Two of the sherds decorated in this manner are tall collar sherds; other information on form is lacking. The punctations are elongated jabs or slashes, generally arranged in vertical rows below the lip (pl. 14, *a*).

10. Linear punctation. One red-slipped rim sherd with a horizontally flattened lip had rows of semicontinuous shallow punctations arranged diagonally across the lip. They give the appearance of having been executed with a toothed implement (pl. 14, *l*).

11. Shell edge stamping. Fifteen sherds are recorded with this form of decoration including two recognizable shapes: a pedestal base, and a jar form with a short outcurving collar. Some of the sherds are red slipped. On the pedestal, the shell edge stamping is arranged in three vertical bands of two rows each (each impression is also oriented vertically), the bands separated by scored panels. A collar sherd shows horizontal rows of vertically placed shell edge impressions; others are stamped on the shoulder, again in horizontal rows. Shell edge stamping also occurred on the exterior of a medium-sized red-banded open bowl (pl. 14, *h*).

12. Applique ridge. One small buff sherd with a short applique ridge about 6 mm. high and 6 mm. wide was recovered (pl. 14, *k*).

13. Applique ridge with notching. At least four sherds with notched applique ridges, generally 6 mm. wide by 2 mm. high, were recovered. All were buff ware and one showed traces of red paint. The ridges are generally applied in parallel and are transversely gashed at closely spaced intervals (pl. 14, *b*). These gashes or notches are sometimes quite open and jagged. Dot punctation was combined with the ridges on one sherd.

14. Pinching. Five sherds were found with raised clay triangular or cuneiform shapes applied in rows. These appear sometimes as though the potter had pinched the wet clay of the vessel wall between two fingers and at other times as though narrow pellets of clay had been applied to the surface and pulled out into elongated nail shapes. This technique was found on rim sherds of incurving bowls with red banded lips, and on pedestal or tall collar sherds (pl. 14, *n*).

15. Fluting. Vertical fluting was found on sherds from shallow bowls with incurved rims, all of which were well weathered. One of these had definite traces of a red lip band on a light buff paste. Others were light buff to brown with evidences

of a polished surface, and may have been examples of Smoked ware which were not fired to the usual brown hue. The flutes are 2–5 mm. deep and the crests between them run 5–10 mm. apart (pl. 14, *o*).

16. Semilunar punctation and scoring. A single sherd, probably of a pedestal base, combined horizontal deep scoring with two horizontal rows of semilunar shaped punctations separated by an incised line, so that the combination of incision and punctations gives the impression of a stem with curved leaves attached evenly on either side. Vestiges of red paint are clearly visible on the interior of the sherd. The punctations are boldly executed; that is, deeply impressed and fairly large, about 1 cm. long by 2 mm. wide (pl. 14, *i*).

17. Fine-line incision with fine scoring. One vessel of unslipped Buff ware washed out of the riverbank and subsequently purchased from Sr. Girón, owner of the site, merits somewhat more detailed description (fig. 65, *a*). Shaped like a slender flower vase with a flared or pedestal base (completely closed at the foot or base rim) and a gently flaring orifice, the vessel measured 23.5 cms. high, had an orifice diameter of 10.8 cms., a base foot diameter of 8.8 cms., and a minimum diameter of 3.5 cms. The upper half of the vessel is smoothed on both the interior and exterior and decorated with vertical shallow-line incision and scoring marks. The central part of the vessel is encircled by two roughened bands which are bordered by incised lines and show traces of red paint. Two applique "buttons" with deep jab punctations are opposed on either side of the vessel near the midpoint. Below the midpoint a series of fine-line incisions run down the sides to the point where the base flares out. These have been smoothed over so that in some areas they are barely visible, and the entire lower half of the vessel has a resultant semipolished surface. The vessel is somewhat similar in shape and possible function to the "pottery drum" recovered at Sitio Conte (Lothrop, 1942, fig. 341), and also resembles the Guacamayan ware vessels illustrated by Feriz (1959, figs. 20, *4*, 21, *10*).

COCLÉ POLYCHROMES

The Coclé Polychrome sherds from the Girón site had the characteristic gray paste noted in sherds of the same type at the El Hatillo site and presumably fairly characteristic of the same type at Sitio Conte. Forms were limited to plates or shallow open bowls with the one exception of one sherd from a collared jar. All plate rim sherds were of the "drooping lip" variety, generally a characteristic of the Early Period polychromes at Sitio Conte.

AZUERO POLYCHROMES

An examination of a representative sample of the Azuero group sherds recovered at the Girón site reveals the absence of the Calabaza and El Hatillo types, a minimal representation of the Parita type through a few Yampí sherds, and a heavy concentration of Macaracas type with Pica-pica, Higo, and Cuipo varieties all present.

RED DAUBED

Vessel shapes present at the Girón site included: large collared jars with tall straight outflared collars; jars with short everted collars;

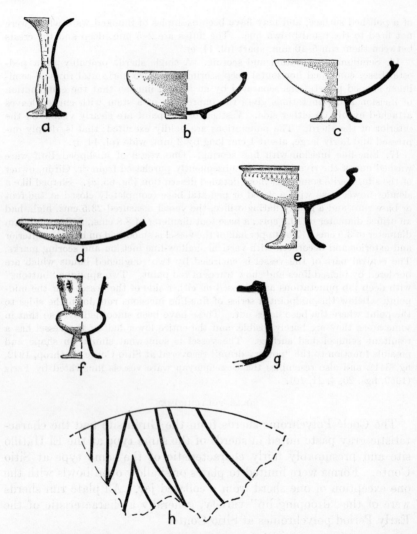

FIGURE 65.—Miscellaneous shapes and design elements. *a*, Purchase, hearsay from Co-2, Guacamayan ware; *b*, Smoked ware, Platanillo variety, Find 5-2 from He-1; *c*, Smoked ware, Sangre variety, Find 14-*f* from He-1; *d*, Smoked ware, Aromo variety, Find 14-*g* from He-1; *e*, Smoked ware, Venado Beach incised, Find 21-*g* from He-1; *f*, Red ware chalice, Find 14-*e* from He-1; *g*, rim of Smoked ware spouted jar, Find 5-*c* from He-2; *h*, Red line ware plate, Find 5-*g* from He-2.

bowls with slightly incurved rims; and plates or shallow bowls (some may have been incensario fragments, especially since small nubbin feet are noted for the plate or open bowl shapes). Decoration consists mainly of irregular smears and dribbles of red with no apparent design pattern. However, some teardrop elements were noted.

STONE ARTIFACTS

Here, as at the other sites, the stone inventory is a relatively simple one which can be broken down into metate fragments, manos, celts, and two flakes of jasper or chert which may have served as scrapers or drills.

Metates.—These and the manos treated below were, for the most part, made from a porous volcanic stone tentatively identified as rhyolite. The edge fragments all reveal a rounded edge with a flattened, slightly concave "upper" surface and a slightly convex lower surface. The fragments are relatively thin, ranging from 1.5–3 cms. in maximum thickness. One fragment of a cylindrical leg was recovered. Many of these fragments were found on the surface and the remainder are largely limited to the upper levels of the excavations.

Manos.—A number of fragments were recovered, all from the upper levels of Pit 2 and all of the long cylindrical variety with one side worn flat, except for a single example in which the two opposing sides are both worn flat, one in a step formation (pl. 21, *a*).

Celts.—All made of a dark igneous basaltic rock, these are of two varieties. In neither group are there any fragments present with clear or definite cutting edges, and all may have been used as hammers or picks rather than celts. In the first group, the celts are markedly petaloid in outline and are unpolished and roughly chipped with a thick triangular or diamond cross section (pl. 21, *b*, *c*). A typical specimen measures 8×6×3.5 cms.; a few others are longer and slimmer.

The second group (pl. 21, *d*, *e*), which may or may not have been celts, exhibits some polished areas, but otherwise is so fragmented that it is impossible to ascertain the original proportions or even shape.

Flakes.—Two fairly large red jasper chips were recovered (pl. 21, *f*, *g*) which may have been intended as scrapers or drills. Neither shows any clear signs of retouching or of use.

WORKED BONE AND SHELL

No worked shell occurred at the site, but two fragments of cut bone tubes (pl. 19, *b*, *c*) were recovered at a depth of 140–150 cms. in Pit 1. One of these was 5 cms. long and unworked except for the cutting at each end. The other, an end fragment of a longer tube, 2 cms. in maximum diameter and 7 cms. long, had three rather crudely cut shallow grooves near the finished end.

SUMMARY

The Girón site, certainly a village or occupied site rather than a cemetery, situated near broad alluvial plains and 7 air miles from the delta, provided a good location for a subsistence pattern combining both agriculture and shellfish. Both are indicated in the cultural remains by manos and by a relatively (compared to He-1 and He-2) heavy concentration of shells. No graves were encountered in the excavations, [14] nor were any pottery caches or single complete pottery vessels found. Probably in part as a result of this lack of grave or cache discovery, scanty worked bone and no metal were recovered, although a number of stone chipped and polished celts were found.

The ceramic sequence of Pit 1 as supported by Pit 3 suggests a high popularity for Aristide group wares and Red Line, Red Daubed variety during most of the period of site occupation, with Coclé and Azuero group sherds appearing only in the upper level as the Aristide group drops off.

---

[14] McGimsey (1959) reports that subsequent excavations revealed three skeletons without cultural association in the lowermost refuse; two (adult and child) were extended burials and one was flexed.

DELGADO (HE-8) SITE

SITE DESCRIPTION

He-8, the Delgado site, is located on the land of Juan Delgado on the north bank of the Parita River near the Parita highway bridge, a few kilometers from the town of Parita. At this point in the river's course small hills abut the rather narrow river lowlands and old terraces. Sherds were revealed by the highway cut through these hills, and graves uncovered by miscellaneous digging suggested the area as a site in 1948. Excavations consisting of two test pits were conducted in March and April of 1952 by Dr. Willey, Dr. McGimsey, and Mr. East.

Pit 1, a 3-meter square cut, was put down on the lower west flank of a small rise about 10 meters west of the Delgado house and 120 meters east of the highway. The pit was excavated through layers of gray soil mixed with shell, in 10-cm. levels to a depth of 130 cms. and produced 3,301 sherds, almost all of which were of the Delgado Red type. The 114 polychrome sherds from this pit were classified in 1954 as El Hatillo. The sample remaining for examination reveals them to be primarily Macaracus in type although there was a scattering of Parita varieties (Yampí and Ortiga). By far the greater proportion of the sherds was concentrated in the first 50 cms.

Pit 2, another 3-meter square cut, located on the flat of the second river terrace about 30 meters west of Pit 1, produced about twice as many sherds (6,784) as Pit 1, thus suggesting that the main habitation area lay along the river terrace rather than on the hills behind it. As was the case with Pit 1, the sherds were almost entirely either Delgado Red or Azuero group polychromes, and most of these were concentrated in the uppermost 40 cms. in a gray soil mixed with oyster and small clamshells. No Coclé Polychrome sherds were classified for either pit. A few sherds of red paste with a heavy white to cream slip, probably of the same type as those recovered in Mound III at He-4, were found.

CERAMIC REMAINS

DELGADO RED

This type, the characteristic red ware at the Delgado site, was apparently absent at the Girón site. However, its similarity to Girón Red should be noted. For comments on the type at He-4, see the Red-buff section of the He-4 typology.

Paste.—Color of paste ranges from dark orange to light orange (Maerz and Paul colors, "persimmon," plate 6, E–12, to "agate," H–12, and "cognac," plate 4, J–11) and sometimes is fired reddish throughout. Often there is a lighter core present. Temper is of crushed white rock and sand with occasional hematite particles. Hardness rates at about 4 on Mohs' scale. Thickness ranges from 5–9 mm. with an average of about 7 mm. The paste is distinguishable from the Aristide group wares by the presence of more sand in its temper, and its slightly harder surface, redder firing, and relative thinness.

Shapes.—Forms included those found at the El Hatillo site, e.g.: globular or subglobular constricted orifice jars with unmodified lips and often with loop handles horizontally placed on the shoulders; globular or subglobular jars with collars that are generally short and out-curved; small open bowls; and plates or shallow open bowls.

Bases recovered which may belong to any or all of these forms include ring and pedestal forms. Both tall (15 cms.) and short (3 cms.) pedestal bases were recovered. At the El Hatillo site most of the jars, collared or collarless, had round unmodified bases, and the ring and pedestal bases (with the exception of a few pedestal bowls and pedestal effigy bowls) were limited to the plate and shallow open bowl forms.

Surface.—Surfaces are well smoothed, but do not have a polished appearance despite the noticeable marks of a polishing stone. Generally the entire exterior surface is red slipped except for the handles, collar, and often the base. Slip color corresponds to Maerz and Paul, "tawny," plate 13, D–10.

Appendages.—Appendages include most prominently loop handles horizontally placed on the shoulder just below the rim. These are usually unslipped. A very few of these were of the roped variety. Occasionally plain loop handles (as distinct from the rope form) were decorated with dash punctations. Somewhat flattened loop handles also occurred on plates as an extension of the rim. Several high, narrow strap handles (or legs) were also recovered, but these were not as common as the loop shoulder handle.

Additional appendages include horizontal flanges (rounded triangular shape when viewed from above) placed just below the rim, lugs with grooves and deep incision, crudely done untapered spouts, squarish nodes placed just below the rim on incurved wall bowls, and small buttonlike nodes, also placed just below the rim on incurved wall bowls.

Geographical range.—The type thus far appears limited to the Parita area occurring at He-4, He-8, and at the additional sites in the Parita Bay area listed for the La Mula Complex (Willey and McGimsey, 1954, p. 113).

Chronological position.—Herrera Phase and possibly the Late Coclé Phase.

Relationships of type.—As discussed on page 22, I believe the type is so similar to the Red-buff ware of the La Mula Complex that the latter should be subsumed within the former.   In addition, Delgado Red shares collared jar and collarless constricted-orifice jar forms with the Girón Red variety.

Bibliography.—Willey and Stoddard, 1954, and Willey and Mc-Gimsey, 1954.

STONE ARTIFACTS

Worked stone at He-8 is limited to a celt, a lag fragment, and two mano fragments.   The celt is of the pointed poll variety with flattened oval cross section and measures roughly 9×5×2.5 cm.   Polishing is confined to the blade and some outstanding areas of the body.   The lag fragment resembles a celt, in the early stages of manufacture before polishing, with the cutting edge broken off.   The surface is very rough, but there are no signs of battered or pecked areas.

Of the mano fragments, the larger one appears to be the broken end of an oblong tool 8 cm. wide and 4 cm. thick with a flattened oval cross section.   It is made of granite and both sides are worn. The second, smaller, fragment exhibits a rounded edge and a worn and flattened surface on one side; the remaining surfaces are rough.

SUMMARY

The Delgado site, He-8, is a shallow habitation site with exclusively Azuero group pottery and thus a period of occupation apparently limited to the Late Coclé and Herrera phases.   Mano fragments and marine shells in the refuse suggest a subsistence dependence on corn and shellfish.   Since no graves or caches were recovered, the site adds nothing to our knowledge of ceremonial practices for the phases concerned.

SIXTO PINILLA PLACE (HE-1) SITE

SITE DESCRIPTION

The site, about 1.25 kilometers south of the modern town of Parita, lies on a hill 200 meters northwest of the Parita River in an area characterized by numerous rolling hills and intervening lowland flats. Trees are scattered, but small growth is luxuriant even in the dry season. The central portion of the site is a hilltop 100×50 meters in total area, well above the flood level, with two knolls which rise 2-3 meters above the hilltop proper.

When the 1948 excavations were undertaken by Dr. Stirling and Dr. Willey, a small farmhouse stood on the southeast knoll with an old well or excavated pit near it. Numerous large boulders averaging 50 cm. in diameter were present on the two knolls and on the flanks of the hill.

Excavation was undertaken in the saddle between the two knolls and on the northwest knoll, and various test pits were dug in the lower slopes. These excavations revealed that the occupational layers are quite shallow. In general, the area was covered by a thin layer (20-30 cm.) of humus, then a layer of mixed red clay and organic material extending down to a depth of 1 meter and underlain by sterile yellow-white clayey soil. In view of this uniform picture of natural stratigraphy and the lack of evidence of any artificial layering such as floors or ash layers, profiles of the excavations are omitted.

The shallowness of cultural remains is reflected in the sherd counts of the two test pits and two trenches bearing statistically relevant material. In all four cases the total sherds, especially polychrome sherds, are concentrated in the upper two levels of excavation; the humic and red clay zones.

The first of these test pits, Pit 1, a 2×2 meter cut in the west flank of the southeast knoll, was excavated in 25 cm. levels to a depth of 175 cms., although no cultural material was found below the 75 cm. mark. The lower two levels, with only 2 and 12 polychrome sherds each, provide too small a sample for valid statistical analysis. The dominant ceramic type within the upper two levels is Girón Polychrome, which gains in popularity from the second level (25-50 cms.) to the first level (0-25 cms.) (chart 12). Coclé Polychrome also increased in popularity from the second to the first level, while the percentages of the Azuero types, and Red Daubed and Red Line all decrease from the second to the first level. The only Azuero group type represented is Macaracas. Almost all of these sherds were of the faded black and purple on red, rather than on cream or orange, technique. The El Hatillo, Parita, and Calabaza varieties were not represented. Within the Girón type, the Interior Banded and

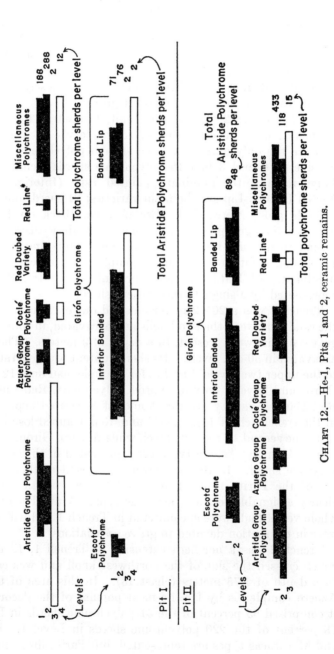

CHART 12.—He-1, Pits 1 and 2, ceramic remains.

Radial Banded Lip are by far the most popular varieties in both levels; of the total of 151 Aristide group sherds only 12 were decorated on the exterior and could tentatively be classed as Escotá type. The sequence of this pit suggests that while the Macaracas type was declining in popularity, the Girón type, Interior Banded variety and Coclé Polychrome were gaining. In this instance, the Red Daubed and Red Line wares appear more closely related to the Macaracas type than to the Aristide group.

Pit 2, another 2×2 meter test pit, located at the south end of Trench 1, was also excavated in 25-cm. levels, of which the upper two are the only ones with large enough polychrome samples to be considered (Level 3 had 15 polychrome sherds) (chart 12). Girón Polychrome is the dominant painted type (Interior Banded and Radial Banded Lip are the main varieties; 21 sherds out of 137 total Aristide group were of the Escotá type, Black on Red variety). The Aristide group and Red Daubed variety decrease from the second to the first level, Azuero remains stable and Coclé and Red Line gain. Within the Azuero complex, Macaracas type is again dominant. El Hatillo is not represented, and the Parita type is represented by a single Ortiga variety sherd.

Trench 1 was a 20×2 meter cut laid out on a north-south axis in the saddle between the two knolls and excavated, in some areas where graves or pits were present, to a depth of 3 meters. The trench was excavated in 50-cm. levels. Its sherd content was geneially restricted to the upper two levels; Level 3, for example, had only 12 polychrome sherds and Level 4 only 6. Girón Polychrome, Red Line type, and Red Daubed variety are the dominant decorated types represented in the trench (chart 13). Coclé and Red Daubed lose in popularity from the second to the first level, while Azuero, Girón, and Red Line gain. Actually, Azuero types are represented in the second level by only one sherd. In the first level, 23 percent of the Azuero sherds are of the Parita type (Yampí and Ortiga varieties) and none is clearly assignable to the Macaracas type. A number of graves and whole vessel finds were encountered in Trench 1 and will be discussed later in the section devoted to grave associations.

Trench 2 was a northern extension of Trench 1, 12 meters long, which crossed the side of the northwest knoll and was carried down to a depth of 1.75 meters (chart 13). In this area of the site, the Azuero complex is by far the most popular of the decorated wares; it comprised 55 percent of the 51 polychrome sherds in Level 2, and 58 percent of the 220 polychrome sherds in Level 1. Both Parita and Macaracas types are represented, but Parita drops in popularity from 18 percent of the Azuero sherds in Level 2, to 2 percent in Level 1, while Macaracas increases from 21 percent in Level 2 to 66 percent

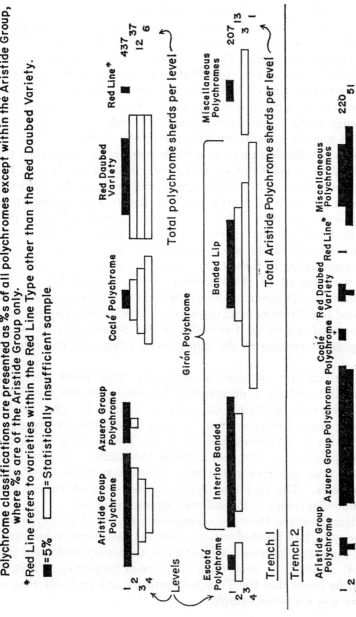

CHART 13.—He-1, Trenches 1 and 2, ceramic remains.

in Level 1. Parita type is represented by the Yampí and Ortiga varieties, Macaracas by the Pica-pica variety. Coclé, Girón, and Red Daubed and Red Line all are, at most, 6 percent or under in both levels and thus of negligible proportions.

On the basis of the above, one can only say that it is difficult to draw valid conclusions concerning the relative chronologies of the various types considered. The Girón type, the dominant type in three of the four stratified excavation units, increases in popularity from lower to upper levels in Pit 1 and Trench 1, decreases in Pit 2, and is present in inconclusive numbers in Trench 2. This increase in frequency in the more recently deposited levels in two of the four excavation units is at variance with the results of the Co-2 excavations where the Aristide group as a whole was clearly earlier than the Coclé and Azuero polychromes, and serves to highlight, if true, the continued popularity of the Girón type beyond the Santa Maria Phase.

It should be noted that even here the Escotá type makes up as much as 15 percent of the total Aristide group sherds in Pit 2, 8 percent of those in Pit 1, and 7 percent of those in Trench 1 (total Escotá sherds for these pits is 48, see charts 12 and 13). Within the Girón type, as represented in these three excavations, there is a consistent pattern with regard to the varieties. Thus, the Interior Banded variety gains in frequency in the upper level in all three cases, while the Banded Lip decreases in all instances. This finding disagrees with the vague tendency at the Girón site for the Banded Lip variety to show higher frequencies in the upper levels relative to the Interior Banded.

Coclé polychrome increases in frequency from lower to upper levels in Pit 1 and Pit 2, decreases in Trench 1 and, like the Girón type, is present in negligible amounts in Trench 2. The Azuero group increases in frequency from lower to upper levels in Trench 1, is stable in Pit 2, and decreases in Pit 1. In Trench 2 it is by far the dominant polychrome, but, contrary to the findings at He-4, the Macaracas type increases in the upper levels here while the Parita type decreases. The Red Line type and Red Daubed variety also show conflicting trends in the different stratigraphic units.

It is clear, however, from gross frequencies that the Girón type and Red Line type, Red Daubed variety, were the most popular decorated wares at the site, a conclusion reinforced by the unstratified sherd lots (chart 14) although in some cases the Azuero proportion is higher. It should be noted that the Trench 3 material, and probably that of Pit 9 also, was a selected sample.

	Pit 4	Pit 5	Pit 6	Pit 9	Trench 3	Trench 4	Trench 5	Surface collection
Azuero Group	*Percent*	*Percent*	*Percent*	*Percent*	*Percent*	*Percent*	*Percent*	*Percent*
Polychrome_____	5. 3	1	16	10	7. 3	5	6	18. 6
Coclé Group								
Polychrome_____	14. 5	1	0	2	1. 8	3	2	10
Aristide Group								
Polychrome_____	1. 4	0. 5	0	0. 2	1. 8	3	8	0
Red Daubed								
Variety_____	18	2	0	5	5. 5	0	6	4. 7
Sherd total_____	76	433	37	858	219	37	64	129

CHART 14.—He-1, unstratified sherd lots (percentages are based on the total of all sherds, decorated and other, recovered in each excavation unit).

CERAMIC REMAINS

The following comments on the pottery types represented at He-1 are based primarily on complete or almost complete vessels. Since most of these have been described in the literature (Lothrop, 1942; Willey and Stoddard, 1954) or in this report in the sections dealing with He-4 and Co-2, only significant variations occurring will be mentioned.

AZUERO CERAMIC GROUP

As noted earlier in the section devoted to stratigraphic results, the Macaracas type was the most heavily represented in the sherd counts. The Parita type is also present in smaller proportions, represented by the Ortiga and Yampí varieties. No El Hatillo type sherds were found and no complete Azuero group polychrome vessels were recovered.

However, Delgado Red constricted-orifice jars with unmodified rims and loop handles were represented both in the sherds and by a number of complete vessels (Finds 19-*b*, 25-2, 30-*b*, and 47-*b*). Class "c" collared jars of the same type were also present (Finds 9, 19-2, 25-1, 41, and 47-*a*, and one example with a lobed shoulder, Find 30-*a*).

COCLÉ POLYCHROME

A number of Coclé vessels were found, most of them probably assignable to the Late Period at Sitio Conte (Finds 11, 14-*d*, 16-17-*c*, 16-17-*d*, 17-*a*, 17-*b*, 18-*a*, 18-*b*, and 19). However, the polychrome vessels of Find Unit 24 (Finds 24-1, 24-19–24-22, and Find 23-*e*) all appear to correspond to Early Period vessels at Sitio Conte. Find 24-21 is an example of Early Period Coclé Black on Red. Finds 16-*a* and 16-17-*b* should probably be classed as Paneled Red ware, similar in shape but not design to the vessel illustrated by Lothrop (1942) in figure 303, *a*.

ARISTIDE GROUP POLYCHROMES

The Aristide group at He-1 was represented almost entirely by the Girón type; only 51 Escotá type sherds were recovered and 20 of these are of questionable identifications. Of the remainder, however, 29 are fairly typical examples of the Black-on-red variety and 2 are equally typical of the Crosshatch variety. No complete Escotá vessels were found.

Within the Girón type, the Interior Banded variety had the highest frequency in all three excavation units containing a significant number of Aristide Group sherds (charts 12 and 13) and increased in frequency from lower to upper levels as the Banded Lip variety declined. One complete Interior Banded variety vessel (Find 8-a), a small (diameter 11 cm.) open bowl with a rounded base and a ski-tip lip, was recovered.

Although the pottery at He-1 assigned to the Girón type is, I believe, sufficiently similar in paste, shape, surface color, and design to the varieties at the Girón site to be treated as an extension of them, certain peculiarities should be noted. First, the vessels at He-1 are generally thinner-walled (thickness for the Interior Banded ranged from 6–8 mm.) and tend toward the lower size limit for the type. Although a few Banded Lip variety sherds at He-1 indicate a vessel diameter of 42 cms., most of them fall within the 20–30 cms. range. Those of the Interior Banded are fragments of vessels with estimated diameters between 12–24 cms. Second, in addition to the usual rim types illustrated for the vessels at the Girón site, the ski-tip rim (figs. 59, s, and 61, b) is a common type, particularly on bowls with circumferential banding. Third, the shade of red slip falls at the darker pole of the range of variation for the type at the Girón site. The slip is not only thicker, but normally covers the entire vessel except for the extreme basal portion of the exterior. Thus the thin, washlike appearance and the buff unslipped areas characteristic of many of the vessel exteriors at the Girón site are seldom present at He-1. Fourth, design elements occur at He-1 and He-2 which were not present at the Girón site. These include the scroll (fig. 60, c), and a serpent motif (fig. 60, b). Circumferential banding below and parallel to the lip (fig. 60, e), although present at the Girón site, is much more common at both He-1 and He-2, often with a row of black dots appended to the lowest band, and constituted the only decorative motif of the Girón type at He-4.

MISCELLANEOUS TYPES

RED LINE TYPE

RED DAUBED VARIETY

Vessels of this variety, provisionally described by Willey and

Stoddard (1954), were quite common at the site. In general, they conform to Willey and Stoddard's description (that is, buff vessels with red daubs, dribbles, teardrop designs and bands around the lip), but the red often verges on purple at the He-1 site. Also at He-1, collar exteriors and vessel interiors usually showed signs of brushing or scoring. The vessels differ from the Red Line type examples illustrated by Lothrop in that Sitio Conte vessels often had loop handles whereas the handles of the Red Daubed variety at He-1 invariably were of the strap shape. The following four shapes were characteristic of the variety at He-1:

1. Wide-mouthed collared subglobular jars without handles (pl. 10, c). Bases are rounded. The lip is usually banded with red, often the only decoration, and the shoulders or upper body of the vessel are decorated with paired or triple teardrop elements. Size of the vessel ranges from small (about 7 cms. in diameter) to medium (15–20 cm in diameter) with heights about one-half to two-thirds of the diameter. Complete vessels (Finds 14-c, 14-j, 16-17-a, 24-4, 24-8, 24-9, 26-4, 45-c, and 48-b). Additional examples (possibly unfinished) in buff but without decoration are 14-b, 16-b, and 23-a. This shape has both Early and Late associations at this site.

2. Wide-mouthed collared jars with strap handles (pl. 10, d). The jar body, especially in the large examples, is high shouldered with a somewhat pointed base, although squat in overall dimensions. Handles, usually two opposed, are placed vertically on the shoulders almost touching the rim. In the large examples, the collars are relatively high and straight. Decoration consists of a red band around the lip and a series of red dribbles of paint running vertically from the lip down both the interior and exterior of the collar and over the shoulder.

Large vessels (diameters of 40–60 cms. and heights of 25–30 cms.; Finds 1 and 21-f) and small to medium sized vessels (with diameters of 14–20 cms.; Finds 21-c, 24-24, and 44-a) both occur. Associations of strap-handled jars at He-1 are Early.

3. Plates and incensarios. The one complete plate had an unmodified lip and was round based with a diameter of 16 cms. and a height of 4 cms. (Find 14-b). The incensarios range in size from small (diameter 9 cms.) to medium (diameter 20 cms.) and are identical in shape to those illustrated from Sitio Conte (Lothrop, 1942, figs. 354–355, a); that is, with two luglike feet and fishtail handles. The find numbers of the He-1 incensarios are Finds 21-e, 24-11, 24-15, 24-23, and 42. The Red Daubed incensario form associations are Early at He-1.

4. Constricted orifice collared jars. These may be variations of the wide-mouthed shape since the two examples (Finds 18-c and 24-5)

are similar to the former shape in all features except in the proportion of collar diameter to body diameter. This shape was found with both Early and Late Period Coclé polychromes at He-1 (see pl. 11, *a*).

PITO VARIETY

This variety, represented by four vessels at He-1 (Finds 13, 22, 24-25, and 24-26) consists of globular vessels with relatively high and constricted collars and four vertical loop handles placed equidistantly around the collar on the shoulder (pl. 11, *b*). Bases are rounded. Decoration consists of a red (or purple) band around the lip, and red or purple bands arranged vertically in open chevron design or a ladder pattern on the body and shoulders. The paint was applied in definite bands, not drips or daubs. Ground color varies from a creamy buff to orange red slip. The vessels are small to medium in size (diameters 12–17 cms.). This variety also had Early Period Coclé polychrome associations at the site.

RED LINE PATTERNED AND MODELED SHAPES

This category was set up as "catch-all" for residual vessels decorated in simple red or purple patterns on a buff or light red slip. Two of these vessels (Finds 12-*a* and 23-*d*) are jars which have modeled effigy face collars, red-banded rims, and red applied on the faces as well as on the bodies. Find 24-27 is a collared jar with a scroll motif in red encircling the upper body. Finds 12-*b* and 23-*c* are also collared jars with plain bases decorated in one case with three parallel vertical lines in red, in the other with a red band around the shoulder with four deep scallops in effect, or four graduated points extending well downward toward the base. Find 24-6 is a small jar with a rounded base and a reverse flared collar. The lip is red banded and a red band encircles the vessel body at its midpoint with four long curved teeth or fanglike projections of red paint extending upward toward the collar. Another jar, Find 40, round-based and with a short outflared collar, was decorated with a crudely drawn horizontal red band encircling the vessel just above the shoulder. Find 48-*a* was a miniature trilobed collared jar with a rounded base decorated by thin smearings of a purple-red paint about the lobes and, in some cases, running down to the base. No clear pattern is evident. Finds 44-*b* and 48-*c* are both round-based and round-lipped plates with red band decoration on the upper surface arranged in radiating lines. These lines extend from a red hub, in the former case, and in parallel red bands across the entire plate exterior in the latter case. Except for Find 44 and 47 unit, all associations of this amorphous group were Early Period vessels at He-1.

RED OR RED/BUFF WARE

In addition to the collared jars and constricted-orifice collarless jars mentioned in connection with the Azuero ceramic group, five vessels (Finds 14-*a*, 14-*e*, 24-7, 24-10, and 24-16) of plain red ware but of a distinctive chalice shape were found (fig. 65, *f*). These may be described as subglobular jars on short pedestal bases with high straight collars on which are appended, near the rim, three pairs of equidistant vertical nodes, each of which has three or four deep impressions. Of the vessel exterior surface only the body is red slipped and polished; both the pedestal base and the collar are unslipped and roughly finished. However, the collar or neck interior is red slipped and polished and, in at least one case (Find 24-7), the interior body base is also red slipped and polished. Heights range from 11 to 16 cms.

Two vessels from He-1 which were red-slipped both on their exteriors and interiors, were Finds 24-2 and 29. The former is a medium-sized (diameter 15 cms.; height 10 cms.) insloping bowl with an unmodified lip and a plain base. The latter is the rim fragment of an open bowl (diameter estimated at 17.5 cms.) with an obliquely flattened lip slanting downward and toward the interior in a fashion similar to that of Finds 45-*b*, 24-13, 21, and 21-*c*.

In addition, two plates (Finds 3 and 4) with rounded lips, plain bases, and no decoration other than a red slip on the upper surfaces, were recovered.

BUFF WARE

A plain crudely modeled buff open bowl (Find 44-*c*) with rounded base and a lip which curls inward slightly to overhang the interior was recovered in Trench 5. It is of small to medium size (diameter 15 cms.; height 7 cms.) and has no direct counterpart at the site. A large, light buff, deep, open bowl (Find 14-*i*) with a ring base and a thickened lip which curls in a similar fashion to that of Find 44-*c* was also found. Its diameter is 38 cms., and its height is 22.5 cms.

Additional buff vessels from He-1 included:

Find 2.—A small incomplete buff jar or bottle, the collar or neck of which is missing. Surface is rough and eroded. Maximum diameter is 11 cms. An especially rough circular area on the shoulder appears to indicate the place of attachment of a lug or vertical loop handle.

Find 21-*a*.—A medium-sized, plain-based, buff-slipped plate or shallow dish with a rounded lip (diameter 16.5 cms.; height 4 cms.).

Find 43-*a*.—A small, roughly finished buff jar with collar missing and a rounded base. The diameter is 8.5 cms. and the height is 8 cms.   The exterior, although rough and lumpy, is covered with a red slip.

SMOKED WARE

PLATANILLO VARIETY

The most common shape among the examples of Smoked ware was that of a ring-based open bowl with a modified gutter rim, usually slanted slightly inward and downward (fig. 65, *b*).   These vary considerably in size; Find 45-*b* is 16 cms. tall with a diameter of 35 cms. while Find 12-*c* is 5 cms. tall with a diameter of 18 cms.   Eight of these vessels were found at He-1 (Finds 5-*a*, 12-*c*, 21-*h*, 23-*b*, 24-3, 26-2, 45-*b*, and 48-*d*).   The shape apparently did not occur in Smoked ware at Sitio Conte, although similar rims on pedestal-based vessels were recovered at He-4.   This variety was associated with Early Period Coclé polychromes in Find Units 23 and 24, but its popularity may have extended on into Late Period times.

SANGRE VARIETY

Another fairly consistent shape, represented however by only two whole vessels (Finds 14-*f* and 26-1), is that of a shallow open bowl on a low pedestal.   The pedestal rim is flanged outward, and the bowl rim or lip has a double flange, one extending outward and the other on the interior extending upward (fig. 65, *c*).   The lip may be incised. The sizes of these two examples range from small (diameter 12.5 cms.) to medium (diameter 27.5 cms.).   Smoked ware bowls similar to these in shape and rim treatment, but with ring bases, were found in Early Period graves at Sitio Conte (Lothrop, 1942, fig. 320, *b*) and at He-4, Find 378.   At He-1, the variety is associated in Find Unit 14 with a Late Period Coclé polychrome plate and the Red ware chalice shape.   Find 26-1 is associated with a Red Daubed variety wide-mouthed collared jar and a Platanillo variety Smoked ware dish. Thus, it may have extended from Early to Late Periods.

AROMO VARIETY

Three vessels (Finds 14-*g*, 26-3, and 45-*a*) share a plain open shallow bowl shape with a rounded base and a rim which is thickened and obliquely flattened on the outer edge (fig. 65 *d*).   Polishing marks are generally clear on the interiors.   Diameters range from 18–24 cms.; heights are 3–4 cms.   The variety is associated at this site with a Late Period polychrome plate (Find 14-*d*).   Platanillo variety bowls in Finds 26 and 45, however, give it a range over both Periods.   The shape is not illustrated for Sitio Conte, nor have I seen examples of it elsewhere in the literature.

VENADO BEACH INCISED VARIETY

Although represented at this site by only two examples (Finds 21-*g* and 24-29) and at He-2 by only one example, the particular combination of shape and surface treatment appears stable enough and frequent enough at Venado Beach to warrant varietal status.   Find 21-*g* (fig. 65, *e*) is a shallow pedestaled bowl with an everted and horizontally flattened lip on which are incised a number of circumferential grooves and a series of dashes.   The shoulder is fluted and the surface color is dark brown with reddish tinges apparent in some areas.   The diameter is 22.5 cms. and the bowl height is 7.5 cms. (pedestal missing).   This vessel is practically duplicated (except for size variation) by three vessels from Venado Beach (Peabody Mus. cat. Nos. 51-25-20/20704, 51-25-20/20308, and 51-25-20/20851).   Find 24-29 consisted of fragments of a vessel similar but without the fluting on the shoulder, and Find 5-*b* at He-2, with a complete short pedestal, is similar in all respects including size.   Although the one complete pedestal present at He-2 was unperforated, several of the examples at Venado Beach had rectangular or square apertures.   An exotic shape probably assignable to the same variety is illustrated from Los Santos (Lothrop, 1942, fig. 459, *b, b′*).

Other miscellaneous shapes in the Smoked ware type represented at the site by one vessel each include a small open bowl with a ring base and a horizontally flattened lip (Find 21-*d*; diameter 14 cms.), a miniature ring-based plate with unmodified lip (Find 24-12), and a collared, unfluted, and spouted jar (Find 44-*d*; 10 cms. in diameter). Similar Smoked ware spouted jars (Lothrop, 1942, fig. 325) were recovered at Sitio Conte in Early Period graves, although the shape in other wares there was generally more characteristic of the Late Period (ibid., p. 162).

PINILLA BLACK-LINE-ON-RED

Classification of this type (pl. 11, *c, d*) is based entirely on three complete vessels (Finds 7, 10, and 20-*a*) and one additional complete vessel (Find 49) on which all decoration has disappeared, but which is assigned to this group because of its shape.   All four examples are subglobular collared jars with rounded bases of medium size (diameter 16–23 cms., height 11–17 cms.).   Orifices range from constricted (one quarter of total diameter) to medium-sized (about one half of total diameter) and collars are characteristically straight with an outward flare.   Decoration consists of relatively narrow black lines applied in geometric patterns (concentric circles or squares) on the upper shoulder or shoulder and neck of the vessel.   Ground color is a red slip.   The painting is uneven and sloppy.

Paste is fired a brick red, except for a gray core, and thickness ranges from 5–8 mm. The chronological position of this type is unknown and I have been unable to find examples from other sites. The closest similarity noted in the literature (and it is not very close) would be two vessels from Sitio Conte Grave 37 (Lothrop, 1942, fig. 290, *a* and *b*), an undated grave.

WHITE-AND-BLACK-ON-RED WARE

This type which occurred at Sitio Conte (Lothrop, 1942, figs. 287, 288, and 289) is represented at He-1 by only one complete vessel (pl. 12, *a*) (Find 24-14), an open bowl with incurved rim and somewhat pointed base. The vessel is fairly large (diameter 33 cms.; height 18 cms.) and has a rounded lip. Decoration consists of a panel of closed arcs in white paint running around the upper shoulder of the vessel and separated by an undulating black band which is bordered in white. These black bands terminate in frog or turtle legs. Unfortunately, the design opposing these, presumably a head or face, is missing. The shape then, is quite similar to the Early Period Grave 14 vessel of Sitio Conte figure 287 (Lothrop, 1942) without the modeled portions, and its closest similarity to the He-4 material would be with the Macaracas type closed arc design.

EL TIGRE PLAIN

All of the 31 sherds of El Tigre Plain, many of them from the same vessel, were found in the topmost level of Pits 1 and 2; 15 sherds from the former and 16 from the latter. Most of these, in both pits, were from thick-walled (1.5 cm.), deep, open bowls with large, plain, horizontal lugs just below the rim (pl. 17, *a*, *b*, and *e*). The surface color of these was a cream buff. A few sherds from vessels of the same basic shape were thinner (1 cm.), with red-buff surfaces and notched lugs (pl. 17, *c*, *d*, and *g*).

UNCLASSIFIED SINGLE VESSELS

Find 5.—A large open bowl with a somewhat pointed rounded base and ski-tip lip. Interior and most of the exterior are covered with a purplish red slip which easily washes off. Diameter is 40 cms.; height is 14 cms.

Find 8.—A small open bowl with slightly incurving sides and a flattened base. The rim is broadened at the lip to form an interior flange and is flattened at an oblique angle slanting inward and downward. Traces of white slip occur on both the exterior and the upper lip where there is also a faint indication of black radial lines. Otherwise the surface is buff. Diameter of the vessel is 9.5 cms.; height is 4 cms.

Find 15.—A high collared jar with a ring base and an exterior flange just below the horizontally flattened lip. The upper half of the vessel exterior is covered with an orange-pink slip over which black horizontal bands and an open crosshatch pattern have been arranged. The lower half is red slipped. Diameter is 13.5 cms.; height is 16.5 cms. (See pl. 12, *b*.)

Find 20-*b*.—A medium-sized open bowl (diameter 15 cms.; height 7 cms.) which is similar in shape to Find 21-*d*, with a ring base and a modified gutter rim. Vessel was buff slipped, then red slipped with black bands placed transversely on the lip as ticking.

Find 21-*b*.—A flat medium-sized plate (diameter 19 cms.; height 2.5 cms.) with a plain base, rounded lip, and somewhat upcurved rim. A red overslip covers the interior, lip, and about 2 cms. of the outer rim; otherwise the vessel is buff slipped.

Find 24-17.—A wide mouthed jar (diameter 18 cms.; height 11.5 cms.) with a round base and short, straight collar. Two flattened lugs jut out horizontally from opposite shoulders of the vessel. Most of the vessel is buff slipped, but a broad red band encircles it just below the lugs, and a narrower one runs around the lip. The vessel is similar in shape to Find 377, He-4.

STONE ARTIFACTS

Metates.—Two complete metates, both of the table type, were recovered at He-1. The first, a simple table type (pls. 22, *a*, *b*, 23, *a*) with a slightly concave platform and three unadorned conical legs, two flush with the sides and one along the center axis but well inside the edge, measured 52 cms. long by 42 cms. wide by 14 cms. high. The legs are flattened at the tips and slant inward toward the center of the platform. Platform edges are flattened and beveled. This specimen was associated in Find 14 with Late Coclé Phase polychromes. Combining this with the evidence at He-2, it is apparent that the simple table type metate extended at least through both Coclé phases. The second metate, associated in Find 49 with a probable Pinilla Black-line-on-red jar, is considerably more ornate (pl. 23, *b*). The slightly concave platform is rectangular with rounded corners and flattened and beveled edges. Three tall (height 22.5 cms.) legs support the platform which measures 46.5×35 cms. The latter's underside is decorated with 13 stone "rings" resembling birds' heads attached to the platform by neck and beak. A lizard in low relief is also present on one side.

Manos.—None. Two smoothed, rounded, and flattened pieces of sandstone were found in the top level of Trench 2. Because of their shape and softness, however, I believe that they probably were used for polishing rather than grinding.

Celts. No definite beveled-edge or ovoid celts were found at He-1;

all those recovered were, or had originally been, of the chipped-poll type.   The one possible example of the beveled-edge type is a miniature 3.5 cms. long found in probable association with Find 24.   Most of those recovered in the refuse showed evidence of postmanufacture battering or pounding on both the cutting face and the poll tip (pl. 20, *a, b*).   A few complete celts with sharpened edges were found in the trenches and a group of 10 was part of Find 24.   All of these were generally similar to those of He-4; that is, with polished cutting edges, polishing on the outstanding portions of the body part way up to the poll, and termination in roughly chipped polls.   In a few cases, there was a marked transition from broad blade to narrow poll (pl. 20, *c, d*) a feature which is duplicated in the one example from He-2 and in certain of those illustrated by Lothrop for Sitio Conte (Lothrop, 1937, figs. 53, *b*, and 54, *a, b*) from an Early Coclé Phase grave. With the exception of a small, atypical example (pl. 20, *e*) from Find 24 of a multicolor baked sedimentary rock, all the celts were of poorly polished schist or basalt altering to serpentine.   Sizes vary from small to large; $6\times4\times1$ cm. to $13\times7\times3$ cms.   The cross section is generally a flattened oval.

Hammers.—All the examples at He-1 of stones showing signs of hammering appear to have been originally celts.   Evidence of postmanufacture battering was present on both the cutting edges and the polls.

Points and drills.—Three chert or jasper points were recovered in the uppermost layers of Trench 1 and Pit 2 (pl. 20, *f–h*) and two were probably associated with Find 24.   Of those found in the refuse, two exhibit rudimentary shoulders, one has a broad haft, and all are approximately the same size, $5.5\times2.5\times1$ cm.   One of those with Find 24 is made of slate (pl. 20, *i*) and is somewhat larger, measuring $8.5\times3\times0.8$ cm.   The other is a small quartz point $3.2\times1.8\times0.3$ cm. These are shouldered, roughly chipped without retouching and are similar to those illustrated by Lothrop for Sitio Conte (Lothrop, 1937, fig. 64, *r, t, b'*, etc.).   One probable drill fragment (pl. 20, *j*) with triangular cross section was recovered in the uppermost layer of Pit 2.   The point is apparently broken off and the tool lacks retouching except possibly on the broader or haft end.

Scrapers and chisels.—As at He-4, but in greater frequency at this site, a number of chert flakes were found which may have been used as scrapers (pl. 20, *k–n*).   No objects resembling the "chisel" of He-4 were found.

Rubbing stones.—A number of elongated, probably river-smoothed stones, usually fairly soft, were found which showed definite signs of grinding or polishing (pl. 20, *o–s*).   Often these were vaguely spatulate in shape, with the broader end polished.   They varied from approximately 5–9 cms. in length. Larger stones, already mentioned under the category of manos, may also have served as polishers. One round hard stone was recovered with what appears to be blue pigment on the worked surfaces.

Jewelry and miscellaneous.—No stone ornaments were found. One sandstone net sinker or "plummet stone" (Find 27, pl. 20, *t*) was recovered. This measures 4×3×2.5 cms. and is unique for the five sites.

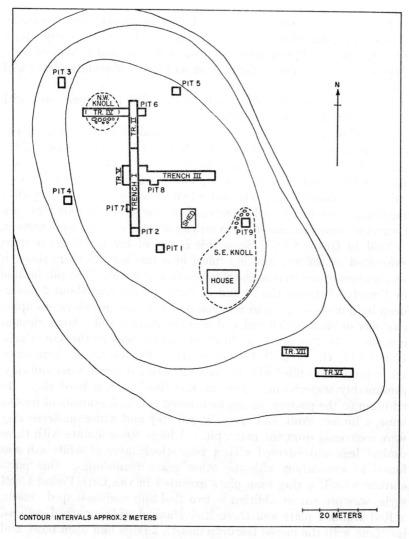

CONTOUR INTERVALS APPROX. 2 METERS   20 METERS

FIGURE 66.—He-1, 1948.

WORKED BONE AND SHELL

The only object in either of these categories recovered at He-1 is a bone or antler harpoon point (pl. 19, *a*) associated in Find 24 with Early Coclé Phase pottery. This measures 8.5 cms. long by 1.5 cms. maximum width by 0.6 cms. maximum thickness. The haft is perforated.

FIND INTERPRETATIONS AND SITE CHRONOLOGY

Find 1-5 cache contained no polychrome vessels, but associated a large strap-handled Red Daubed bowl with plain red slip plates, the large purple slipped open bowl, and a fragment of a Smoked ware, Platanillo variety dish. There were no objects of stone or bone with these vessels.

Find 8 cache combined a small, unclassified buff open bowl with a Girón, Interior Banded bowl.

Find Unit 12 associates a Platanillo Smoked ware dish with two examples of the Patterned and Modeled Red Line ware. One of the latter, Find 12-*a*, is an effigy collared jar with lobed shoulders and painted red decoration; the other, Find 12-*b*, is a collared jar with painted red decoration. The latter two vessels were found very close together, the lobed vessel inverted, but the Smoked Ware dish was recovered somewhat lower. No articles of bone or stone were present.

Find 14 Grave Unit. Since this is one of the larger grave units excavated at the site and is typical of a number of others there, it seems appropriate to describe the pit in some detail. The pit, located in Trench 1 between the 14 and 16 meter points, was about 2 meters deep by 2 meters wide and was composed of two chambers; an upper chamber or shaft which widened near the surface and a lower circular chamber. In this grave, as in other similar ones at the site (Cache Unit 16-17, Grave Unit 18, Grave Unit 19), the lower chamber or grave proper was filled with horizontally bedded brown sand and clay, presumably waterborne. The pit was lined with a hard clay. In addition to the pottery vessels mentioned below, fragments of human bone, a human skull, and lumps of red clay and white plastered clay were recovered from the grave pit. A large stone metate with three conical legs and covered with a 2-cm.-thick layer of white ash was found in association with the other grave furnishings. One polychrome vessel, a ring base plate executed in the Late Period Coclé style, was present in addition to two Red Slip chalice-shaped vessels, a Red Daubed plate and three Red Daubed wide-mouthed collared jars (one with the paired teardrop motif), a large buff open bowl, and two Smoked ware vessels; one Aromo variety plate and a Sangre variety bowl. This association places the distinctive chalice shape

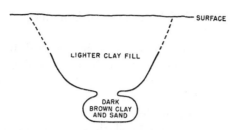

FIGURE 67.—Idealized diagram of grave pit, Find 14, He-1.

in the Late Coclé Period.   No artifacts of bone or stone were present in the grave unit.

Find 16-17 Cache Unit, located in Trench 1 at a depth of 2–3 meters, is similar in shape to Find 14 grave pit, except for the occurrence of three small pits in the floor of the lower grave chamber of the 16-17 unit.   These latter measured roughly 15 cms. in diameter and were 10–12 cms. deep.   Red clay, charcoal, and burned earth were found in association with some of the vessels of the unit, in addition to a flint chip.   An entrance shaft is suggested in the upper southeast corner of the chamber by a tentative upward continuation of the chamber about 50 cms. in diameter.   No bones or other artifacts are mentioned in the field notes, but the following vessels were found with the unit: two open bowls with ring bases which I have classed as Paneled Red ware; three Coclé polychrome cups of the Sitio Conte Later Period style; one polychrome collared jar with a design layout similar to a vessel from the Late Period Grave 26 at Sitio Conte (Lothrop, 1942, fig. 192, e) and a collar design which is duplicated by a sherd from the Rio Estibana, Macaracas (ibid., fig. 466, a); and two wide-mouthed collared jars, one of which is definitely Red Daubed with a triple teardrop motif, and the other of which is probably an unfinished Red Daubed specimen.   Thus this cache, like Find Unit 14, can be considered as coeval with the Late Period at Sitio Conte. The Coclé cups are illustrated in Stirling, 1949, p. 376, center row (Find 17-a left, Find 17-b center, Find 16-17-c right).

Find 18 Grave Unit is another grave pit shaped similarly to that of Finds 14, 16-17, and 19, also lined with burned clay which apparently served as a domelike lining or roof for the burial chamber.   Only three pottery vessels were encountered in the grave, a complete Coclé polychrome plate (Late Period), fragments of another which is also probably of the Late Period, and a Red Daubed collared jar.   In addition to the vessels, a white ash layer was present in the grave chamber along with a fragment of a stone metate, fragments of a stone disk or mirror, and two hemispherical pieces of earth which were shaped like the earthfills of vessels and may represent decayed gourds or bowls.   A few human bone fragments were noted, but no complete skeletons. Find 24, a notched bone harpoon point, may be from the fill of Grave 18.

Find 19 Grave Unit is also domed or bell shaped, but was not lined with red clay. Fragments of human bone, including a cranium and an adult femur, were recovered. The pottery of the unit consists of a Late Period Coclé Polychrome plate, a miniature Red ware pedestal plate or pot stand, and two Delgado Red vessels, namely: a class "c" collared jar and a loop-handled collarless jar containing several pieces of charcoal. This grouping tends to ally two characteristic Azuero Red ware shapes with Late Polychrome styles at Sitio Conte.

Find 20 Unit. It is difficult to determine from the field notes whether the two vessels of Find 20 actually were associated. They consist of a Pinilla Black-line-on-red collared jar (Find 20-*a*) and a shallow open red-slipped bowl with a ring base and black ticking on the lip.

Find 21 consists of a cache of pottery vessels, several of which were found within a large collared jar (Find 21-*f*) from Trench 3 at a depth of about 40 cms. No polychrome vessels were present. Complete specimens consist of three Red Daubed vessels (one medium-sized strap-handled collared jar, one large strap-handled collared jar, and one incensario), three Smoked ware vessels (one Platanillo variety bowl, one small open ring-based bowl with a flat lip, and one Venado Beach Incised open bowl) and two additional vessels; a buff plate or shallow bowl, and a flat plate with a red slip over a buff slip.

Find 22–23 Unit was a cache of only pottery vessels located in Trench 3 at a depth of approximately 1–1.2 meters. Associations consist of two Red line Patterned and Modeled variety jars, a Red Line, Pito variety collared jar, an undecorated wide-mouthed collared jar (unfinished Red Daubed?), a Smoked ware, Platanillo variety open bowl, and a Coclé Polychrome plate with a "bird-which-looks-back" design, probably of Early Period vintage. Thus, here, the Red Line, Pito variety and Red Line Patterned and Modeled appear contemporary with the Early Period at Sitio Conte.

Find Unit 24, a multiple grave and the largest grave excavated at the site in terms of number of skeletons and vessels, included parts of four skeletons. Burial 1 contained the flexed skeleton of a young adult with a harpoon point, two flint points, some green-stained bone awls, a copper chisel, seven stone celts, and a shark's tooth. Most of these artifacts were found near the chest of the individual. Grouped around the bones were pottery vessels, Finds 24-1 through 24-12, including a Coclé Polychrome flaring bowl with scroll design which, on the basis of design layout and drooping lip, would be placed in the Early Period at Sitio Conte; a Red Daubed incensario; and a number of vessels which in other graves or caches at He-1 have Late Period associations.   These include two red slip chalices, a number of Red Daubed wide-mouthed collared jars, a Red Line Patterned and Modeled specimen, and a Smoked ware Platanillo variety bowl.

Burials 2 and 4 (the former adult, the latter a female or adolescent), with associated long bones, were close together with a small chipped and polished stone ax between the two skulls.   Definitely associated with these were Finds 24-23 through 24-27 which include a Red Daubed incensario, a Red Daubed strap-handled collared jar, two Red Line Pito variety vessels, and a Red Line Patterned and Modeled collared jar.   Probably associated with these   particular skeletons were Finds 24-13 through 24-15 and 24-18 through 24-22, which include a Red Daubed incensario, a definite Early Period Coclé shallow dish (illustrated in Stirling, 1949, p. 376, bottom row center) with turtle god design (Lothrop, 1942, fig. 91, a), two probable Early Coclé Polychrome shallow bowls or plates, an Early Period Black-on-red ware shallow dish, and a White-and-black-on-red ware pear-shaped bowl with incurving rim and the closed arc design so common on Macaracas type vessels.

The third burial, a semiflexed adult skeleton with a copper nose ornament, five chipped stone celts, and some clamshells, was found with a red slip chalice and an unclassified bowl (Find 24–17) in association.

Fragments of two incomplete vessels (Finds 24-28, 24-29) were also present, both Smoked ware open bowls or dishes, one of the Platanillo variety and the other of the Venado Beach Incised variety.   Occasional pieces of bird bones were found with the burials of Find Unit 24.

Find 24, then, provides a number of associations of unmistakably Early Period Coclé polychromes with other types (including Red Line, Pito variety, Red Line Patterned and Modeled, the Red ware chalice, and the Smoked ware Platanillo variety dish), some of which are associated with Late Period polychromes in other Finds at the same site.   Although it is true that Find 18, with its Late Period polychromes, and Find 24 were situated close together in the trench with the consequent possibility that some of the vessels of Find 24 may belong to Find 18, there seems no reason to doubt the validity of the ceramic associations of Find 24, Burial 1, since these vessels were found clearly grouped around the skeleton.   Thus, at the very least, there is one definite instance of an Early Period Coclé Polychrome (Find 24–1) associated in a grave lot with the Red ware chalice, Smoked ware, Platanillo variety, and Red Line Patterned and Modeled.

Find Unit 25 is a cache comprised of two Azuero group Delgado Red type vessels.   One is a class "c" collared jar, the other a collarless jar with loop handles.   No polychrome vessels or other artifacts were associated.

Find Unit 26, a cache of broken vessels from Trench 5, consists of three Smoked ware open bowls, a Sangre variety bowl, a Platanillo variety bowl, an Aromo variety plate, and a large Red Daubed wide-mouthed collared jar.

Find Unit 30, consisting of two Delgado Red vessels of the Azuero ceramic group, may have been associated with a badly crushed skeleton found in the same excavation pit. One of the vessels is a class "c" collared jar with lobed shoulders, the other is a collarless jar with loop handles.

Find Unit 43 contained a small, crude, unclassified, buff jar with rim or collar missing, and the only spindle whorl found at the site.

Find Units 44 and 47. Find 44 was made up of four vessels arranged in a straight line with some bone fragments under one of them and charcoal and burned earth associated. The vessels include one Red Line Patterned and Modeled open bowl, one Red Daubed strap-handled collared jar, one Buff open bowl, and one small Smoked ware spouted jar, a shape which in Smoked ware occurred only in Early Period graves at Sitio Conte (Lothrop, 1942, p. 162) although the shape in other wares at that site generally occurred in the Late Period. Find 47, just below and "in the same grave as Find 44" (Field Notes) was comprised of a skull and two Azuero group Delgado Red vessels, a class "c" collared jar, and a collarless jar with loop handles. Three rubbing stones were found with the skull. Thus, we have the two Find 47 Delgado Red vessels, which appear to have late affinities at the He-4 site, associated with the vessels of Find 44 which are placed in the Early Period at Sitio Conte or have early associations at this site.

Find Unit 45 was a cache of three vessels; a large (diameter of collar lip is 38 cms.) Red Daubed wide-mouthed jar containing a Smoked ware Aromo variety plate and covered by a large inverted Smoked ware Platanillo variety open bowl.

Find Unit 48, a cache in Trench 6, associated a Red Daubed wide-mouthed jar with two Red Line Patterned and Modeled vessels and a Smoked ware Platanillo variety open bowl.

Momentarily disregarding the evidence of Finds 44 and 47, the grave lots of He-1 suggest that the Red Daubed wide-mouthed jar, the Red Daubed constricted-orifice collared jar, and the Red ware chalice extended through both the Early and Late Periods. The Red Line Patterned and Modeled, Red Line, Pito variety, Red Daubed jars with strap handles, and Smoked ware of the Platanillo variety all appear to be Early Period types or varieties. These relative positions, based on associations with the more easily dated polychrome vessels, are reinforced in some cases where no polychrome association was present. For example: On the basis of polychrome associations in

Finds 22-23 and Find 24, we conceivably may assume that the Platanillo variety, with its modified gutter rim shape in Smoked ware, is
a diagnostic of the Early Period. If this is so, then the Find 1-5
and Find 21 association between Platanillo variety vessels and Red
Daubed strap handled jars emphasizes the Early position of the
Red Daubed variety. This is also true for the Red Line Patterned
and Modeled ware.

The Smoked ware Sangre and Aromo varieties both are associated
with a Late Period Coclé polychrome vessel in Find 14, but in Finds
26 and 45 are associated with the Platanillo variety and thus may
have appeared in the Early Period. Pinilla Black-line-on-red had no
clear associations at the site and remains a chronological floater.

Finds 44 and 47 combine a unit of Early Period types (Red Line
Patterned and Modeled, Smoked ware spouted jar, Red Daubed
strap-handled vessel) with a unit comprised of two presumably Late
Period vessels, the Delgado Red jars of the Azuero ceramic group.
It may be that the latter shapes spanned both periods. The loop-
handled collarless jar is a useful simple shape which could have been
developed early in ceramic history and lasted throughout, but I am
inclined to believe that the two finds were not part of the same grave.

SUMMARY

He-1 is a shallow village or occupational site with burials in the
occupied area. No evidence of dwellings or structures was found,
but the number of plain or red-slipped sherds without decorations
suggests a predominance of utilitarian wares over ceremonial. Agriculture is assumed to be the main subsistence activity. This assumption is based on the relative absence of shell or animal bone in the
midden, the inland location of the site, and the presence of metates,
although the latter with the relatively "expensive" design (three legs
and, in some cases, carved) may have had a primarily ceremonial
function. No manos were found. Weaving is suggested by the
probable spindle whorl of Find 43.

Ceremonial practices included placing single vessels or caches of
two or more pottery vessels in the ground and using chamber graves
for burial. Bowls were inverted and used as covers for jars (Finds
1-5 and 45). Chambers were lined with clay or plaster (Finds 14,
16-17, and 18) and showed evidence of fire in connection with the
burials or caches (Finds 14, 16-17, 18, 19, and 44). There is no evidence of cremation, although charcoal pieces were found in Find 19-b.
One example of a mass burial was present: Find 49. Here the skeletons of 32 individuals and a three-legged metate with carved decoration were found at the base of a deep shaft (almost 4 meters deep)
which included a layer of boulders placed immediately over the burial.

Grave 24 contained four skeletons; three adult and one adolescent or female adult. The remaining graves were probably single, since only a few bone fragments were found. Grave furniture included pottery, worked bone and stone (Finds 18-24, and 47), copper objects (Find 24), bird bones (Find 24), three-legged metates (Finds 14, 49), and a shark's tooth (Find 24).

The graves and caches include types present in both the Early and Late Periods at Sitio Conte, while the sherd lots include Aristide group types of the Santa Maria Phase (both Escotá and Girón, but especially the latter), of the Azuero group and 31 sherds of the El Tigre Complex. Although the Macaracas type, presumably coeval with Late Coclé, is the dominant one, the probably later Parita type is represented by a few (33) sherds. The period of occupation would appear to be contemporary with both Early and Late Coclé periods at Sitio Conte with indication of both an earlier and later occupation. The few El Tigre sherds present suggest that during early Colonial times, the site may have been used occasionally as a camping spot by salt boiling parties traveling to and from the coast.

LEOPOLDO AROSEMENA (HE-2) SITE

SITE DESCRIPTION

The Leopoldo Arosemena site lies on the west bank of the Parita River (actually the south bank at this point in the river's course) about 2 kilometers from the town of Parita and 600–800 meters from He-1 across the river.   The 1948 excavations were located on a flat hilltop or spur which rises immediately above the riverbank at a point where the river makes an oxbow, and about 15–20 meters above the present river level.   Like He-1, the river cuts sharply through

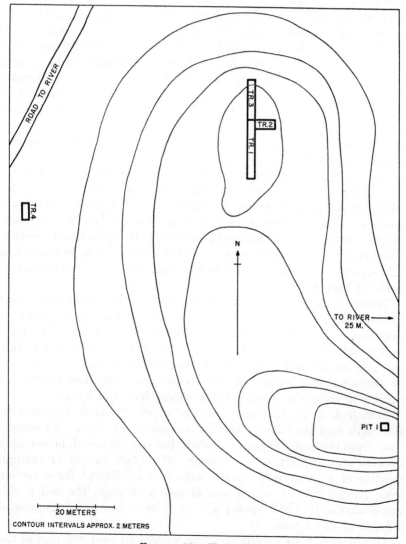

FIGURE 68.—He-2, 1948.

the rolling hills leaving little room for a broad alluvial plain such as that of the Santa Maria River to the east. Sites, therefore, tend to be on the hills rather than on the riverbanks.

Four trenches and one test pit were excavated at the site in 1948 by Drs. Stirling and Willey. Due, however, to the shallowness of the cultural deposit, except for the occurrence of occasional grave pits, the stratigraphic results are meager to nonexistent. Thus, descriptions of the excavations can be brief and profiles will be dispensed with.

Trench 1, a north-south cut of 15×2 meters, extended diagonally across the top of the spur mentioned above and, as digging proceeded, divided into two sections; a southern section running from the 0 meter or southernmost point to the 11 meters point, and a northern section extending from the 11 to the 15 meters point. The soil profiles of the southern section were fairly uniform, beginning with a gray organic layer with cultural remains running from 0–50 cms. Beneath this was an irregular stratum of clean tan sand of from 25–50 cms. in thickness which, in turn, was underlain by the basal gray-white clay rock. The southern part of the trench was carried down into this clay rock for total depths of 1.3–1.8 meters and thus well down into sterile soil. In the northern section, where the greatest number of sherds were recovered, the gray humus layer was separated from the basal gray-white clay rock by a stratum of red-brown clay with streaks of dark brown to black mineral deposit in its lower portions. This red-brown clay stratum was thickest at the north end of the trench but continued throughout the 11–15 meters section. This section of the trench was excavated in some areas to a depth of 2.1 meters. A grave, a few pottery caches, and 320 sherds were excavated in Trench 1.

Trench 2, a 2×5 meters cut at right angles to Trench 1 and joining it at the 13–15 meters point section, was an extension to the east begun primarily to follow out the Find 4–6 Unit. The main part of this trench was carried to a depth of 1.4 meters; that is, into the gray-white rock. Test holes were carried down to 1.9 meters in the northwest corner of the trench with negative results. A number of complete vessels were recovered from this trench.

Trench 3, a 2×10 meters cut, in effect extended Trench 1 to the north over the brow of the hill and down the slope. All pottery came from the upper 50 cms. of the cut, but was not saved, presumably because of its amorphous character. No whole vessels or cultural remains of a nonceramic nature were found. Except for a section from 1.7–5.0 meters, which was almost pure rock, the soil profile was similar to that of Trench 1 with gray-white clay rock beginning at a depth of 70–90 cms.

Trench 4, a 2×4 meters cut, was excavated near the foot of the west slope of the hill quite close to the road to Parita. The upper layer of humus extended downward to as much as 50 cms., averaging 25 cms. in depth, and it was from this layer and the upper portions of the clay just below it that about 300 sherds were recovered. Below the humus layer lay a zone of red-brown clay which was most pronounced at the north end of the trench where it extended to a meter below the surface (at the south end it extended down to 60 cms.). Below this was undisturbed yellow-white soil. Find 18 was recovered from the trench.

Pit 1, a 2×2 meters test pit, was excavated on the flat top of a hill to the southeast of the Trench 1 hill. The hill, which was roughly rectanguloid in shape and had a number of stones on the surface, apparently appeared promising. The pit, however, going through a very thin humus layer, yielded only a few sherds and was closed at a depth of 50 cms. in gray, semidisintegrated granite.

CERAMIC REMAINS

As was the case with He-1, practically all of the ceramic types and varieties have been fully described elsewhere in this report or in the literature so that my comments here will be restricted to significant additions, absences, or variations which occurred at He-2.

The most striking point is the relative absence of either of the great polychrome groups near the area, the Coclé or the Azuero. Although the total number of sherds analyzed is low, only about 600, it is still surprising that only 1 Coclé polychrome sherd was recovered and only 10 Azuero group sherds were found, none of them indisputable. No complete polychrome vessels of either group were recovered, although both Smoked and Red ware spouted jars duplicating those at Sitio Conte were present.

COCLÉ GROUP

COCLÉ POLYCHROME

One sherd, a "drooping lip" sherd from a shallow bowl, too fragmentary to determine chronology from design, but presumably Early Period on the basis of the lip shape.

COCLÉ RED WARE

Coclé Red ware was represented at He-2 by 11 sherds and 2 vessels; a spouted jar (Find 4-c) similar in shape to the one illustrated by Lothrop (Lothrop, 1942, fig. 272, a,), but without incision or fluting, and an open bowl. The junction of the neck and shoulder of the jar was sharply angled, but there was no flattening of the shoulder at the junction point. The lip treatment is similar to that of the Smoked ware spouted jars. Maximum diameter was 17–18 cms. and total height (to rim, not spout tip which extends upward another 1.5 cms.) was estimated at 16.5 cms. The open bowl or dish (Find 11-2) with a diameter of 27 cms. and a height of 7.5 cms. was ring based and had a "drooping lip." The upper or interior surface and the lip exterior were covered with a soft red slip (hardness rating of 2 or less on Mohs' scale); the rest of the exterior was unslipped and retained the orange-buff color of the paste. The paste had a light gray core.

ARISTIDE GROUP

All 29 sherds of this group were classified as Girón type within which 16 were Interior Banded and 13 were Banded Lip. Two Banded Lip open bowls were recovered (Finds 1-a and 2-b). One had eared projections from the rim and both were marked with radially arranged parallel black lines on the lip. Find 1-a had a diameter of 11 cms., and Find 2-b an estimated diameter of 36 cms. Two additional complete or almost complete Girón type Interior Banded variety vessels were recovered, Finds 5-a and 8. Find 5-a, 28 cms. in diameter by 12 cms. high, is an open bowl with rounded base and a ski-tip lip. Decoration consists of a series of black bands running horizontally around the interior of the bowl from just below the lip to about 4 cms. below the lip. Black-banded scroll and V-elements depend from the lowest of these bands (fig. 60, c; pl. 10, a). Find 8 (diameter 30 cms., height 9.5 cms.) has the same shape and rim band decorations, but the base interior bears a black undulating band or snake design bordered on either side by panels of crosshachure (fig. 60, b; pl. 10, b). These scroll and serpent design elements were not apparent at the Girón site, and the other peculiarities in the type noted for the He-1 site concerning size, ski-tip rim, and slip characteristics, apply to the type as it occurs at He-2.

AZUERO GROUP POLYCHROME

Ten sherds, seven of which were classified as faded black-on-white and could just as easily be placed in the Coclé group, one classified as Azuero miscellaneous, and two classified as Coclé-like. Distinctive shapes were not evident.

MISCELLANEOUS TYPES

SMOKED WARE

This type is represented by a very few sherds, even if one includes some of those classified as Buff, no more than four or five at the most, but seven complete or almost complete Smoked ware vessels were recovered. Two examples of the Platanillo variety (Finds 4-e and

10-2) were present, ranging from 17–30 cms. in diameter and from 5–8 cms. in height, and four spouted and collared jars were found (Finds 5-*c*, 7-1, 11-1, and 14-2). Heights of these jars ranged from about 15–19 cms., and diameters from 15.5–20 cms. One example, Find 5-*c*, was fluted. Lips had a broad, shallow groove and a low ridge running around the upper surface (fig. 65, *g*). A pedestal bowl with shoulder flutings and a broad, flat, incised lip similar to examples found at Venado Beach and at He-1 was also recovered. This vessel, Find 5-*b*, was 13 cms. tall, 17.5 cms. in maximum diameter and its pedestal was not perforated as were some of those at Venado Beach. One other possible example of the same variety consists of a plain pedestal only (Find 17), which has a surface treatment and shape similar to others of this variety, but cannot be positively identified.

RED LINE WARES

The Red Line type is represented at the site by 14 sherds and a number of complete vessels. Find 4-*a* is a Pito variety jar. The Red Daubed variety is represented by three vessels: a wide-mouthed, collared and strap-handled jar (Find 10-1); an incensario with handle missing (Find 16); and a wide-mouthed collared jar with red dribble decoration on the collar exterior and shoulder and with rounded points of attachment on the shoulders for two opposed loop handles or adornos. The loop handles, which were missing, are not characteristic of the variety as represented at He-1, Co-2, or He-8, but they are illustrated by Lothrop for Sitio Conte (Lothrop, 1942, fig. 254, *b*). A further possible Red Daubed vessel, Find 1-*b*, was left unclassified due to its eroded and fragmentary condition.

Three vessels were classified as of the Patterned and Modeled variety and, again, the vague and tentative nature of this variety should be stressed. Find 5-*d* is a collared jar with rounded base and a relatively high straight collar which flares out slightly (collar height 2.5 cms. compared to a total vessel height of 8 cms.; diameter 10 cms.) with a faint red slip applied to the lip and collar exterior. An eroded, pointed lug, possibly representing a bird's head and beak, is appended to the shoulder. Its probable opposite is missing, but the point of attachment for another lug is clearly visible on the other side of the vessel. Another collared jar (Find 5-*e*), with rounded base and a high straight collar (collar height 5 cms. compared to a total vessel height of 13 cms.; diameter of 15 cms.) is decorated with a red band on the lip and a second one around the collar base. Rims on both vessels are unmodified. Places for attachment of two opposed loop handles are present on the shoulders of Find 5-*e*. The third vessel of this variety (Find 5-*g*) is a large plate (diameter esitmated at 46 cms.) with an unmodified lip and rounded base. Decoration consists of red bands in a broad chevron design on the upper surface of the plate and a red band around the lip, all on a cream-buff ground slip (fig. 65, *h*). I know of no other examples similar to this.

MISCELLANEOUS RED SLIPPED VESSELS

One example (Find 11-3) of the chalice shape, so common at He-1, with an estimated height of 17.5 cms. and a diameter of 12 cms. was recovered. Other shapes included collared jars and plates. Find 3 was a straight-collared jar with a rounded base, two opposed strap handles on the shoulder, and a short collar which extended upward vertically from the shoulder and terminated in an unmodified lip. The orifice is wide (10.5 cms. compared to an estimated total diameter of 18 cms.) and the vessel is 16 cms. in estimated height. The vessel interior is smoothed and brushed, the exterior and lip interior are red slipped, and the base is fire blackened. Three medium to large squat-collared jars were recovered, two of which (Finds 4-*d* and 15) are similar enough except in overall size to be described as one. Body interiors and collar exteriors are smoothed and brushed and are unslipped, retaining the buff-orange color of the paste. Collar interiors and body exteriors are red slipped with a thin slip or wash. The collars are relatively short and are outcurved with a rounded lip. The bases are rounded, and the orifices are relatively wide. Find 4-*d* has a diameter of 25 cms., an orifice diameter of 15 cms., and an estimated height of 17 cms. Find 15 had a maximum diameter estimated at 38 cms., an orifice diameter estimated at 24 cms. and an estimated height of 27 cms. A third vessel (Find 4-*b*) is considerably more globular (estimated diameter 34 cms., estimated height 30 cms.), has a more constricted orifice (diameter 8 cms.), and a tall straight collar with an outward flare and a lip which is flattened and flanged outward. Surface treatment, however, is the same for this vessel as for Finds 15 and 4-*b*, and the base is rounded. Find 12, another round-based collared jar, has a tall straight collar with an outward flare and an unmodified lip; its shape is roughly globular with a diameter estimated at 20–25 cms. The body interior is smoothed and brushed. The collar interior is unslipped and apparently intentionally decorated with more or less evenly spaced dribbles of red paint or slip. The lip and entire exterior including the collar has been treated with a soft, fugitive red slip or wash. The interior of the base is fire-blackened.

Plates were rare at He-2; only one example, Find 14-1, was found. This is a fairly flat vessel (diameter estimated at 20 cms., height at 3.5 cms.) with a round lip and unmodified base. The upper surface, the lip, and that part of the under surface within 5 cms. of the lip, are covered with a thin red slip or wash.

PLAIN WARE

One vessel (Find 18), possibly an unfinished Red ware vessel, comprises this category. It is a small, unslipped, collared jar with a round base and an outcurving collar. Surfaces are rough and the paste is fired to an orange-buff.

UNCLASSIFIED VESSELS

Find 1-*b*, a badly weathered and eroded jar with a round base, fragments of a strap handle, and an estimated diameter of 15–20 cms. was not classified due to its inconclusive nature. The strap handle and traces of red paint, however, suggest that it may have been a Red Daubed jar.

Find 9 is another badly weathered jar, but with a distinctive shape which has no counterpart in the materials covered in this study. The body is globular with a rounded base and the collar is tall with a widely outcurved neck and rim and an unmodified lip. Total height is 15 cms., diameter is 14 cms., orifice diameter is 5.5 cms., and lip diameter is 10.5 cms. The surface is smoothed and buff-colored with faint traces of red paint or slip on the body and upper lip surface. There are also traces of a black paint or stain on the body exterior.

Another collared jar (Find 13), with an estimated diameter of 26 cms., also appears unique. The base is round, the collar widely outcurving (orifice is 7.5 cms. and lip diameter is 16 cms.), and the upper lip surface is decorated with red paint and a series of shell edge impressions arranged radially. The paste and surface of the vessel are fired an orange-red and the surface is soft (Mohs' scale rating of No. 2) with a waxy feel to it.

STONE ARTIFACTS

Worked stone, consisting only of a few rubbing or polishing stones, a stone celt, and a metate, was very rare at He-2. The metate stands 16 cm. high and is of the table variety, and has three conical legs; two opposing and flush with the sides of the platform, and one along the long axis of the platform but located well inside the edge. The edges of the platform are beveled. The surface is smoothed and worn and is slightly concave along the long (57 cm.) axis but virtually flat along the short (43 cm.) axis. In view of the Girón type and other pottery associations of Find Unit 4–6, this variety of metate can be placed in the Early Coclé Phase in addition to the Late Coclé Phase associations of the variety at He-1.

The celt, Find 7–2, also probably Early Coclé Phase, belongs in the chipped poll category discussed earlier for He-4 and has a broad, fully curved and well-polished blade and a thick, narrow, roughly chipped poll. It most closely resembles one illustrated by Lothrop

for Sitio Conte (Lothrop, 1937, fig. 53, *b*) except that the example from
He-2 has a somewhat thicker cross section.

FIND INTERPRETATIONS AND SITE CHRONOLOGY

He-2 appears to be a site which bridges the later types of the Santa
Maria Phase and the Early Period at Sitio Conte. No Late Period
vessels were recovered either in sherd or complete form, and the only
evidences of Azuero group pottery are the 10 rather vague sherds
mentioned in the section on typology. On the other hand, Girón type
vessels and sherds were represented as were Early Period Coclé vessels
and Red Line and Smoked ware varieties which had Early Period
associations at He-1 and Sitio Conte. Pinilla Black-line-on-red vessels
were absent, but most other varieties which were either definitely or
probably of Early Period vintage at the Pinilla site were represented.

Turning to those finds which either present significant associations
or conditions of excavation, Find 1 associates a large fragment of a
Girón type, Banded Lip variety bowl with a Red Line, Red Daubed
variety strap-handled jar, an association which concurs with the
findings at He-1. Since the field notes make no mention of the bowl
fragment, it is possible that the Girón fragment was not deposited with
the jar but was accidentally included from the surrounding fill. Its
inclusion, however, does no violence to the relative chronology at the
present time.

Find 4-6 was a more complicated unit. Find 4, a cache of pottery
and some badly decayed human bone, was located slightly west of the
center of Trench 1 at a depth of 0.85-1.25 meters. Associated with the
find were a Pito variety jar, a Platanillo variety bowl, two red-slipped
collared jars, and a Coclé Red ware spouted jar. The latter shape
occurred more commonly in the Late than in the Early Period at Sitio
Conte (Lothrop, 1942, pp. 138-139), but in view of the Pito and Platanillo associations and the absence of Late period vessels here, I am
inclined to place this example in the Early Period.

Find 5, a group of six vessels with associated decayed human bone,
apparently adult, was located in the same longitudinal position as
Find 4 but at a depth of 1.08-1.20 meters and somewhat separate in
that it lay against and in the east profile. Immediately above the
unit were 10-15 tightly packed boulders, roughly 15 cms. in diameter,
and the grave pit for the unit showed up clearly as clay and midden fill
in the east profile. Nothing comparable to this was noted in the west
profile for Find 4, but field observations suggested that the two units
may be one. The vessels of the Find 5 unit all may be appropriately
placed in the Early rather than the Late Period consisting as they do
of a Girón type Interior Banded variety bowl, a Red Daubed wide-
mouthed jar, two Red Line Patterned and Modeled variety vessels,

a Smoked ware spouted and fluted jar, and a Venado Beach incised bowl.

Find 6 is a three-legged metate.

Field observations suggested that Find 7 (a Smoked ware spouted jar and a spatulate celt) may be part of the 4–6 Unit placed as grave goods in the upper part of the Find 5 Unit shaft.   The spouted jar would fit chronologically with such an interpretation.

Find 10 associates a Red Daubed strap-handled jar with a Platanillo variety bowl and, again in line with the situation at He-1, would be placed in the Early Period.

Find 11 could also be classified as an Early Period cache on the basis of the Smoked ware spouted jar.   The other two vessels have both Early and Late affiliations; a Coclé Red ware plate with drooping lip (Lothrop, 1942, pl. 14) and a Red ware chalice (Early associations in Find 24 at He-1 and Late in Find 14 at the same site).

Find 14 consisted of two vessels; a Red slipped plate and a Smoked ware spouted jar.   The presence of the latter vessel suggests an Early Period timespan for the find unit.

Glancing briefly at special circumstances connected with the finds, it is apparent that many of them were single complete vessels or caches of two or more without evidence of burial.   In one instance, Find 10, a jar was found with an inverted bowl cover, a practice also found at He-1.   No human remains were associated with this find. Finds 4 and 5 were accompanied by decayed human bone, apparently one individual each.   Find Unit 5 was placed in a clearly delineated pit under a layer of stones and included evidence of fire (Find 5-*f* showed fire clouding over the design and had carbon on both interior and exterior surfaces of the base).   At least one vessel was obviously placed in the grave in a broken condition (the fragments of Find 5-*g* were found stacked on top of each other).   Units 4 and 5 also were associated with nonceramic grave furniture; the three-legged metate of Find 6, and possibly the stone celt of Find 7.   Other burials are represented by the presence of powdered human bone in association with Finds 11 and 15.   The only other evidence of fire uncovered at the site was exterior base burning and blackening of Finds 2–*a* and 3, neither of which was a burial.

SUMMARY

In summary, it appears that He-2 was a hill and valley occupation site during the Early Period as represented at Sitio Conte and contemporaneous, in part, with the Girón site.   The particular hilltop of Trenches 1, 2, and 3 may have been a graveyard, but the number of undecorated and presumably utilitarian sherds suggests a site occupied by people who buried their dead in their living area and also deposited caches of a ceremonial nature.   A dependency on agriculture as the major source of subsistence is suggested by the location of the site at some distance from the sea, by the absence of shell refuse, and by the presence of metates.   It is also possible that the "brushing" noted on the interiors and collar exteriors of some of the vessels, e.g., Finds 4-d and 15, was produced with corncobs.

CHRONOLOGICAL SUMMARY OF THE COCLÉ REGION

SANTA MARIA PHASE

In summarizing the chronology of the five sites treated in detail in this report and consolidating it with the previously existing sequence for the region, it seems most useful to arrange the material in terms of phases beginning with the earliest recognized among the sites; the Santa Maria Phase (see chart 2, p. 19, for chronology).

Like all of those which follow, this phase is based primarily on its pottery content and, in this case, especially on the ceramic stratigraphy of the Girón site. At this site, the Girón and Escotá types, along with a gamut of plastic decorative techniques, were found concentrated in the middle and bottom layers of what was an essentially three-layered Pit 1. Coclé and Azuero sherds representing later phases were restricted to the upper levels; Red Daubed variety sherds maintained a fairly steady but low percentage in all three layers. This pattern was reinforced in Pit 3 at the same site, but is not as clear at other sites. The Aristide group was present at Sitio Conte, but there its polychromes were only gradually replaced by Coclé polychromes. At Venado Beach both the Girón and Escotá types appear along with Early Coclé styles. The phase is represented at He-1 by both Girón and Escotá types, but the latter is present in very small quantity. At He-2 only the Girón type is present, again associated with Early Coclé styles. Thus the Santa Maria Phase, as distinct from the following Early Coclé Phase, is firmly located at only two sites: the Girón site and Sitio Conte.

Little is known about the phase aside from its ceramics. The sites are inland, and agriculture along with some shell fishing is assumed as the subsistence base. Although burials were subsequently excavated at the Girón site by McGimsey (McGimsey, 1959), they were without cultural associations, and Santa Maria graves have not been excavated with the possible exception of Venado Beach. Absolute dates for the phase are unknown.

EARLY COCLÉ PHASE

Following immediately on the Santa Maria Phase, the Early Coclé Phase (corresponding to Lothrop's Early Coclé Period at Sitio Conte) is represented at that site, at He-1, He-2, Co-2, and Venado Beach and by a few sherds at He-4. Associated with the Early Coclé polychromes at Sitio Conte were various Smoked ware shapes and Red Line, Red Daubed variety vessels. This association, in general terms, is repeated at He-1 where varieties were tentatively distinguished in both Red Line and Smoked ware types, and is supported by the grave associations at He-2. Specifically, the

Patterned and Modeled variety, the Pito variety and strap-handled jars within the Red Daubed variety, all within the Red Line type, had consistent Early Coclé associations as did the Platanillo variety of the Smoked ware type. Likewise, the Girón type is definitely associated with Early Coclé vessels in graves at He-2 and was heavily represented in the sherd lots at He-1 where Early Coclé polychromes were also present. However, the stratigraphic situation at the latter site is not clear. Girón type vessels were also common at Venado Beach along with Early Coclé polychromes, but detailed information on the grave associations of these vessels is not now available. Girón pottery, either of this phase or the preceding one, has also been found in the Pearl Islands and near the Gulf of San Miguel in southern Darien.

Thus far, the only evidence available for dating the phase are two carbon-14 dates, A.D. 210 and A.D. 960, obtained at Venado Beach for apparently identical burials. My tendency would be to favor the later of these two, placing the phase in the second half of the first millennium A.D.

On the basis of the rich grave furniture at Sitio Conte and the more subdued remains at He-1, it is clear that the phase represents a major cultural florescence as compared to the relatively simple Santa Maria Phase. Ceramics show considerable artistic imagination and technical excellence. Elaborate jewelry in gold, tumbaga, serpentine, and agate and intricately carved bone are abundant in the larger graves. Bark cloth and woven textiles are indicated by impressions. The monumental stone pillars and carvings of Verrill's Rio Caño "temple" site may have been erected in this phase, for Lothrop notes that although pottery of both the Early and Late Periods at Sitio Conte was collected at Rio Caño, the bulk of it was Early (Lothrop, 1942, p. 212). The nature of the graves at Sitio Conte suggests the development of wealthy chiefdoms and the possible practice of retainer burial, although none of the Early Coclé graves (Grave 32, with six skeletons, is the largest) contains mass interments comparable to the 22 individuals buried in Grave 26 of the succeeding phase. Evidence of the use of fire in connection with burial practices, another characteristic of the following phase, was present in some of the graves at Sitio Conte but absent at He-1 and He-2. The inland site locations, the high development of the more sophisticated crafts such as metallurgy, and the presence of manos and metates in the graves, clearly imply an agricultural base for the society. The continuing importance of the hunt, however, is suggested by the frequent bundles of stone and bone points and stingray spines found with the burials. Incidentally, the practice reported by the Spaniards of using dogs in game drives (Lothrop, 1937, p. 18) may have begun at this time, for numerous perforated dog teeth were recovered from Early graves at Sitio Conte.

LATE COCLÉ PHASE

The Late Coclé Phase, like its predecessor, was first outlined by Lothrop as the Late Coclé Period at Sitio Conte, and typical Late Coclé polychromes have since been recovered at both He-4 and He-1. Red Line and Smoked ware types continued into this phase, although different varieties such as the Aromo and Sangre become popular within the Smoked ware type. Aristide group pottery ceases, but the Azuero group, represented in polychrome by the Macaracas type, first appears in this phase, both at He-4 and at Sitio Conte where it was known as Foreign Style A or the Fine Line Style of Grave 5. Miniature vessels are common in the Late Coclé and Azuero style polychromes. Typical Delgado Red collared and collarless jars occur in association with both Macaracas and Late Coclé polychrome vessels at He-1 and He-4. Macaracas sherds were also found at Co-2 and were the dominant polychrome at He-8. Outside of the Coclé region the phase is represented by Late Coclé style polychromes and, especially, Macaracas type vessels. The latter occur fairly frequently in Veraguas graves, have been reported for Chiriquí and the islands off the Chiriquí coast, but so far have not been unearthed east of Coclé Province. Data for absolute dating is absent for this phase.

The funerary evidence at Sitio Conte and He-1 indicates that the phase is culturally much like its predecessor, but with greater elaboration. The crafts continued to be of very high quality in ceramics, metal, stone, and bone. The earliest burial mounds at He-4 with Macaracas type grave vessels probably belong to this phase and the occupation of Verrill's Rio Caño site is apparently still active. Mass burials occur at Sitio Conte with the principal occupant seated under a canopy (Grave 5) surrounded by his wealth. Evidence of fire in the burial ceremony is more frequent both at Sitio Conte and He-1 where Late Coclé burials were characterized by circular clay-lined pits. Two graves (Graves 9 and 19) at Sitio Conte with Late Coclé pottery contained possible urn burials as well, and at least one urn burial at He-4 was associated with Macaracas pottery.

HERRERA PHASE

The Herrera Phase follows the Late Coclé Phase but is present in force only at the He-4 site, although a few sherds of the Parita type were also present at He-1, He-8, and Co-2. As indicated in the discussion for He-4, the later chronological position assigned to the Parita and El Hatillo types is based, in part, on the stratigraphy at that site (reversed at He-1) and, in part, on the lack of association of these two types with either the Macaracas or the Late Coclé polychrome style. Stylistic interpretation also suggests the development of some Parita design elements out of Macaracas elements. Delgado Red modes, especially the oblique lip of the class "c" collared jars, are characteristic of the phase. With the possible exception of a late carbon-14 date for a deep grave at He-4 (see p. 151), no evidence for absolute dating of the phase has yet come forth. Geographically, the phase is represented on the Parita River, in Veraguas (both El Hatillo and Parita types) and in Chiriquí (Parita type only). The Sitio Conte Period of Decline (Lothrop, 1942) may be contemporaneous. Few, if any, vessels have come to light east of the region adjacent to the Parita River, although similarities to both Parita and El Hatillo types have been noted for the Pearl Islands.

Aside from the ceramics, the phase content so far is scanty. Very few Herrera Phase burials have been excavated; most of the El Hatillo and Parita vessels at He-4 were scattered singly or in caches of two or three vessels throughout Mound III. The few burials which have been excavated, all in Mound II, were urn burials both of adults and children with El Hatillo type vessels, ash, and burned bone in association. Grave furniture consisted of perforated human teeth and delicately carved manatee bone which, aside from the highly developed carving technique, do not indicate the richness or variety of the preceding two phases. On the other hand, the massive amounts of "killed" pottery which comprise the bulk of Mound III, and the existence of the mound itself, certainly indicate a surplus economy.

EL TIGRE AND LA ARENA PHASES

The final two phases, El Tigre and La Arena, remain as described by Willey and McGimsey in 1954 and occur, respectively, around the time of the Conquest or shortly post-Conquest and in recent times. El Tigre, consisting of large coarse vessels found among the coastal salt flats and probably representing the remains of salt boiling operations, may or may not be contemporary with the final part of the Herrera Phase. La Arena pottery was made within the memory of the local inhabitants when visited by members of the 1952 expedition.

In view of the varying geographic limits of the phases as noted above, it is difficult to establish new regions for Panama although the old ones of Veraguas, Coclé, and Darien are now in need of qualification, if not revision. The Canal Zone region is valid, I think, as a transition area between the predominantly plastic-decorated pottery sites of the tropical forest zone to the east and the polychrome tradition of the savanna zone of the west. Beyond that, however, any further differentiation rests on circumstances which have changed through time. Thus, the Santa Maria Phase appears at the present time to have been concentrated in the area between the Santa Maria River and the Rio Grande de Coclé. The Early Coclé Phase shows considerable expansion to the east at Venado Beach, and, on the basis of Girón type, Interior Banded variety finds, possibly as far as the Gulf of San Miguel and the Pearl Islands.   To the west it extends as far as the Parita River, and possibly into Veraguas.   The following two phases, on the other hand, have a more westerly distribution: Late Coclé Phase vessels occur sporadically as far west as Chiriquí and its islands and, in quantity, in Veraguas graves; and Herrera Phase ceramics are limited to the Parita River region with occasional examples farther west.

In view of the foregoing, it seems apparent that Veraguas loses some of its identity in these later phases and that the Parita River region, possibly the whole northern base of the Azuero Peninsula, gains in distinctness from the Coclé region.   Nevertheless, I believe these shifts are too transitory to warrant either the creation of a new Parita region or the inclusion of Veraguas within the Coclé region.   Further excavation may suggest modification of the existing breakdown, especially along the lines of a consolidation of parts of Veraguas with Parita as distinct from Coclé.   At the present time, however, I believe that Parita is best represented as part of the Coclé region, recognizing its differences in the later phases.

COMPARISONS WITH REGIONS BEYOND PANAMA

Among the earlier pottery phases of the Coclé region, the Mona-grillo Phase (Willey and McGimsey, 1954) is that most often cited as having interareal similarities and possible contact with other "formative" phases in both South and Middle America, especially the former.[15] In a temporal sense, Monagrillo, dated at about 2000 B.C., certainly belongs in such a general period. However, when the term "formative" is used in a developmental sense, Monagrillo, except for its ceramics, lacks the typical arts, crafts, accomplishments, and implied agricultural subsistence base of the formative cultures of either Middle America or the Andean areas.

The Monagrillo Phase as it is now known represents an apparently simple culture despite the sophistication of its incised designs on pottery and stone. Basically, the material culture preserved is un-complicated. Pottery shapes (primarily bowls and beakers) are simple, and decorative techniques are limited to incising and simple red paint designs on plain ware. It is true that excised areas are combined with incision and that the latter is often terminated in a dot or punctation, but neither excision nor punctation are used as major techniques in their own right. No worked bone was recovered in definite association with Monagrillo artifacts, and the stone in-ventory, with one exception, more closely resembles that of Cerro Mangote than anything else. The exception to the characteristic assemblage of pebble choppers, grinders, a few crude boulder metates, and chipped stone scrapers, is a fragment of a stone bowl with finely executed incised designs identical to those on the pottery. It is in these designs, with their relatively complex swirls, scrolls, interlocking elements, and excised areas, that the only indications of aesthetic development lie. The painted designs are restricted to well-executed but simple bands, rectangles, pendent triangles, and semicircles. Paint combinations (bichromes or polychromes) are absent as are such forms of plastic decoration as applique, rocker stamping, zoned punctation, reed punctation, adornos, handles, or supports. Rims are simply treated without any apparent attempt at consistent modi-fication. Pottery figurines are lacking. Articles of personal adorn-ment must have been limited to easily worked organic material since no stone, bone, or shell jewelry was found, although the stone bowl fragment mentioned above suggests that this absence may be fortui-tous rather than due to a lack of technical competence. Thus, the general impression is that of a culture considerably simpler than those

---

[15] At a preceramic level the similarities between the pebble or edge grinders of Cerro Mangote in Panama, Pedro Garcia, Cabo Blanco and El Heneal on the Venezuelan coast, and Loiza Cave in Puerto Rico, are noteworthy, while the few examples of fluting and lanceolate-shaped points from Madden Lake indicate general affinities to Paleo-Indian material in both North and South America.

represented by Momil or even Valdivia, and appears closer to that represented by the complexes at Barlovento and possibly Isla de los Indios.

The Valdivia assemblages (Estrada, 1956, 1958; Evans, Meggers and Estrada, 1959), located in shell middens on the south coast of Ecuador, have been dated by carbon-14 methods at between roughly 2500–2000 B.C. and thus are contemporaneous, at least in part, with Monagrillo. Agriculture, if practiced at all, was a minor activity and worked bone and shell are rare. Also like Monagrillo, rough chipping characterizes the stone industry. But the total impression, including ceramics and viewing the four subperiods (Valdivia A, B, C, and D) together, is one of considerable elaboration.[16] For example, pottery shapes include collared jars, insloping and outsloping bowls, thickened and modeled rims, and tetrapod supports. Surfaces are occasionally treated with a polished red slip and, although painted designs are lacking, a variety of plastic decoration fills the gap. This variety includes incision (both with and without rubbed-in pigment), punctation in zones bordered by incision, finger indentation, rocker stamping, excision, striation or brushing, and the use of applique fillets. Designs, often nested rectangles, are unlike the curvilinear motifs which dominate Monagrillo Incised, and the termination of a line by a dot was certainly rare if present at all. Although worked bone and shell objects are uncommon, bone labrets or earplugs, awls, and drilled shell are present. Finally, pottery female figurines are common in the last three of the four subperiods and so characteristic of the complex or phase as a whole that they may be considered diagnostic. In short, although both Valdivia and Monagrillo represent coastal peoples at roughly the same cultural stage and time in history, Valdivia includes so many related traits not shared by Monagrillo while excluding some of the more characteristic elements of the latter, that any marked period of contact or shared influence between the two must be repudiated.

Further to the north much the same conclusion is called for with regard to Momil I of the Sinú River sequence in Colombia (Reichel-Dolmatoff, G. and A., 1956, and Reichel-Dolmatoff, 1957). The sites lie in a lowland riverine region favorable to a subsistence pattern combining hunting and agriculture, and the frequency of pottery griddles along with mammal bones in the refuse implies that such a pattern existed. Unlike Monagrillo, the evidence here suggests considerable reliance on manioc agriculture. Vessel shapes are far more varied and specialized than those of Monagrillo; for example, Momil I forms include dishes, ollas, composite silhouette bowls, pottery stands,

---

[16] This point is also made in the detailed comparison presented in Evans, Meggers, and Estrada, 1959, pp. 80–87.

griddles, and bowls with divided interiors. Surfaces are decorated with a variety of both plastic and painting techniques, the latter ranging from the use of a simple red slip through resist dye painting to bichromes (red on white, black on white, and black on red) and polychromes (black and red on white). Among the plastic decorative techniques, not only do the incised designs for the most part differ from those of Monagrillo,[17] but they extend beyond the use of simple incision and excision to include pigment-filled incision, dentate roulette stamping and zoned crosshatching. Additional proliferation in the crafts is evident in the clay human figurines, bar-shaped clay pendants, pottery rattles, clay disks with designs, and the numerous articles of worked bone including awls, disks, antler tools, and a carved bone monkey from Momil I-b levels. Shell was fashioned into cups, spoons, picks, and buttons, although it is not clear whether these shell objects may be assigned to the Momil I Period. The stone industry, as at Monagrillo, includes the category of pebble tools, but unlike the Panama site also included microlithic points.

The general impression given above is certainly that of a more fully developed culture than at Monagrillo, an impression supported in some ways by the chronological position of 1,000 B.C. to the time of Christ suggested by Reichel-Dolmatoff for Momil I on the basis of comparative materials. However, even if this dating should be shifted back in time as a result of carbon-14 analysis, I do not believe there are sufficient significant resemblances between Monagrillo and Momil I to indicate cultural diffusion between the two.

To the east, on the Isla de los Indios, a small island far in from the coast on the lower Magdalena River, the Reichel-Dolmatoffs excavated 64 badly eroded sherds, 22 of which were decorated (Reichel-Dolmatoff, G. and A., 1953, pp. 61–62). Most of these were incised in a fairly broad line technique with rectangular designs, parallel lines, or crosshatching, none of which particularly resembles Monagrillo Incised. One sherd had a combed surface. Apparently no other cultural remains were found and the chronological position is unknown. Since the only similarity between this admittedly meager assemblage and the Monagrillo pottery is the ubiquitous trait of incised decoration, there is no reason to postulate a connection between the two, and to do so unnecessarily clutters up the search for more reliable affinities.

On the other hand, the shell heap at Barlovento on the Colombian coast near Cartagena in a general way parallels Monagrillo (Reichel-Dolmatoff, G., 1955, pp. 249–272). The coastal shell heap sites are

[17] Examples of both fine line incision and engraving ("Incisa Grabada") which are reminiscent of Monagrillo designs, but do not include the dot termination of lines, may be seen in plate 7, 8, 10–13, and in plate 14, 1, 3, of Reichel-Dolmatoff, G. and A., 1956.

similar, the worked stone shows some similarities, and ceramic decoration limited to incision-punctation and zoned red paint also represents a general resemblance between the two. Furthermore, such traits of the more elaborate Formative cultures as dentate stamping, figurines, basal flanges, tripod or tetrapod supports, and carved bone or shell ornaments are missing at both sites. Carbon-14 dates place the material from Barlovento in a fairly close but somewhat more recent position than the one date for Monagrillo, i.e., from 1500 B.C. to 1000 B.C. (Evans, Meggers, and Estrada, 1959, pp. 90–91).

At a different level of comparison, however, the similarity ends. The incised and punctated designs convey an impression very different from the Monagrillo incision. Not only is the incision very broad, but it usually encloses or borders punctated zones. Reed punctation, finger pinching, and pigment-filled incisions are also present in Barlovento pottery; all characteristics foreign to Monagrillo. Barlovento paints apparently were applied in patches and splotches rather than in the clearly defined geometrical forms of the Monagrillo Red. The stone industries of the two complexes do not share major emphases. Thus, pebble choppers or grinding tools are a major item in the Monagrillo inventory, but are minor if duplicated at all at the Barlovento site (see Reichel-Dolmatoff, 1955, pl. 6, 7, 9, 12, for the closest similarity to Monagrillo pebble choppers), and the characteristic stone artifact of Barlovento, an irregular-shaped stone with small circular depressions hollowed out of the surface, is missing entirely at the Monagrillo site.

It appears that Monagrillo and Barlovento, when compared with the more fully developed Valdivia and Momil, share a craft simplicity or lack of elaboration along with a certain sophistication of ceramic design, but that below this level of generalization the two are so unlike in both stone and ceramics as to represent quite distinct cultures which did not influence each other.

For detailed comparisons further afield, the reader is referred to Willey and McGimsey (1954, pp. 128–132). Their survey concluded that the noteworthy resemblances between Monagrillo and other phases were vague ones in both incision technique and design elements and were evident in such widely separated examples as Los Barrancos of Venezuela, Miraflores of Guatemala, early incised pottery of the Ulua Valley in Honduras, some of the simpler Chavin types of Peru, and incised styles in southeastern United States. As they point out (p. 132), at this level of comparison it is certainly questionable whether one is dealing with the same historical phenomena.

Since the publication of the Monagrillo report, one Middle American site, La Victoria on the western coast of Guatemala, has been excavated and should be noted here. At this lowland riverine site, Coe (1960, 1961) set up a number of phases, the earliest of which, the Ocós, he believes shows definite similarities to the Sarigua Phase of Panama. With regard to Monagrillo, as Coe notes (1960, p. 383), about the only specific similarity is the use of cobbles as milling stones. Certainly, like most of the Formative examples of South America discussed above, Ocós with its figurines, tripod supports, zoned punctation, and irridescent paint is considerably more elaborate than Monagrillo. Moreover, it lacks the designs and the line-dot combination so characteristic of the latter.

Although Ocós and Sarigua share a number of ceramic traits, I am not convinced after an examination of the illustrations for the two phases that they are sufficient to "strongly suggest a connection" between the two as Coe believes (ibid., p. 383). The similarities cited by him consist of thin-walled pottery and such modes as zoned simple shell stamping and zoned punctation. However, zoned impressions, either stamped or punctated, are common to many Formative sites, as we have seen, and do not necessarily imply a connection other than the sharing of a very broad tradition. Moreover, the dominant technique of Sarigua is the use of raised ridges, in some cases true fluting, and it is these rather than incised lines which form the zone borders. Illustrated Ocós material, on the other hand, demonstrates incised borders for the punctated and shell stamped zones as the dominant form, while ridging appears to be confined to the gadrooned and fluted rims (Coe, 1961, figs. 21, *f*, *g*, and 19, *a*). As Coe points out in his comparison, most of the characteristic Ocós shapes do not occur in Sarigua, and, in general, I think the same comment applies to Sarigua as to Monagrillo—that it just does not carry out the degree of elaboration of the Ocós Phase. There may have been a connection between the two, but I do not believe that the evidence for this is particularly convincing.

In the post-Monagrillo phases, most of the Coclé and Canal Zone region pottery affinities appear to be with northeastern South America. Coe sees some similarities between the Zoned Bichrome Period of northwestern Costa Rica and the Scarified ware of Chiriquí, and other similarities between the Early Polychrome A of Costa Rica and the black line styles of the Santa Maria Phase. In the later periods, however, similarities are only of a broad nature, and Costa Rica returns once more to the influences of Mesoamerica (Coe and Baudez, 1961).

A few similarities exist between plastic decorated wares of Momil I and II and those of the Santa Maria Phase, Aristide group pottery. Likewise, some of the painted sherds illustrated for Momil look like both Girón and Coclé pottery in a vague fashion,[18] but the discrepancies between the Momil assemblage with its mammiform supports, basal flanges, figurines and other Formative traits and the Santa Maria-Early Coclé phases which lack these traits are too great to argue for any strong influence between the two regions. The same conclusion holds true for contact between the Betancí Complex and Santa Maria and/or Early Coclé phases, but in this case, the probable time gap argues more definitively against diffusion.[19]

Proceeding eastward, the affinities between Early Coclé vessels at Venado Beach and Sitio Conte and those of Reichel-Dolmatoff's First Painted Horizon (La Loma and El Horno Periods) in the Rancheria region are more realistic chronologically. A few design elements featured in the polychromes of both Colombian periods and shared by Panamanian vessels are quite specific,[20] while the slate pendants and shell beads of the El Horno Period are reminiscent of jewelry of the Early Coclé Phase. Other general resemblances include red on white painting for both Colombian periods (comparable to the Red Line varieties of Panama) and the Black Incised wares of La Loma and El Horno (comparable to the Smoked ware varieties of Panama). Later in the Rancheria sequence vague similarities between the Portacelli Period pottery and Coclé and Azuero polychromes are apparent. But, with the possible exception of the rendition of birds and the sharing of a checkerboard design motif,[21] very few of the similarities are close.

Moving farther eastward, most of the similarities noted are between the Late Coclé and Herrera Phase pottery of Panama and the Period

---

[18] Both groups share an emphasis on plastic decoration, but the Panama pottery lacks the zoning, patterning, and designs which are characteristic of the Momil plastic decoration. The similarities noted in painted wares are based on the Momil black on red sherds illustrated in Reichel-Dolmatoff, G. and A., 1956, plate 12, *1* and especially *2*, to Aristide pottery and the Momil polychrome and black on white sherds of plate 13, especially *2*, which could easily be lost in a Coclé sherd lot. It may be noted that although the polychrome has its greatest popularity in the lower levels of Momil II, it and the bichromes both begin in the middle of Momil I, probably earlier than either Santa Maria or Early Coclé.

[19] The similarities are between the general appearance of Betancí Bichrome vessels illustrated by Reichel-Dolmatoff, G. and A., 1957, plate 6, *3*, *4*, and the black line geometric patterns of Aristide group ceramics and more specifically between the hachure of plate 9, *3*, and designs on Escotá, Crosshatched variety. The associated types of the Betancí Complex, light gray, Modeled incised and excised, all look very different from Santa Maria or Early Coclé Phase pottery, and the Bichrome itself shows different shapes as well as the use of black and red lines for the design. Moreover, Betancí also included copper bells, mounds, and tumuli, all absent in the Panamanian phases, and it occupies the most recent position in the Sinú River sequence with probable historic contact (Reichel-Dolmatoff, G. and A., 1957, p. 130).

[20] Two specific design elements (Reichel-Dolmatoff, G. and A., 1951, pl. 8, *1*, *3*, *6*) of La Loma polychrome are present in Early Coclé vessels at Venado Beach and Sitio Conte and are illustrated by Lothrop for Early polychrome cups and carafes at Sitio Conte (Lothrop, 1942, figs. 311, *h*, 110, and 107). The scroll motif, although quite differently executed, is common for both La Loma and Early Coclé. In the El Horno Period the "volute sigmoid in the form of comb" (Reichel-Dolmatoff, G. and A., 1951, pl. 21, *1*, *2*, *4*) is practically duplicated on an Early polychrome effigy jar at Sitio Conte (Lothrop, 1942, fig. 122).

[21] Compare plate 11, *9*, *11*, *13*, of Reichel-Dolmatoff, G. and A., 1951, with the "pelican" of the El Hatillo variety, figure 10, *c*. The checkerboard pattern is found in the Macaracas type, figure 40, *k*, in true three-color polychrome and also on the burial urns of Cut No. 2 at Los Cocos which Reichel-Dolmatoff believes are probably contemporary with the second phase of the Portacelli Period (ibid., p. 164 and pl. 26, *10*, *14*, *15*). In the latter case the design is in bright red on a white ground.

IV styles of northwestern Venezuela. Cruxent and Rouse (1959) have determined a chronology of five periods for Venezuela based on the coordination of a series of carbon-14 dates with a number of ceramic styles. Only the last three periods concern us here: Period III (A.D. 350–1150); Period IV (A.D. 1150–1500); and Period V (A.D. 1500 to the present). Spatially, the styles with the greatest number of Panamanian affinities are limited, with one exception, to the Lake Maracaibo region, a roughly triangular low-lying area bounded on the north by the coast from the Guajira Peninsula to the Paraguana Peninsula, on the west by the Cordillera Oriente, and on the south and east by the Cordillera de los Andes. The exception mentioned above is located eastward on the coast on the Golfo Triste.

Dealing first with the probably earlier similarities, the La Pitia style along the western coast of the Gulf of Venezuela shows some general similarities to Early Coclé Phase pottery in its curvilinear style, and two specific design elements; an S-scroll and the white ovate in a black rectangle (Cruxent and Rouse, 1958, figs. 32, *13*, and 32, *12*). Additional general similarities include black on white and red on white painting as well as plastic decorative techniques. Unlike the Panamanian pottery, La Pitia includes engraving and bulbous tripod legs but lacks handles and pedestal bases. La Pitia does not have a firm chronological position, and Cruxent and Rouse, although noting especially its close relationships to the Tocuyano style of Period II, conclude that other stylistic resemblances give La Pitia a possible range extending from the second half of Period II to the end of Period IV.

The Debajuro style, centered on the east coast of the Gulf of Venezuela with an apparently solid dating in Periods IV and V, shows many more specific similarities to Herrera Phase pottery, and Cruxent and Rouse compare it with various modes present at Sitio Conte. Unlike the late Panamanian sites, Dabajuro sites are shell middens along the coast. However, they share with Panama the characteristics of urn burial and stone celts with polished blade areas but roughly chipped polls. Pottery shapes include collared jars, shallow open bowls with incurved rims (casuela shape), and open bowls. All the pottery was painted, most of it with designs in red and black on a white or plain ground. Specific modes shared with Late Coclé and especially Herrera Phase pottery include the very frequent use of T-elements in rows and boxes (like the Jobo variety), the angular scroll (El Hatillo variety), undulating line with closed arcs (Macaracas and Calabaza types), solid triangles pendent from a line (Achote variety), double looped vertical handles, rim loop handles, and applique ribbons or "worms" (all unassigned as to type or variety, but present in Red-buff ware or Red and Cream ware in Mound III at He-4).[22]

It is interesting to note in passing that all the examples, illustrated by Cruxent and Rouse, of double loop vertical handles and rim loop handles occurred in styles of northwestern Venezuela which were either limited to Period IV or had a span including Periods IV and V,[23] a distribution which would equate with the Herrera Phase of Panama. Although there are numerous differences between the Dabajuro style and Herrera Phase archeology, there appear to be sufficient specific similarities both in decorative modes and other characteristics, such as the celts and urn burials, to indicate possible diffusion. However, the lack of any similar archeological evidence in the area between Venezuela and the Azuero Peninsula presents an obvious obstacle to this theory.

Two other northern Venezuela styles should be mentioned in this connection; the Palmasola style, located to the east along the coast of the Golfo Triste, and the Tierra de los Indios style inland in the Barquisimeto region. The use of red bordered by black, median flanged collars, pedestal bases with cutout sections, and double loop vertical handles of the Palmasola style are characteristics which are present in either the Late Coclé or Herrera phases of Panama. In the Tierra de los Indios style, two design elements are shared with Panama; the fairly complex "clawed swastika" (Lothrop, 1942, p. 90), which is a characteristic of Late Coclé polychrome at Sitio Conte, is practically duplicated on a Tierra de los Indios vessel (Cruxent and Rouse, 1958, fig. 132, *2*), and the closed arc element of the Macaracas and Calabaza types appears carved on a piece of lignite illustrated by Cruxent and Rouse (ibid., pl. 63, *9*). Similarities with Coclé have also been noted by Osgood and Howard (1943). Painted wares in the style include red on plain, a black on plain, and a red and black on white.

Reviewing this brief section, it is apparent that there are a number of specific ceramic modes as well as more general traits which are shared by Panamanian, Colombian, and Venezuelan archeology in the later periods. Among these the most striking are the affinities between the First Painted Horizon of the Rancheria region in Colombia and the Early Coclé Phase in Panama, and the Herrera Phase-Dabajuro style similarities manifested in the Lake Maracaibo region of Vene-

---

[22] For illustration of these modes see Cruxent and Rouse, 1958, as follows: T-element in figure 42, *4*, *9*, *10*, *11*, and figure 43, *2*, *5-a*, *10*; angular scroll in figure 42, *8*; undulating line with closed arcs in figure 42, *3*, *4*, and plate 21, *10*; solid triangles pendent from a line, figure 43, *4-b*; double looped vertical handles in plates 19, *3* and 22, *12*; rim loop handle plate 22, *2*; applique ribbon or "worm" in plate 22, *22*.

[23] Double loop vertical handles occurred in the following styles: Dabajuro (Pds. IV and V), Aroa (Pd. IV), Palmasola (Pd. IV), and Betijoque (Pds. II–V). Rim loop handles are illustrated for the Mirinday Style (Pd. IV) and the Dabajuro (Pds. IV–V.)

zuela.   In each of these cases, the design elements shared are sufficiently
specific yet uncommon enough in general South American archeology
to suggest diffusion.   How this diffusion took place, if in fact it did,
without leaving more evidence in the intervening areas, is a question
which has yet to be answered.   For the present, it is noteworthy that
within the intervening area the Sinú River valley is about the only
region which has been subjected to intensive archeological survey.
With the exception of some coastal sites and a few others along
Balboa's probable route, most of Darien is archeologically unknown.
It is possible that further work in this region would produce corrobora-
tive evidence of an East-West diffusion such as that postulated above.

LITERATURE CITED

ADAMS, ELEANOR B., and STONE, DORIS, TRANSLATORS AND EDITORS.
  1950. Conversion of Guaymí and Darién and its Indians, by Adrian de
      Santo Thomas. Appendix II, pp. 97–103, in S. K. Lothrop, 1950.
BIESE, LEO P.
  1964. The prehistory of Panamá Viejo. Bur. Amer. Ethnol. Bull. 191,
      Anthrop. Pap. No. 68, pp. 1–52.
BOLLAERT, WILLIAM.
  1860. Antiquarian, ethnological, and other researches in New Granada,
      Equador, Peru, and Chile . . . . London.
BULL, THELMA H.
  1959. Preliminary report on an archaeological site, District of Chame,
      Province of Panama. Panama Archaeol., vol. 2, No. 1, pp. 91–137.
COE, MICHAEL D.
  1960. Archaeological linkages with North and South America at La Victoria,
      Guatemala. Amer. Anthrop., n.s., vol. 62, No. 3, pp. 363–393.
  1961. La Victoria, an early site on the Pacific Coast of Guatemala. Harvard
      Univ. Peabody Mus. Archaeol. and Ethnol. Pap., vol. 53.
COE, MICHAEL D., and BAUDEZ, CLAUDE F.
  1961. The zoned bichrome period in northwestern Costa Rica. Amer.
      Antiq., vol. 26, No. 4, pp. 505–515.
CRUXENT, JOSÉ M.
  1958. Reconocimiento arqueológico en el Istmo del Darién. Bol. Mus.
      Cien. Nat., 1956–1957, vols. 2–3, Nos. 1–4, pp. 102–195.
CRUXENT, JOSÉ M., and ROUSE, IRVING.
  1958. An archaeological chronology of Venezuela. Vol. 1.   Pan American
      Union, Soc. Sci. Mono. No. 6. Washington, D.C.
  1959. An archaeological chronology of Venezuela. Vol. 2.   Pan American
      Union, Soc. Sci. Mono. No. 6. Washington, D.C.
DADE, PHILIP L.
  1959. Tomb burials in southeastern Veraguas. Panama Archaeol., vol. 2,
      No. 1, pp. 16–34.
  1960. Rancho Sancho de la Isla, a site in Coclé Province, Panama: A pre-
      liminary report. Panama Archaeol., vol. 3, No. 1, pp. 66–87.
ESTRADA, EMILIO.
  1956. Valdivia, un sitio arqueológico formativo en la costa de la provincia
      del Guayas, Ecuador. Mus. Victor Emilio Estrada. Publ. No. 1.
      Guayaquil.
  1958. Las culturas Pre-Clásicas, formativas o arcaicas del Ecuador. Mus.
      Victor Emilio Estrada. Publ. No. 5.   Guayaquil.
EVANS, CLIFFORD; MEGGERS, BETTY; and ESTRADA, EMILIO.
  1959. Cultura Valdivia. Mus. Victor Emilio Estrada. Publ. No. 6. Guayaquil.
FERIZ, HANS.
  1959. Zwischen Peru und Mexico. Koninkluk Instituut voor de Tropen,
      No. 134. Amsterdam.
GIFFORD, JAMES C.
  ———— Certain pottery types from Barton Ramie, British Honduras. MS.,
      Harvard Univ., 1961.
GREENBURG, J.
  1956. The general classification of Central and South American languages.
      In Selected papers of the Fifth International Congress of Anthropo-
      logical and Ethnological Sciences, pp. 791–794.   Philadelphia.

HABERLAND, WOLFGANG.
1956. Research in Central America. Archaeol., vol. 9, No. 3, p. 218.
1959. A re-appraisal of Chiriquian pottery types. *In* Actas del XXXIII
       Congreso Internacional de Americanistas, San José, July 1958,
       vol. 2, pp. 339–346.
1960. Villalba, Part I. Panama Archaeol., vol. 3, No. 1, pp. 9–21.
HOLMES, WILLIAM H.
1888. Ancient art of the Province of Chiriquí, Colombia. Sixth Ann. Rep.
       of the Bur. Amer. Ethnol. for 1884–1885, pp. 1–187.
JOHNSON, FREDERICK.
1948. The Caribbean lowland tribes: the Talamanca Division. Bur. Amer.
       Ethnol. Bull. 143, vol. 4, pp. 231–251.
KEEN, A. MYRA.
1958. Sea shells of tropical west America. Stanford Univ. Press.
LADD, JOHN.
1957. A stratigraphic trench at Sitio Conte, Panama. Amer. Antiq., vol. 22,
       No. 3, pp. 265–271.
LINARES, OLGA.
——— The archaeology and ethnohistory of Panama. Seminar paper,
       Harvard Univ., 1962.
LINNÉ, SIGVALD.
1929. Darién in the past: the archeology of eastern Panama and northwestern
       Colombia. Göteborgs Kungl. Ventenskap-och vitterhets-Sam-
       hälles Handlingar, Femte följden, ser. A, vol. 1, No. 3, Göteborg.
1936. Archaeological field work in Chiriquí, Panama. Ethnos, vol. 1, No. 4,
       pp. 95–102. Stockholm.
LOTHROP, SAMUEL K.
1937. Coclé; an archaeological study of Central Panama, Part I. Harvard
       Univ. Peabody Mus. Archaeol. and Ethnol. Mem., vol. 7.
1942. Coclé; an archaeological study of Central Panama, Part II. Harvard
       Univ. Peabody Mus. Archaeol. and Ethnol. Mem., vol. 8.
1950. Archaeology of southern Veraguas, Panama. Harvard Univ. Peabody
       Mus. Archaeol. and Ethnol. Mem., vol. 9, No. 3.
1959. A re-appraisal of Isthmian archaeology. Amerikanistsche Miszellen,
       Mitteilungen aus dem Museum für Völkerkunde, pp. 87–91. Ham-
       burg.
1960. C-14 dates for Venado Beach, Canal Zone. Panama Archaeol., vol.
       3, No. 1, p. 96.
MACCURDY, GEORGE G.
1911. A study of Chiriquian antiquities. Connecticut Acad. Arts, Sci.,
       Mem. vol. 3.
1913. Note on the archeology of Chiriquí. Amer. Anthrop., n.s., vol. 15,
       No. 3, pp. 661–667. [*also in* Heye Mus. Contr., vol. 1, No. 4, 1913–
       1915.]
McGIMSEY, CHARLES R., III.
1956. Cerro Mangote: a preceramic site in Panama. Amer. Antiq., vol. 22,
       No. 2, pp. 151–161.
1959. A survey of archaeologically known burial practices in Panama. *In*
       Actas del XXXIII Congreso Internacional de Americanistas, San
       José, July 1958, vol. 2, pp. 347–356.
MAERZ, A., and PAUL, M. R.
1930. A dictionary of color. New York.

MAHLER, JOY.
  1961. Grave associations and ceramics in Veraguas, Panama. *In* Essays in
    Pre-Columbian art and archaeology, by S. K. Lothrop and others.
    Harvard Univ. Press.
MARSHALL, DONALD S.
  1949. Archaeology of Far Fan Beach, Panama Canal Zone. Amer. Antiq.,
    vol. 15, No. 2, pp. 124–132.
MASON, JOHN ALDEN.
  1942. New excavations at the Sitio Conte, Coclé, Panamá. Proceed. 8th
    Amer. Sci. Cong., Washington, D.C., 1940, vol. 2, pp. 103–107.
MERRITT, J. KING.
  1860. Report on the huacals or ancient grave yards of Chiriquí. Amer.
    Ethnol. Soc. New York.
MITCHELL, R. H.
  1959. Projectile points from Panama. Panama Archaeol., vol. 2, No. 1, pp.
    70–82.
  1960. Panama projectile points. Panama Archaeol., vol. 3, No. 1, pp.
    22–34.
MUNSELL COLOR COMPANY.
  1954. Munsell soil color charts. Baltimore.
OLSSON, AXEL A.
  1961. Mollusks of the tropical eastern Pacific. Paleontological Research
    Institution. Ithaca.
OSGOOD, CORNELIUS.
  1935. The archaeological problem in Chiriquí. Amer. Anthrop., n.s., vol. 37,
    No. 2, pp. 234–243.
OSGOOD, CORNELIUS and HOWARD, GEORGE D.
  1943. An archeological survey of Venezuela. Yale Univ. Publ. Anthrop. No.
    27.
PINART, ALPHONSE L., EDITOR.
  1875–82. Franco. Noticias de los indios del departamento de Veragua, y
    vocabulario de las lenguas guayami, norteño, sabanero y doras-
    que. *In* Bibliothéque de linguistique et d'ethnographie américaines,
    vol. 4. San Francisco.
REICHEL-DOLMATOFF, GERARDO.
  1955. Excavaciones en los conchales de la Costa de Barlovento. Rev.
    Colombiana Antrop, vol. 4, pp. 249–272. Bogotá.
  1957. Momil: a formative sequence from the Sinú Valley, Colombia. Amer.
    Antiq., vol. 22, No. 3, pp. 226–234.
REICHEL-DOLMATOFF, GERARDO, and REICHEL-DOLMATOFF, ALICIA.
  1951. Investigaciones arqueologicas en el Depto. del Magdalena, Colombia—
    1946–1950. Parts I–II. Bol. Arqueol., vol. 3, Nos. 1–6. Bogota.
  1953. Investigaciones arqueologicas en el Depto del Magadalena, Colombia—
    1946–1950. Part III. Univ. Atlantico Divulgaciones Etnologicas,
    vol. 4, No. 4. Bogota.
  1956. Momil, excavaciones en el Sinú. Rev. Colombiana Antrop., vol. 5, pp.
    109–333. Bogota.
  1957. Reconocimiento arquelogico de la hoya del rio Sinú. Rev. Colombiana
    de Antrop., vol. 6, pp. 31–160. Bogota.

SANDER, DON.
    1959. Fluted points from Madden Lake. Panama Archaeol., vol. 2, No. 1,
        pp. 39–51.
    1960. Report on pottery stamp, Chiriquí Province, Panama. Panama
        Archaeol., vol. 3, No. 1, pp. 99–104.
SMITH, ROBERT E.; WILLEY, GORDON R.; and GIFFORD, JAMES C.
    1960. The type-variety concept as a basis for the analysis of Maya pottery.
        Amer. Antiq., vol. 25, No. 3, pp. 330–340.
STEWARD, JULIAN H.
    1948. Circum-Caribbean Culture. In Bur. Amer. Ethnol. Bull. 143, vol.
        4, pp. 2–15.
STEWARD, J. H., and FARON, L. C.
    1959. Native peoples of South America. New York.
STIRLING, MATTHEW W.
    1949. Exploring the past in Panama. Nat. Geogr. Mag., vol. 95, No. 3,
        pp. 373–399. [R. H. Stewart, photographer.]
    1950. Exploring ancient Panama by helicopter. Nat. Geogr. Mag., vol. 97,
        No. 2, pp. 227–246. [R. H. Stewart, photographer.]
STONE, DORIS.
    1958. Introduction to the archaeology of Costa Rica. Museo Nacional,
        San José.
STOUT, DAVID B.
    1948 a. The Cuna. In Bur. Amer. Ethnol. Bull. 143, vol. 4, pp. 257–268.
    1948 b. The Choco. In Bur. Amer. Ethnol. Bull. 143, vol. 4, pp. 269–276.
TAX, SOL.
    1960. Aboriginal languages of Latin America. Current Anthrop., vol. 1.
        Nos. 5–6, pp. 430–436.
VERRILL, ALPHEUS HYATT.
    1927 a. Excavations in Coclé Province, Panama. Heye Foundation Indian
        Notes, vol. 4, No. 1, pp. 47–61.
    1927 b. The Pompeii of ancient America. The Worlds Work, January, pp.
        279–288. New York.
WASSÉN, S. HENRY.
    1960. A find of Coclé-style pottery in a single Veraguas grave, Panama.
        Reprinted from Etnografiska Museet, Göteborg Årstryck for 1957
        Och 1958, pp. 62–81. Göteborg.
WHEAT, JOE BEN; GIFFORD, JAMES C.; and WASLEY, WILLIAM W.
    1958. Ceramic variety, type cluster, and ceramic system in southwestern pot-
        tery analysis. Amer. Antiq., vol. 24, No. 1, pp. 34–47.
WILLEY, GORDON R.
    1951. A preliminary report on the Monogrillo culture of Panama. In The
        civilization of ancient America, edited by Sol Tax, pp. 173–180.
        Selected papers of the XXIXth International Congress of Ameri-
        canists, New York, 1949.
    1958. Estimated correlations and dating of South and Central American cul-
        ture sequences. Amer. Antiq., vol. 23, No. 4, p. 353.
WILLEY, GORDON R., and McGIMSEY, CHARLES R., III.
    1952. Archaeology in western Panama. Archaeol., vol. 5, No. 3, pp. 173–181.
        Cambridge.
    1954. The Monogrillo culture of Panama. Harvard Univ. Peabody Mus.
        Archaeol. and Ethnol. Pap., vol. 49, No. 2.

WILLEY, GORDON R., and STODDARD, THEODORE L.
  1954. Cultural stratigraphy in Panama: a preliminary report on the Girón
        site. Amer. Antiq., vol. 19, No. 4, pp. 332–343.
ZELTNER, A. DE.
  1865. Sepulturas indias del Departemento de Chiriquí en el Estado de
        Panama. El Felix, ca. August 15, Panama. [Lothrop, 1937, notes
        that the only copy of which he knew was in the Musée d'Ethnographie
        du Trocadéro, Paris.]
  1866. Note sur les Sépulturas indiennes du départment de Chiriquí (Etat de
        Panama). Panama.

APPENDIX 1

SITE DISTRIBUTION OF CERAMIC GROUPS, TYPES, AND VARIETIES

Group, type, variety	He-4 site	Co-2 [1] site	He-1 site	He-2 [2][3] site	He-8 site
Aristide:					
Escotá polychrome:					
Black on buff		X			
Black on red		X	X		
Chevron		X			
Crosshatched		X	X		
Plain		[4] X			
Red		X			
Girón polychrome:					
Banded lip		X	X	X	
Interior banded	X	X	X	X	
Plain		X			
Red		X			
Azuero: [2]					
Calabaza polychrome:					
Calabaza	X				
Ceritó	X				
Delgado red	X		X		X
El Hatillo polychrome:					
Achote	X				
El hatillo	X				
Espalá	X				
Jobo	X				
Macaracas polychrome:					
Cuipo	X	X			X
Higo	X	X	X		
Pica-pica	X	X	X		X
Parita polychrome:					
Anón	X				
Caimito	X				
Níspero	X				
Ortiga	X		X		X
Yampí	X	X	X		X
Coclé:					
Coclé black-on-red			X		
Coclé paneled red			X		
Coclé polychrome: [3]					
Early	X	X	X		
Late	X		X		
Coclé red ware	X			X	
Paneled red ware	X		X		

See footnotes at end of table.

SITE DISTRIBUTION OF CERAMIC GROUPS, TYPES, AND VARIETIES

Group, type, variety	He-4 site	Co-2[1] site	He-1 site	He-2[2,3] site	He-8 site
Miscellaneous:					
Black-on-white lip	X				
Buff ware	X		X		
Cream ware	X				
Pinilla black-line-on-red			X		
Plain ware				X	
Red and white ware	X				
Red-buff ware (incl. Delgado red)	X				
Red line ware:					
Patterned and modeled			X	X	
Pito			X	X	
Red daubed	X	X	X	X	
Red ware:					
Chalice shaped			X	X	
Smoked ware:					
Aromo			X		
Coclé spouted				X	
Coclé spouted and fluted				X	
Platanillo	X ?		X	X	
Sangre	X ?		X		
Venado Beach incised			X	X	
White and black on red ware			X		

[1] In referring to Willey and Stoddard (1954) on Co-2, Girón site, read "Santa María" for "Girón" and "Escotá," "El Hatillo" for "Macaracas" and "Parita."

[2] At the He-2 site the few Azuero sherds found were tentative and could be classified only by group.

[3] One Coclé polychrome sherd was found at the He-2 site but its period is unknown.

[4] Plastic decoration on plain includes: lip grooving, broad line incision, fine parallel line incision, lip engraving, rough scoring, punctation, reed punctation, linear punctation, slash punctation and scoring, fingernail impression, shell edge stamping, applique ridging both with and without notching, and pinching and fluting.

APPENDIX 2

HE-4 FINDS OF MORE THAN ONE VESSEL

MOUND I

Find 1. Located in Trench 1, superficial depth; 8.0 m. north; 1.7 m. west.

1-*a*. A class "b" Red-buff collared jar with an angled shoulder; diameter 1.7 cm.

1-*b*. Sherds from a polychrome bird effigy jar with Achote variety shape, but rectangular scroll design.

Find 5. Located in Trench 1, depth 2.4 m.; 3.0 m. north; in west profile, in the fill of a sub-mound pit.

5-*d* and 5-*b*. Large Red-buff collarless jar with blackened interior of base; diameter 38 cm.

5-*i*. Small Red-buff collared jar; class "a"; height 8 cm.

5-*f*. Fragments of a Red-buff plate; base missing; diameter 28 cm.

5-*h*. Polychrome collar and rim; collar and lip are banded and the lip is obliquely flattened in a fashion similar to class "c" Red-buff collared jars; Ortiga variety miscellaneous sherds including an Ortiga variety frog handle.

Comment. 5-*i* was found inside 5-*d*; 5-*h* and the Ortiga frog handle may come from the surrounding fill.

Find 6. Located in Mound I, Trench 1, same location as Find 5.

6-*a*. Buff ware plate with plain base and thick rounded lip; diameter 17.5 cm.

6-*b*. Large (diameter 45 cm.) Red-buff jar with base blackened on the interior; collarless rim fragments of same paste and with loop handle (6-*c*) probably are part of the rim of this jar.

6-*d*. Smoked ware Sangre variety pedestal shallow bowl with diameter 15.2 cm.; paste is fired buff-gray and vessel surface is slipped except for base.

Comment. The pedestal bowl and the plate were found inside the larger jar; on the basis of the similarity of this find and Find 5, and the proximity of their location in the fill of a sub-mound pit, it seems probable that they are contemporary.

Find 8. Located in Mound I, Trench 1, depth 2.4 m.; 3.5 m. north; 2.0 m. west.

8-1. Fragmentary pedestal Pica-pica variety plate with coral snake rim and ray design; lip unmodified in shape; pedestal missing; diameter 26 cm.

8-2. Medium-sized Buff or Smoked ware plate, 20 cm. in diameter; flattened lip; plain base; similar to Find 9-4.

8-3. Medium-sized Red-buff collared jar; class "a" but collar is slipped and lip is flattened horizontally; diameter 18.5 cm.

8-4. Rim fragment of small (12 cm. diameter) reverse flare collared jar; Red and White ware with evidence of modeling on collar.

8-5. Large Red-buff collared jar, class "a" with shoulder handles; diameter 43 cm.

8-6. Small Red-buff collared jar, class "a"; diameter ca. 7 cm.

Comment. The field notes describe Find Unit 8 as a large upright cooking pot with a plate and three red ollas inside. On the basis of this description it is probable that the Pica-pica plate and the reverse flare collared jar are sherds from the surrounding fill.

Find 9. Located in Mound I, Trench 1, depth 2.4 m.; 2.5 m. north; 2.5 m. west.

9-1. Sherd fragments showing a purplish-red scroll design without a black border; paint peeling and no black visible; unclassified.

9-2. Fragments of a large Red-buff vessel of unknown shape.

9-3. Large (43 cm. diameter) collarless jar with loop handles, rounded base, and high shoulder; interior of base is blackened with carbon.

9-4. Well polished gray-buff ware (Smoked) dish with plain base and flattened lip; diameter 17 cm.; similar to Find 8-2.

Comment. Inasmuch as the field notes describe the find unit as a large cooking pot, red rimmed vessel, with a black plate inside it, it is probable that Finds 9-1 and 9-2 above are sherds from the surrounding fill.

Find 346. Located in Mound I, Trench 1, southeast corner in a pit hollowed out of the clay rock at a depth of 3.5 meters.

346-1. Large (45 cm. diameter) open bowl with pear-shaped body and incurving rim; Pica-pica variety.

346-2. Red-buff collared jar, class "a"; 27 cm. diameter.

346-3. Red-buff collarless jar with horizontal loop handles and a lip diameter of 28 cm.; fragments only.

346-4. Miniature ring-based Smoked ware plate; unpolished surface and unmodified lip; diameter 6 cm.

346-5. Pica-pica variety polychrome collared jar, 25 cm. in diameter; decorated with claw elements in closed arc panels and a black line design on the collar exterior; one of the few examples of this kind of collar decoration in the collection.

346-6. Red-buff collared jar, class "a"; diameter range 12.5–15 cm.

346-7. Red-buff collared jar, class "a" with two horizontal loop handles; diameter 8.5–12 cm.

346-8. Large Red-buff ring-based dish or open bowl; diameter 34 cm.

Burials. Find 346-3 contained the remains of an adult. Find 346-1 contained the remains of a child, the Smoked ware plate (Find 346-4), three doglike animals modeled in a resinlike substance, nine gold beads, several stone beads, a pearl, and several concretions or bezoar stones.

Find 364. Located in Mound I, Trench 1, southwest corner of trench at depth of 4.5 meters.

364. Miniature polychrome collared jar; diameter 6.3 cm.; Pica-pica variety.

364-1. Miniature Red-buff collared jar, class "a"; diameter range 5–7.5 cm.

364-2. Miniature Red-buff ring-based plate; diameter range 3.5–8 cm.

Comment. These three miniature vessels were found together in the fill of a pit surrounded by gray-brown waxy clay. No other vessels or artifacts were found with them.

Find 384. Located in Mound I, Trench 1, southeast corner of trench at depth of 6.7 meters.

384-1. Miniature polychrome collared jar; diameter 5.5 cm.; Pica-pica variety.

384-2. Small pedestal polychrome plate; diameter 11.6 cm.; Pica-pica variety.

Comment. In addition, a small roughly made polished stone celt measuring 6.5 cm. long by 2.5 cm. wide by 1.3 cm. thick was found with these vessels.

Additional single or sherd finds for Mound I:

Find 2. Stone mortar.

Find 3. Stone mortar.

Find 4. Modeled polychrome "dog" head and a bone awl.
Find 7. Large Ortiga variety sherd with frog handles.
Find 349. Red-buff collared jar, class "a"; diameter 22 cm.
Find 352. Two collars, one for a polychrome vessel, probably Ortiga variety.
Find 380. Small collarless jar with horizontal loop handles; diameter range 8.5–
12 cm.; Red-buff ware.

MOUND II

Find 10. Located in Mound II, Trench 2, at depth of 40–70 cm. or more; north
2.3–1.5 m.; west 1.2–1.3 m.

10-1–10-8 and five additional specimens in Panama (Finds 10-36–10-41);
were 13 globular bottles, Jobo variety; diameters 14–15 cm.

10-9–10-16 and nine additional specimens in Panama (Finds 10-27–10-35);
16 wingless bird jars, Jobo variety; diameters 12–14 cm.

10-17. Bird jar with wings, Jobo variety; diameter 14 cm.

10-18. Collared jar, Red-buff, class "a"; diameter 21 cm.

10-19, 10-20, 10-22–10-26. Seven miniature (diameters ca. 8 cm.) jars with
flared or straight collars; chalky buff ware with rough gritty surface.

10-21. Red-buff collarless jar with loop handles; diameter in 8.5–12 cm.
range.

Olla 1. Red-buff class "e" collared jar with four vertical loop handles;
diameter ca. 60 cm.

Olla 2. Red-buff class "e" collared jar with at least two horizontal loop
handles; interior of base is carbonized; diameter ca. 50 cm. *Cover:*
open bowl with flared rim and short flaring base; diameter 26.5 cm.;
interior blackened and vessel found inverted over mouth of olla;
no other vessel like this is known from the site.

Olla 3. Large jar with an estimated diameter of 80 cm.; so badly crushed in
situ that it was not saved; probably a Red-buff class "e" jar.

Olla 4. Large unslipped collared jar (height 56 cm.; diameter 42 cm.)
with four vertical double loop handles placed equidistantly about the
shoulder.

Olla 5. Red-buff class "e" collared jar with four horizontal loop handles;
diameter estimated in 50–60 cm. range. *Cover:* open bowl or dish 34
cm. in diameter; 10 cm. deep; unmodified lip and rim; rounded base;
from near center of base exterior two loop handles extended at right
angles to each other; base interior not blackened and both interior
and exterior surfaces are roughly smoothed but unslipped, retaining
the brick-red color of the pastel; found inverted over Olla 5.

Bone. Carved manatee bones (pl. 1, *a–c*), burned bones, necklace of perforated human teeth.

Comment. Find 10 is one of the larger find units of the site, containing
about 50 pottery vessels, ornaments, and the remains of at least 15
individuals. All the bird jars and bottles were found inverted in a
group at a level of 40 cm. or slightly above the 60 cm. level of the urns.
The carved manatee bone batons were also recovered at the 40 cm.
level, about half way between the group of small vessels and Olla 1.
The latter contained the bones of apparently three individuals and a
necklace of 737 perforated human teeth and was surrounded by a
pile of ashes and some burned bones.

Olla 2 was crammed full of bones, apparently the remains of two
adults and one young person and, in addition, contained a small
necklace of perforated human teeth and a conical bone object; included
among the bones were three jaws but no skulls.

Olla 3 contained two adult skulls and many bones, but no artifacts.

Olla 4 contained the bones of one adult including a mandible but no skull; no artifacts were in the urn.

Olla 5 contained the bones of three individuals including three skulls, but no artifacts.

Olla 6 contained the bones of two adults and one infant but no artifacts.

This find unit represents a burial assemblage which, with the exception of other similar but smaller finds in Mound II, is rare at the site. Class "e" urns were not recovered outside of Mound II and the only Jobo variety pottery outside of Mound II consisted of 19 sherds from the uppermost level of Trench 7.

Find 14. Located in Mound II, Trench 2, at depth of 1.2 m.; north 3.3 m.; east profile.

14-1, 14-2, and 14-8. Three miniature ring-based plates or shallow bowls with red-slipped interiors but buff colored and roughly finished exteriors; diameters in 10–11 cm. range.

14-3–14-7. Five miniature Red-buff class "a" collared jars; diameters in 7–12 cm. range.

14-9. A large Red-buff class "e" collared jar with four loop handles placed vertically on the shoulder.

14-10. Olla cover; open bowl about 30 cm. in diameter and 9 cm. deep with two loop handles crisscrossed on the center of the convex surface; entire exterior including handles is red-slipped as is the interior lip; remainder of interior is polished buff-brown; lip unmodified.

Comment. The large urn or jar contents included a stone bead, perforated teeth which were presumably part of a necklace, a piece of white lime, and a burial. Thus the unit is very similar to Find 10, especially in the close resemblance between Find 14-9 and Find 10, Olla 1, and between Find 14-10 and the cover of Olla 5 in Find 10.

Find 15. Located in Mound II, Trench 2, at depth of 30 cm. in southwest corner.

15-1. Collared jar, class "e" with probably two horizontally placed loop handles; diameter 38 cm.

15-2. Ring-based collared jar with shoulder bosses (see fig. 56, i–j); vessel too fragmentary to reconstruct the diameter, but diameter of ring base is 16 cm.

Additional sherds. A few fragments of a deep, 32 cm. wide bowl with a plain lip, blackened interior, and unslipped gray-buff exterior were present as well as sherds from a large Red-buff ware collared jar; it is not clear whether these sherds belong to the find unit or were from the surrounding fill.

Comment. Both urns were inverted and apparently were not burial urns. Find 15-2 appears to be almost a duplicate of Find 17-2 and, according to field observations, the two finds were probably part of the same cache.

Find 16. Located in Mound II, Trench 2, adjoining Find 14.

16-1. Wingless bird effigy jar, Jobo variety.

16-2–16-3. Two small (diameter 11 cm.) ring-based shallow dishes, one with a highly polished red-slipped upper surface and an unslipped rough under surface; entire surface of other is unslipped and rough.

16-4–16-5. Two small Red-buff collared jars (diameter 10 cm.), class "a"; both are roughly finished and have a lumpy surface; bases almost flat.

16-6. Large collared class "e" jar with four vertically placed loop handles on the shoulder; height 55 cm.; diameter 55 cm.; collar is short and straight.

16-7. Rim fragments of an open bowl or dish, presumably pot cover; Red-buff ware; red-slipped outer surface; diameter ca. 30 cm.; interior smoothed and polished light chocolate brown.

Comment. The urn contained the bones of one individual but no artifacts. No mention was made in the field notes of the pot cover.

Find 17. Located at a depth of 40 cm. in the southwest corner of Trench 2, apparently as part of Find 15.

17-1. Wingless bird effigy vessel, Achote variety.

17-2. Collared jar with ring base and modeled bosses, apparently duplicate of Find 15-2.

Comment. The olla was inverted. No mention was made in the field notes of the Achote vessel, which was badly broken. According to field observations, the unit is probably part of Find 15.

Find 18. Located in Mound II, Trench 2; the top of the urn was 1.2 m. below the surface, just outside the main trench, at point 3.6 m. north.

18-1, 18-5. Two small collared jars (diameters 10–14 cm.); Red-buff ware, class "a" with unslipped collar exteriors.

18-2, 18-6. Two miniature ring-based plates (diameters 10–14 cm.) with slipped interiors and unslipped exteriors; Red-buff ware.

18-7, 18-8. Two small ring-based plates (diameters 10–10.5 cm.) of rough unslipped gray ware.

18-4. Red-buff dish (diameter 29 cm.; estimated 6 cm. deep); interior unslipped but smoothed; exterior has polished red slip; base missing; fragments probably represent the pot cover with crisscross handles mentioned in the field notes.

18-3. Straight-sided bottle with spout missing; surface design almost obliterated, apparently by heat; El Hatillo polychrome, El Hatillo variety.

18-9. Pedestal dish (diameter 28 cm.); Smoked ware; unmodified rim.

18-10. Burial olla, class "e" with four vertical loop handles; base missing.

Comment. The burial urn contained two adult remains; the four small pots were found around its base.

Additional single vessel finds for Mound II:

Find 11. A small, unslipped buff ware jar similar to Find 10-19.

Find 12. Bird effigy bottle, diameter 11 cm.; atypical Jobo variety.

Find 13. Bone point.

MOUND III

Find 19. Located in Mound III, Trench 3; at depth of 15 cm.; north 10.4 m.; west 1.0 m.

19. Red-buff collared jar, class "a"; diameter 20.5 cm.

19-*a*. Calabaza variety bottle; diameter 15 cm.

Find 21. Located in Mound III, Trench 4; 1.3 m. north; in east profile.

21. El Hatillo variety globular bird jar.

Comment. Field notes describe the find unit as "A bird effigy jar, painted, a black pedestal based bowl, a red bottle." The second two vessels were not present in the collection nor could photographs or further description of them be located.

Find 22. Located in Mound III, Trench 4, at depth of 1.0 m.; north 1.60 m.; west 2.0 m.

22-1. El Hatillo variety globular bird bowl; diameter 17.5 cm.

22-2. Níspero variety bird bowl; diameter 20.5 cm.

22-3. El Hatillo variety large bird jar; diameter 22.5 cm.

Comment. Field notes list Find 22 as a "bird effigy pot." Due to confused labeling, the association of these vessels could not be considered certain.

Find 24. Located in Mound III, Trench 4, at depth of 1 m.; north 60 cm.; west 3.6 cm.

24-1. Anón variety bowl with pedestal missing; diameter 17 cm.

24-2. El Hatillo variety "dovelike" bird bottle; width 10 cm.

Comment. Field notes describe the find unit as "bird effigy, small olla."

Find 27. Located in Mound III, Trench 4, at depth of 1 m.; south 30 cm.; west 1 m.

27. El Hatillo variety "dovelike" bottle; width 7.5 cm.; length 20.5 cm.

27-*a*. Red-buff ware collared jar, class "a"; diameter 7–12 cm.

Comment. Field notes describe the unit as "Four pots." Information on the other two vessels was lacking, although Find 22-3 may be one of the Find 27 "pots."

Find 30. Located in Mound III, Trench 4, at depth of 1.3 m.; north 30 cm.; west 1 m.

30-1. El Hatillo variety straight-sided bottle with spout missing; diameter 16 cm.

30-2. El Hatillo variety "dovelike" bottle; width 10 cm.; length 19 cm.

30-3. Anón variety bowl; pedestal missing; diameter 17.5 cm.

30-4. El Hatillo variety straight-sided vessel (bottle ?); diameter 14.5 cm.

30-5. El Hatillo variety globular bird bowl; diameter 19.5 cm.

30-6. Red-buff collared jar; class "b"; diameter 19.5 cm.

30-7. Red-buff globular bird effigy bowl; diameter 20.5 cm.

30-8. Number omitted.

30-9. El Hatillo variety pyramid-shaped bottle; diameter 16 cm.

30-10. El Hatillo variety globular bird bowl; diameter, including wings, 19 cm. (see below).

30-11. Red-buff collared jar, class "a"; diameter 12.5–15 cm.

Comment. Vessel 30-10 may not belong in this find unit since the field notes, on which the description is based, question the find number.

Find 39. Located in Mound III, Trench 3, at depth of 1.2 m.; north 5.2 m.; west 2.0 m.

39-*a*. Níspero variety bird effigy bowl; diameter 17 cm.

39-*b*. No record.

Comment. Field notes describe the find unit as "two bird effigy pots."

Additional Mound III finds.:

So many single finds were made in the Mound III trenches that no attempt will be made here to list them all. For the most part they were Níspero, Anón, or El Hatillo variety vessels, especially the former two categories.

MOUND IV

No finds were made in Mound IV.

MOUND V

Find 219. A stone celt.

MOUND VI

No finds were made in Mound VI.

MOUND VII

Find 347. Located in Mound VII, Trench 7, at depth of 1.30–1.75 m.; north
8.4 m.; west 1.3 m.

347-1–347-6, 347-49–347-74. Eight small Red-buff ring-based plates;
diameter range 10–14.7 cm.

347-7–347-14, 347-16–347-48. Forty-two small Red-buff collared jars,
class "a" often with slightly flattened bases; diameter range 7–12.5
cm.

347-15. Small Red-buff plate with low pedestal base; diameter 12–15 cm.

Comment. Four partially cremated burials were found partly encircled by
the small collared jars listed above. The jars did not appear to be
individually placed in any special position, although most of them were
upright. Of the four skulls, one was definitely an adult and another
a child. Find 347-15 probably belongs with the 347-1–347-6 and
347-49–347-74 group of ring-based plates.

Find 348
and   350. Located in Mound VII, Trench 7, at depth of 1.3 m.; north 6.3 m.;
west 5 cm.

348-1, 348-3–348-11. Ten small Red-buff collared jars, class "a"; diameter
range 7–12 cm.

348-12. Small Red-buff ring-based plate; diameter 10–14.7 cm.

348-2. Caimito variety effigy vessel fragment; estimated diameter 16 cm.

350-1–350-5. Five small Red-buff ring-based plates; diameters in 7–12
cm. range.

Comment. Find 348-2, the only decorated vessel in the unit, consists of a
large fragment only, the numbering on it is not clear and there is no
mention of it in the field notes. Under the circumstances, its inclusion
in this unit must be made with reservations. Two fragments of bone
batons were recovered with Find 348, and field observation noted that
Find 350 "may be related" to Find 348.

Find 351. Located in Mound VII, Trench 7, at depth of 1.5 m.; north 3.7 m.;
west 55 cm.

351-1. Small Cuipo variety collared jar; diameter 11.5 cm.

351-2, 351-6, 351-7. Three small Red-buff collared jars, class "a"; diameters 7–13 cm.

351-3. Small polychrome collared jar; Pica-pica variety; diameter 9.5 cm.

351-4, 351-5. Two small Red-buff collared jars, class "a" with loop handles;
diameter range 8–12 cm.

Comment. No other artifacts or vessels were reported for the unit.

Find 354. Located in Mound VII, Trench 7, at depth of 1.7–2.0 m.; north 8.5 m.;
west 31 cm.

354-1. Red-buff ring-based plate; with handle from center to rim; diameter
18.5 cm.

354-2, 354-7, 354-8. Three small Red-buff collared jars, class "a"; one with
a straight collar; diameter range 5–7.5 cm.

354-3. Miniature pot cover; Red-buff; loop handle; diameter 5 cm.

354-4, 354-5. Two small Red-buff collared jars with ring bases; class "b";
diameters 9–10 cm.

354-6. Small Red-buff collarless jar, two loop handles; diameter range
8.5–12 cm.

354-9–354-13. Five miniature collarless jars; two loop handles; diameter
range 5.7–7.2 cm.

354-14. Miniature ring-based plate; Red-buff ware; unpolished; diameter range 3.5–8 cm.

Comment. Associated with the unit was a considerable amount of black decayed organic matter.

Find 357. Located in Mound VII, Trench 7, at depth of 2.4 m.; north 1.45 m.; west 2.8 m.

357-1, 357-2. Two small Red-buff collarless jars with horizontal loop handles; diameter range 8.5–12 cm.

357-3–357-7. Five small Red-buff collared jars, class "a"; diameter range 7–12 cm.

Comment. Burned earth was associated with two of the jars of this find unit.

Find 359. Located in Mound VII, Trench 7, at depth of 2.4 m.; north 4.4 m.; west 2.8 m.

359. Small Red-buff collarless jar with two horizontal loop handles; diameter range 8.5–12 cm.

Comment. Field notes describe the unit as consisting of a medium-sized olla, a small handled olla (presumably Find 359 above) associated with a burial, and crushed bone material.

Find 361. Located in Mound VII, Trench 7, at depth of 2.9 m.; north 9.3 m.; west wall.

No ceramic contents. Consists of several pieces of copper, a long shell bead, and cremated human bone.

Find 362. Located in Mound VII, Trench 7, at depth of 2.5 m.; north 2.4 m.; west 1.09 m.

362. Red-buff plate 12 cm. in diameter; base missing but of raised type.

362-*a*. Red-buff collared jar with ring base, class "b"; diameter 12.5 cm.

362-*b*. Red-buff collared jar, class "a"; diameter range 7–12 cm.

Find 366. Located in Mound VII, Trench 7, at depth of 3.1 m.; north 7.3 m.; west 2.8 m.

366. Small Red-buff collarless jar with loop handle opposed by a lug or node which has a punctated "eye"; diameter 8.7 cm.

366-*a*. Medium collarless Red-buff jar with loop handles; diameter range 15.5–16.5 cm.

366-*b*. Miniature Red-buff pot cover with central lug; diameter 6.5 cm.

Comment. The field notes describe the unit as one small olla and a larger broken vessel; all three vessels described above were unbroken.

Find 368. Located in Mound VII, Trench 7, at depth of 3.1–3.4 m.; north 5.6–5.9 m.; west 2.0–2.9 m.

368-1. Polychrome pedestal plate; Higo variety, dancing crocodile; diameter 27 cm.

368-2. Polychrome pedestal plate; Higo variety, crouching crocodile; diameter 26 cm.

368-3. Polychrome collared jar; Pica-pica variety; diameter 22 cm.

368-4, 368-5, 368-7, 368-12, 368-30–368-32. Seven miniature or small polychrome pedestal plates; Pica-pica variety; diameter range 7–13.5 cm.

368-6. Number omitted.

368-8–368-11, 368-14, 368-15, 368-21–368-27. Thirteen miniature polychrome collared jars; Pica-pica variety; diameter range 4–8.7 cm.

368-13. Red-buff miniature angled shoulder collared jar; diameter 4.5 cm.

368-16. Polychrome pedestal plate; Higo variety, crouching crocodile; diameter 25 cm.

368-17. Polychrome pedestal plate; Higo variety, both crouching and galloping crocodile motifs; diameter 26.5 cm.

368-18. Red-buff pot cover with loop handle in center; diameter 3.4 cm.

368-19. Red-buff miniature collarless jar with two opposed projections from shoulder, one vertical and one horizontal; diameter 4.6 cm.

368-20. Small Red-buff jar with loop handles and short collar; diameter range 8.5–12 cm.

368-28, 368-29. Two Red-buff miniature collared jars, class "a"; diameter 5–7.5 cm.

368-33, 368-34. Two Red-buff miniature pedestal plates; diameter range 6.5–8 cm.

Comment. In addition to the ceramic material listed above, the unit also contained fragments of human bone, a crushed adult male skull ("probably associated") and four jade beads. This seems a surprisingly meager human accompaniment to a grave containing so many elaborate polychrome vessels. The find also included a miniature stone celt with beveled edges.

Find 369. Located in Mound VII, Trench 7, at depth of 2.5–3.0 m.; north 1.0–1.7 m.; west 1.4 m. to east wall.

369-1. Polychrome collared jar with angled shoulder; Cuipo variety; diameter 13 cm.

369-2. Miniature polychrome collared jar; Pica-pica variety; diameter 6 cm.

369-3. Small polychrome collared jar; Pica-pica variety; diameter 7.5 cm.

369-7, 369-21–369-25, 369-34. Seven Red-buff collarless jars with horizontal loop handles; diameter range 5.7–16.5 cm.

369-8, 369-9, 369-12, 369-14, 369-26–369-33. Twelve Red-buff collared jars ranging in diameter from 5–14 cm.; 10 of them fall within the 7–12 cm.

369-20. Red-buff jar with vertical loop handles; rim undescribed; diameter 12.5 cm.

369-11, 369-35–369-40. Seven small Red-buff pedestal plates; diameters 10–14.5 cm.

369-18. Miniature Red-buff open bowl, shallow; diameter 7.2 cm.

369-10, 369-16. Two small Red-buff bird jars, similar in shape to El Hatillo polychrome, Achote variety, examples except for size; diameters 8.5–9.5 cm.

369-4, 369-5. Two small Red-buff globular bottles similar to El Hatillo polychrome bottles in shape; diameters 9–10 cm.

369-6. Small Red-buff pyramid-shaped bottle similar to Ceritó variety polychrome examples in shape; diameter 11 cm.

369-13, 369-41. Two small Red-buff loop-handled pot covers; diameters 9.5 and 4.6 cm.

369-16, 369-17. Fragments of two polished black Smoked ware pedestal open bowls with flattened and/or grooved rims; one is possibly a Sangre variety vessel; diameters estimated ca. 20 cm.

369-19. Miniature Smoked ware tripod open bowl with gutter rim; diameter 4.4 cm.

Comment. The only other contents of the unit mentioned in the field notes consist of a fragment of a spoon or pipe of bone. This unit combines Pica-pica and Cuipo polychrome vessels with Red-buff vessels sharing shapes with the El Hatillo and Ceritó polychrome varieties, a suggested contemporaneity of Macaracas and El Hatillo types which is at variance with the stratigraphic evidence. Possibly these particular vessel shapes, the pyramid bottle, globular bottle, and bird jar shapes, were developed earlier in the Red-buff wares, or the three polychrome vessels may have been heirlooms. Aside from the polychromes, specific similarities to Find 372 include the following: Find 369-18 is almost identical to 372-15 and 372-19. The same comment applies for Find 369-19 and 372-16.

Find 372. Located in Mound VII, Trench 7, at depth of 2.65 m.; north 1.1 m.; west 1.4 m.

372-1–372-3, 372-20. Four small polychrome collared jars; Pica-pica variety; diameters 7.3–12.5 cm.

372-6–372-11, 372-23–372-25. Nine miniature polychrome pedestal plates; Pica-pica variety; diameter range 6.5–10 cm.

372-4, 372-18. Two bowls, black line on white; Pica-pica variety; diameters 6.3 and 10 cm.

372-5. Miniature deep open bowl with projections missing from upper shoulder; black line on white; Pica-pica variety; diameter 5 cm.

372-14, 372-17, 372-21, 372-22. Four miniature Red-buff collarless jars with horizontal loop handles (one has both a vertical and horizontal loop handle); diameters 5.7–7.5 cm.

372-12, 372-13. Two miniature Red-buff pedestal plates; diameters 7.5 and 8.5 cm.

372-26. Red-buff pedestal plate, miniature; diameter range 3.5–8 cm.

372-27. Red-buff plain-based plate with rim handles and nodes; diameter 10.5 cm.

372-15, 372-19. Two Red-buff miniature shallow open bowls with incurving rims; diameter range 7–7.5 cm.

372-16. Miniature tripod Smoked ware open bowl with gutter rim; diameter 6 cm.

372-28. Smoked ware round-based plate with rim handles and nodes; diameter 8.3 cm.

Comment. Two adult skulls and three chipped poll celts were found with the unit, but no other items of significance were noted. Except for the black line on white vessels, the unit is limited to Pica-pica polychromes and ubiquitous Red-buff shapes, although as noted earlier, there are specific resemblances to Find 369.

Find 373. Located in Mound VII, Trench 7, at depth of 3.0 m.; north 2.3 m.; west 2.7 m.

373-1. Polychrome pedestal plate; Pica-pica ray design; diameter 27.5 cm.

373-2. Polychrome pedestal plate; Pica-pica variety; diameter 26 cm.

373-3. Polychrome collared jar; turtle motif, Cuipo variety; diameter 38 cm.

Comment. Find 373-1 merits further description. The design layout consists of three hammerhead sharks or rays with full face treatment. The subject matter and full face treatment suggest Yampí variety, but the angular style of depiction, solid purple bodies except for a red border, and the heavy filler elements all would be out of place alongside Yampí variety plates. Definite Macaracas type elements include the coral snake lip treatment and the diamond base. The plate could be either a Macaracas type copy of a Yampí variety idea or, what is more consistent with other evidence for an earlier chronological position for Macaracas, a prototype for later Yampí elaboration. A number of similar vessels have been found in a Veraguas grave associated with other Macaracas type specimens by Dr. Russel H. Mitchell of the Canal Zone (personal communication from Dr. Mitchell).

No other significant items are reported for the unit.

Find 375. Located in Mound VII, Trench 7, at depth of 3.3 m.; 1.1 m. north; 2.0 m. west.

375-1–375-4. Four miniature polychrome pedestal plates; Pica-pica variety; diameters 9.5–11.5 cm.

375-5. Miniature polychrome collared jar; Pica-pica variety; diameter 7 cm.

375-6, 375-9. Two miniature Red-buff collarless jars (one represented by rim fragments only) with horizontal loop handles; diameters in 5.7–7.2 cm. range.

375-7. Miniature Smoked ware tripod bowl with gutter rim; diameter 4.5 cm.

375-8. Miniature Red-buff collared jar, class "a"; diameter in 5–7.5 cm. range.

375-10. Miniature Red-buff dish or pot cover; no handles; diameter 5.8 cm.

Comment. These vessels were found in a small refuse-filled pocket in the bedrock with no other associated artifacts or remains. Find 375-7 is similar to Finds 369-19 and 372-16.

Find 377. Located in Mound VII, Trench 7, at depth of 2.9 m.; northeast corner.

377-1, 377-4. Two Red-buff globular bottles; diameters ca. 7 cm.

377-2. Red-buff pyramid bottle similar to Ceritó and El Hatillo variety in shapes; diameter 8.2 cm.

377-3. Red-buff collarless jar with two short flat lugs; diameter 11.8 cm.

377-5, 377-7, 377-19–377-26. Ten Red-buff collared jars, class "a"; some with rope handles; diameters in 7–23 cm. range (eight are in the 7–12 cm. range; one is 12–15 cm.; one is 17–23 cm.).

377-6. One Red-buff collared jar, class "b"; diameter in 15.7–16.5 range.

377-9–377-18, 377-29. Ten Red-buff collarless jars with horizontal loop handles; diameters 5.7–16 cm. (eight were in the 8.5–12 cm. range).

377-27. Small Red-buff jar with reverse flare effigy collar; diameter 8.2 cm.

377-28. Red-buff collarless jar with one horizontal loop handle opposed by one effigy lug; diameter 10.5 cm.

377-30. Medium Red-buff ring-based plate; diameter 10–14.7 cm.

377-31–377-36. Six Red-buff pedestal plates; diameters in 10–14 cm. range.

377-37–377-39. Three Red-buff pot covers with lug handles; diameters 6–10 cm.

377-40. Red-buff pot cover with loop handle; diameter 7.8 cm.

Comment. Included in the unit with the vessels listed above were a carved bone baton and cremated burial remains. The unit extended across the entire trench.

Find 378. Located in Mound VII, Trench 7, at depth of 3.6 m.; north 5.8 m.; west 2.2 m.

378-1. Small polychrome pedestal plate; Pica-pica variety; diameter 13.5 cm.

378-2. Miniature polychrome collared jar; Pica-pica variety; diameter 6 cm.

378-3, 378-4. Two apparently identical Smoked ware ring-based open bowls, gutter rims with high interior flange (a Sangre variety rim); diameter ca. 8 cm.

Comment. No other vessels, artifacts, or items of significance were noted for this cache.

Find 379. Located in Mound VII, Trench 7, at depth of 2.9 m.; north 1.4 m.; east profile.

379-1. Small Red-buff collared jar, class "a"; diameter range 7–12 cm.

379-2. Miniature Red-buff collared jar, probably reverse flare collar; beak and nodes for eyes on rim; diameter 6.2 cm.

379-3. Miniature polychrome collared jar; Pica-pica variety; diameter 5 cm.

Comment. No other objects were noted for this unit.

Find 381. Located in Mound VII, Trench 7, at depth of 4.7–5.0 m.; north 2.7 m.; east profile.

381-1, 381-2. Two small collared jars, Red-buff, class "a"; diameter range 7–12 cm.

Comment. The unit also contained a few fragments of gold-plated copper in the pit fill, gold disks with perforations, carved elongated shell beads, numerous shells, and some calcined human bone. The field notes mention "several vessels." Information on only two was available, but it is probable that more vessels were involved in view of the ornaments included.

Find 382. Located in Mound VII, Trench 7, at depth of 4.9 m.; north 2.6 m.; west wall.

382-1. Miniature polychrome collared jar; Pica-pica variety; diameter 6.5 cm.

382-2. Fragment of a Red-buff gadrooned globular vessel; diameter estimated at 18.5 cm.

382-3. Fragment of large Red-buff globular vessel; diameter estimated at 35 cm.

Comment. Field notes describe the unit as a small painted olla and a large plain plate with considerable gray ash in association.

Additional single finds in Mound VII:

Find 344. Listed in field notes as an olla and stand: Two vessels were marked as Find 344: (1) Find 344, gritty cream-slipped dish with vertical sides, diameter 18.5 cm.; (2) Find 344-*a*, small Red-buff collared jar, class "a," diameter 7–12 cm.

Find 345. Red-buff pedestal plate; diameter 20.8 cm.

Find 355. Small Red-buff collared jar, class "a"; diameter 7–12 cm. range.

Find 356. Large Red-buff collared jar, class "e"; diameter 22 cm.

Find 358. Small Red-buff collared jar, class "a"; diameter range 7–12 cm. Included with this were fragments of gold-plated copper and some elongated shell beads (depth 2.35 m.; west 2.1 m.; north wall).

Find 360. Small Red-buff pot cover with loop handles; diameter 7.5 cm.

Find 365. Small fragment of gilded copper.

Find 367. Collared jar, Red-buff body, polychrome collar and lip; probably Pica-pica variety; diameter 22.5 cm.

Find 376. Two copper fragments.

TRENCH 8

No finds were made in Trench 8.

TRENCH 9

No finds were made in Trench 9.

NORTH RIDGE, TRENCH 10

Find 370. Located on North Ridge, Trench 10, at depth of 1.7–2.4 m.; north center 6.6 m.

370-1, 370-2, 370-7. Three Red-buff collarless jars with two horizontal loop handles; handles on one specimen are jab punctated; diameter range 8.5–19 cm.

370-3, 370-5, 370-6, 370-8–370-10. Six Red-buff collared jars, class "a"; diameters in 7–23 cm. range.

370-4. Red-buff jar with two vertical loop handles.

Comment. This unit was in a small grave pit carved out of the gray-white rock and contained fragments of two adult skeletons. No further objects are noted for the unit, except for an ovoid stone celt.

Find 374. Located in North Ridge, Trench 10, at depth of 2.45 m.; 4.4 m. north; 1.0 m. west.

374-1. Medium pedestal-based rattle plate, black on red; Cuipo variety, negative type design; diameter 18.5 cm.

374-2–374-7, 374-22–374-26. Eleven miniature pedestal plates; Cuipo and Pica-pica varieties, black on red, dull polychrome, negative dragons, claws in closed arcs, seed pods; diameters in 7.7–10 cm. range.

374-8–374-11, 374-37–374-45. Thirteen miniature Red-buff pedestal plates; diameter range 6.5–8 cm.

374-12–374-16, 374-27–374-29. Eight miniature collared jars; Cuipo and Pica-pica varieties, black on red; Find 374-12 is high angled shoulder jar with pear-shaped base; diameters in 5–7.5 cm. range.

374-17–374-19. Three Red-buff miniature straight-collared jars; diameter 6–8 cm.

374-20. Miniature collarless jar with horizontal loop handles; diameters 5–7.5 cm.

374-21. Medium Red-buff collared jar, class "a"; diameter 19–20 cm.

374-30, 374-31. Two miniature deep bowls, Red-buff; diameters 2.7 cm.

374-32–374-36. Five miniature collared jars, class "a"; diameters in 5–7.5 cm. range.

Comment. The main portion of the find unit was located in a small chambers about 60 cm. high hollowed out of bedrock near the west wall of the trench. The long bones of an adult were found with the vessels; no other artifacts or significant features were noted. All of the polychrome designs in this unit were executed in the dull finish technique of the Cuipo variety, or the black on red technique, and they combined Cuipo seed pods and negative dragons with Pica-pica split-square-face and closed arc elements. All the vessels were so similar in paste and surface appearance, including style of drawing, as to imply strongly that they were executed by a single potter.

Single finds of Trench 10:

Find 353. Fragment of worked bone.

APPENDIX 3

HE-1 FINDS

Finds 1–5
1. A large (estimated 60 cm. in diameter, 33 cms. in height) Red Daubed collared jar with vertical strap handles extending upward from the shoulder along the jar collar, which itself is almost vertical; base is rounded; vessel is similar to Find 21-*f*.
2. A small buff globular vessel with a somewhat flattened base and collar or spout missing; diameter 11 cms.; place of attachment for handle or lug on shoulder is evident.

3 and 4. Two identical plates; both are shallow (height 2½–3½ cms.; diameters 20.5–21 cms.) with rounded bases and rounded unmodified lips; upper surface and lip is red slipped, lower surface unslipped and smoothed; the slip washes off easily.

5. A large purplish-red slipped open bowl with rounded base and a ski-tip lip; diameter ca. 40 cms.; height 14 cms.

5-*a*. Not listed in field notes; sherds of Platanillo variety open bowl of smoked ware and a large bowl or jar form.

Comment.—Cache located in Trench 1, depth 45 cms., at a point 9.6 meters from south end of the trench.

The large red open bowl (Find 5) was inverted over the Red Daubed collared jar (Find 1) and Finds 3 and 4, standing on their rims, were placed next to the jar. Beside them was Find 2. There was no evidence of bone, nor was there carbon on any of the vessels.

Find 6. A large three-legged stone mortar, inverted and exposed in the center of the trench; roughly circular in shape with a diameter 41×42 cms. and a thickness of about 15 cms.; concavity is well smoothed and between 5 and 10 cms. deep; Trench 1.

Find 7. A squat collared jar (Pinilla black-line-on-red variety) with a straight, somewhat outsloping collar and a rounded base; diameter estimated at 23 cms.; decoration consists of uneven black bands (roughly 2–3 mm. wide) irregularly painted around the base of the collar; pulverized bone powder was found in the earth in immediate association; Trench 1, 0–50 cm. level.

Find 8. A small, plain buff open bowl with slightly incurving walls; diameter 9.5 cms.; traces of white slip apparent; base is flattened; rim is broadened at the lip to form a slight interior flange; Trench 1, 0–50 cm. level.

8-*a*. A small, open bowl with ski-tip lip and plain base; red slipped with black geometric diamond shaped decoration; Girón type; diameter 11 cms.; Trench 1, 0–50 cm. level.

Find 9. Red slipped subglobular olla, rounded base, no handles, obliquely flattened lip; diameter estimated at 20–22 cms.; Trench 1, 50 cm.–1 m. level. Class "c" jar; Delgado red.

Find 10. Squat collared jar with straight outsloping collar and small orifice; rounded base; diameter 16 cms.; decoration in irregular black concentric lines around shoulder from collar base to mid-body height; very similar to Find 7; Trench 1, 50–100 cm. level. Pinilla Black Line on Red.

Find 11. Located at surface near southeast knoll; a Coclé Polychrome open bowl with coral snake lip and ring base; diameter 17 cms.

Find 12. Unit located in Trench 1, level 1.00–1.50 m.; 12.10 m. from the south end.

12-*a*. A small collared jar with three equidistant lobes on the shoulder; collar is straight with a horizontally flattened lip; base is round and unmodified; diameter 12 cms.; height 10 cms.; decorated in vertical pairs of red parallel bands with triangles extending outward from the bands; red orange slip; red banded lip; Red Line ware type; Patterned and Modeled variety.

12-*b*. Small collared jar with an unmodified base; globular in shape with a height of 12 cms.; orange slip; lip is banded with a purplish red, and another red band encircles the shoulder with pendent elongated triangles at wide intervals; Red Line ware type; Patterned and Modeled variety.

12-*c*. Smoked ware open shallow bowl with ring base and modified gutter rim; diameter 18 cms.; height 5 cms.; Platanillo variety.

Find 13. Located in Trench 1, 1.50 m. depth, at a point 15.3 m. from the south end. A collared jar with high straight collar and flattened lip; three vertical loop handles placed equidistantly on shoulder around and up against the collar; diameter 17 cms.; height 17 cms.; vessel is covered with orange red slip and decorated in red-purple bands, one around the lip, one around the collar base with pairs of parallel pointed bands extending down to the round base; Red Line ware type; Pito variety.

Find 14. Grave Unit located in Trench 1; 14.50–16.02 m. from south end; depth 2.00–2.60 m.

14-*a*. Red ware chalice; pedestal base 5.4 cms. high.

14-*b*. Red Daubed plate or shallow bowl; diameter 16 cms.; height 4 cms.; unmodified rim and base; paired teardrop daub decoration.

14-*c*. Red Daubed wide mouthed collared jar without handles; diameter 20 cms.; height 14 cms.; decorated with paired teardrop daubs on shoulder.

14-*d*. Ring-based Coclé polychrome plate; diameter 25 cms.; height 6.5 cms.; opposed full face alligator heads, same style as Find 18-*b*; Late Coclé.

14-*e*. Red ware chalice; diameter 10.5 cms.; total height 10 cms.; pedestal height 4 cms.

14-*f*. Smoked ware pedestal plate or open shallow bowl; flat lip with raised interior flange; decoration consists of four equidistant groups of radially arranged jabs on upper surface of lip; diameter 27 cms.; height 12.5 cms.; Sangre variety.

14-*g*. Smoked ware plate with an unmodified base and a lip which is slightly thickened and definitely flattened at an oblique angle; diameter 24 cms.; height 4 cms.; Aromo variety.

14-*h*. Small collared jar, blackened buff ware, very roughly finished; diameter 12.5 cms.; height 9.5 cms.; interior diameter of orifice is 10 cms.; unclassified as to type or variety; probably is an unfinished Red Daubed vessel.

14-*i*. Large open bowl with slightly incurved lip and ring base; buff to smoked; diameter 38 cms., height 22 cms.; somewhat similar in shape to Find 45-*b*; Buff ware.

14-*j*. Red Daubed collared jar with wide mouth; diameter 15 cms.; height 9.5 cms.; base is round.

Comment.—A flat stone metate with three rounded cones for legs was found with this grave. For further discussion see section on Find Units, pp. 204–205.

Find 15. Located in Trench 2, depth 25 cms., at a point 9.4 m. from south end. A bichrome jar with a double flared neck, flat lip and globular body on a ring base; decoration in black bands, and widely spaced cross-hachure on upper body; diameter 13.2 cms.; height 16.5 cms.; unclassified as to type or variety (pl. 12, *b*).

Find 16–17. Grave Unit located in Trench 1, 1.70–2.30 m. deep, from points 16.45–18.05 m. from south end of trench.

16-*a*. Open bowl on a ring base; diameter 19 cms.; height 7.5 cms.; Paneled red ware.

16-*b*. Wide mouthed collared jar, red and buff slipped; diameter 16.5 cms.; height 12 cms.; unfinished Red Daubed vessel.

16-17-*a*. Wide mouthed collared jar; diameter 15 cms.; height 9.5 cms.; Red Daubed variety with paired teardrop designs.

16-17-*b*. Open bowl on ring base; diameter 11.5 cms.; height 4.5 cms.; Paneled red ware.

16-17-*c*. Small polychrome circular cup on pedestal; diameter 9.5 cms.; height 7 cms.; Late Coclé Polychrome.

16-17-*d*. Polychrome collared jar with round base; diameter 20 cms.; height 19 cms.; Late Coclé Polychrome; (Macaracas? Los Santos?).

17-*a*. Small polychrome circular cup on pedestal; diameter 8.7 cms.; height 7.8 cms.; Late Coclé Polychrome.

17-*b*. Small, square polychrome cup on pedestal; diameter 8.5 cms.; height 5.5 cms.; Late Coclé Paneled red ware.

Find 18. Grave Unit located in Trench 1; depth 2.36–2.75, at about 14.3 m. from the south end and Trench 3.

18-*a*. Polychrome plate fragment, base unknown; rim is between ski-tip and drooping lip types; diameter 32 cms.; Late Coclé Polychrome. Decoration of coral snake rim, alligators in profile, central band of scroll; Late Coclé Polychrome.

18-*b*. Polychrome ring-based plate; diameter 32 cms.; Ski-tip lip; decoration almost identical with 14-*d*, except for center band of scrolls; Late Coclé Polychrome.

18-*c*. Collared jar with plain base medium to small mouth; Red Daubed decoration; diameter 16.5 cms.; height 15.5 cms.

Comment. Also included in the Unit were fragments of white painted plaster of a stone disk, of a stone metate, and of plain plaster.

Find 19. Grave Unit located in Trench 1, point 11.40 m. from south end; depth 2.65 m.

19. A ring-based polychrome plate; diameter 23.5 cms.; height 5.5 cms.; decoration includes coral snake lip, serpent decoration with profile head, purple core along body length; Coclé Polychrome, probably Late.

19-*a*. Medium-sized red-slipped collared jar with a high shoulder and somewhat pointed base and an obliquely flattened lip, i.e., Delgado red; class "c" at He-4; diameter 24 cms.; height 20 cms.

19-*b*. Red-slipped collared jar with plain base and two horizontally placed loop handles on the shoulder; collar so short it might be described as an everted rim forming a flange; diameter 13.5 cms.; height 9 cms.; Delgado red.

19-*c*. Small red-slipped pedestal plate or pot stand; diameter 9 cms.; height 6 cms.

Find 20. Unit located in Trench 3; 55 cms. deep.

    20-*a*. Collared jar, red slipped, with black line decoration on shoulder like Find 10 and Find 7; plain base; diameter estimated at 22 cms.; height 15.5 cms.; Pinilla Black-line-on-red.

    20-*b*. Ring based, slightly incurved sided bowl, 15 cms. in diameter and 7 cms. high; fugitive red slip over buff; general shape is close to that of Find 8, except for base; lip is somewhat flattened and interior flanged.

Find 21. Cache unit located in Trench 3; 40–90 cms. in depth.

    21-*a*. Buff dish or shallow bowl, unmodified base and rim; diameter 16.5 cms.; height 4 cms.

    21-*b*. Red/Buff flat plate with a slightly upcurved rim, a rounded lip and unmodified base; interior, lip, and upper 2 cms. of exterior are red slipped; rest of exterior is buff; diameter 19 cms.; height 2.5 cms.; unclassified as to type or variety.

    21-*c*. Wide-mouthed collared jar with two vertically placed strap handles on shoulder; diameter 19 cms., height 12 cms.; Red Daubed, with irregular lines or drips running vertically (Red Line type, Red Daubed variety).

    21-*d*. Smoked ware bowl with roughly vertical sides and ring base, and a horizontally flattened rim; diameter 14 cms.; height 5 cms.; Smoked ware.

    21-*e*. Red Daubed incensario with fishtail handle; diameter of bowl section is 25 cms.; height of bowl is 6 cms.; height of handle is 13.5 cms.

    21-*f*. Large collared jar with high, almost straight collar, high rounded shoulder, a somewhat pointed base and two vertically placed strap handles on shoulder; diameter estimated at 42 cms.; height estimated 25–30 cms.; Red Line ware type, Red Daubed variety; decoration is drip type.

    21-*g*. Pedestal bowl with fluted shoulder, broad, flattened and incised lip; Smoked ware Venado Beach Incised; diameter 22.5 cms.; height of bowl only is 7.5 cms.; base missing.

    21-*h*. Large ring-based open bowl with modified gutter rim; diameter 35 cms.; height estimated at 10–12 cms.; Smoked ware, Platanillo variety.

Finds 22–23. Unit (cache) located in Trench 3, depth 1.05–1.25.

    22. Collared jar with four vertical loop handles on shoulder and plain base; diameter 14 cms.; height 13 cms.; Red Line type; Pito variety.

    23-*a*. Wide-mouthed collared jar, buff colored, possibly slipped; diameter 14.5 cms.; height 10 cms.; unfinished Red Daubed.

    23-*b*. Open bowl with ring base and modified gutter rim on oblique angle; diameter 22.5 cms.; height 7.5 cms.; smoked ware, Platanillo variety.

    23-*c*. Collared jar with unmodified base and medium-sized orifice; diameter 10 cms.; height 8 cms.; diameter of orifice interior is 6.7 cms.; four groups of vertical red lines on body; Red Line, Patterned and Modeled.

    23-*d*. Small effigy jar, reverse flare collar, human or monkey face, purple line decoration around neck, rim, and face contour; diameter 11 cms.; height 10.5 cms; Red Line type, Patterned and Modeled variety.

    23-*e*. Polychrome plate with ring base; Coclé Polychrome "bird-which-looks-back" pattern with central dividing panel of alternate colored chevrons; probably Early Period Coclé.

    Comment. Field notes suggest that Finds 22 and 23 belong together since they were situated in close proximity in the same fill.

Find 24. Grave Unit located in Trench 3, depth 2.00–2.40.

24-1. Ring-based polychrome plate or open bowl with drooping lip; diameter 28 cms.; height 8 cms.; Early Period Coclé Polychrome.

24-2. Red-slipped bowl with incurving sides and unmodified base and rim; diameter 15 cms.; height 10 cms.; unclassified type or variety.

24-3. Shallow bowl or dish with ring base and modified gutter rim; diameter 14.5 cms.; height 5 cms.; Smoked ware, Platanillo variety.

24-4. Wide-mouthed collared jar with unmodified base; buff surface with purple-red band around lip; diameter 15 cms.; height 10.5 cms.; Red Daubed.

24-5. Wide-mouthed collared jar with unmodified base; red slip on lip, remainder buff; diameter 16 cms.; height 14 cms.; Red Daubed.

24-6. Subglobular jar with reverse flare collar and unmodified base, buff surface; large red claw pattern; diameter 14.5 cms.; height 11 cms.; Red Line type; Patterned and Modeled variety.

24-7. Red-slipped chalice; diameter 8 cms.; height 11.5 cms.

24-8. Wide-mouthed collared jar with unmodified base; diameter 7 cms.; height 7 cms.; Red Daubed.

24-9. Wide-mouthed collared jar with unmodified base; diameter 9.5 cms.; height 6.5 cms.; Red Daubed with paired teardrop motif.

24-10. Red-slipped chalice; diameter 7.5 cms.; height 8.5 cms. (most of pedestal base is missing).

24-11. Miniature incensario; diameter of dish is 9 cms.; height of "fishtail" handle is 4.5 cms.; Red Daubed.

24-12. Red-slipped miniature ring-based plate; diameter 7 cms.; height 2.5 cms.

24-13. Vessel not located; field note description is of large painted bowl; may be Find 24-14.

24-14. Large painted bowl with incurving rim and somewhat pointed base: red slip ground color; decoration in white line and black band; series of closed arcs around shoulder; "turtle" or "frog" feet at one end; diameter 33.5 cms.; height 18 cms.; White-and-black on Red ware.

24-15. Incensario; diameter of dish is 21 cms.; Red Daubed type with fishtail handle.

24-16. Listed in field notes as a small chalice of brown ware.

24-17. Jar with unmodified base, short straight collar and constricted orifice; two opposed flattened lugs on shoulder; traces of red on lip and of a red band around shoulder just below lugs; remainder buff; diameter 18 cms.; height 11.5 cms.; unclassified as to type or variety.

24-18. Listed in field notes as a brown globular olla.

24-19. Polychrome ring-based plate; diameter 31 cms.; Early Period Coclé Polychrome.

24-20. Polychrome ring-based plate; drooping lip; diameter 15.5 cms.; height 4 cms.; Early Period Coclé Polychrome "turtle god." (Lothrop, 1942, fig. 91.)

24-21. Ring-based plate; diameter 18.5 cms.; "Black-on-red ware"; Early Period at Sitio Conte (Lothrop, 1942, p. 142).

24-22. Polychrome ring-based plate with unmodified base and rounded lip; diameter 28 cms.; height 6 cms.; Early Period Coclé Polychrome.

24-23. Large fragment of an incensario; diameter 26.5 cms.; Red Daubed handle missing.

24-24. Wide-mouthed collared jar with vertical strap handles and unmodified base; diameter 17 cms.; height 10.5 cms.; Red Daubed with parallel vertical lines and red lip.

24-25. Collared jar with four vertical loop handles; constricted orifice and high collar; unmodified base; diameter 14 cms.; height 13 cms.; Red Line type, Pito variety; (similar to Finds 22, 13, 24-26).

24-26. Similar to above but smaller; diameter 12 cms.; height 11 cms.; Red Line type, Pito variety.

24-27. Collared jar with unmodified base; diameter 17 cms.; height 14 cms.; scroll elements in purplish-red around shoulder; red lip; similar in feeling to Find 24-6; Red Line type, Patterned and Modeled variety.

24-28. Fragments of a Smoked ware, Platanillo variety open bowl; diameter estimated at 40 cms.

24-29. Fragments of a Venado Beach Incised bowl; unfluted with an estimated diameter of 20 cms.

Find 25. Cache located in Trench 5, depth 30–40 cms.; 67 cms. north.

25-1. Red-slipped collared jar with unmodified base and obliquely flattened lip; class "c" shape; diameter 21 cms.; height 17.5 cms.; Delgado red ware.

25-2. Collarless jar with horizontally placed loop handles; unmodified base; diameter 17 cms.; height 11 cms. (to top of jar only); Delgado red ware.

Find 26. Cache located in Trench 5, 25 cms. depth; 4.24 m. north.

26-1. Small pedestal open bowl with flanged lip; diameter 12.5 cms.; height 6.5 cms.; rim has parallel line incision arranged radially in four groups of seven lines each; Smoked ware, Sangre variety.

26-2. Large open bowl with modified gutter rim; base is missing; diameter estimated at 36 cms.; Smoked ware, Platanillo variety.

26-3. Open bowl with unmodified base and an obliquely flattened lip; diameter estimated at 20 cms.; height unknown, in fragments; Smoked ware, Aromo variety.

26-4. Wide-mouthed collared jar in fragments; base is unmodified; lip has band of red-purple paint; no other decoration on buff-red slip; diameter of lip estimated at 30 cms.; Red Daubed.

Find 27. Two worked stone balls; Trench 5, depth 10 cms.

Find 28. Missing; listed in field notes as a "grooved pottery object."

Find 29. Located in Trench 5; depth 35 cms. Open bowl with unmodified base and a rim which is flat and tilted inward; red slip; estimated diameter 17.5 cms.; height 6 cms.; unclassified as to type and variety, although rim is similar to Smoked ware, Platanillo variety.

Find 30. Grave Unit located in Pit 6; depth of 65 cms.

30-a. Fragments of a red-slipped collared jar with obliquely flattened lip and lobed shoulder; diameter estimated at 22 cms.; class "c" shape; Delgado red.

30-b. Collarless jar with horizontal looped handles on shoulder; unmodified base and somewhat constricted orifice; red slip below handles and on lip; Delgado red.

Finds 31–39. Omitted.

Find 40. Located in Trench 5; depth 70 cms. Globular collared jar with a round, somewhat flattened, base; diameter 10 cms.; height 9 cms.; carmine band encircles vessel just above shoulder, Red Line type; Patterned and Modeled variety.

Find 41. Located in Trench 5; depth 1.10 m. Collared jar with pointed rounded base, high shoulder and obliquely flattened lip; diameter 21 cms.; height 17.5 cms.; red slip; class "c"; Delgado red.

Find 42. Located in Trench 5; depth 1.10 m.   Incensario with fishtail handle; diameter of dish is 22 cms.; height of handle is 13 cms.

Find 43. Located in Pit 7; depth 70 cms.

43-*a*. Small jar with missing collar or neck; red slipped, and rounded base; diameter 8.5 cms.; height to broken collar is 8 cms.; unclassified as to type or variety.

43-*b*. Buff-colored clay "Spindle whorl"; maximum diameter 3.5 cms.; thickness 2 cms.

Finds 44 and 47. Grave Unit located in Trench 5; depth 1.50 m.

44-*a*. Wide-mouthed collared jar with two vertically positioned strap handles and unmodified base; diameter 13 cms.; height 8 cms.; Red Daubed, decorated with vertical red drips.

44-*b*. Open bowl with unmodified rim and base; diameter 18.5 cms.; height 6 cms.; decorated with red bands radiating from center over buff slip; Red Line type, Patterned and Modeled variety.

44-*c*. Open bowl with unmodified base and a rounded lip, the interior edge of which is slightly beveled; diameter 15 cms.; height 7 cms.; slip buff and orange; no decoration.

44-*d*. Spouted jar with horizontally flared rim above a straight collar and a ring base; diameter 10 cms.; height 7.5 cms.; buff to gray-black; Smoked ware.

47-*a*. Collared red ware jar with high shoulder and obliquely flattened lip; unmodified base; diameter 22 cms.; height 17.5 cms.; class "c" shape; Delgado red.

47-*b*. Collarless jar with round base and two horizontally placed loop handles on shoulder; diameter 12 cms.; height 8.5 cms.; Delgado red.

Comment. Three rubbing stones and a human skull were found with these vessels.

Find 45. Cache Unit located in Trench 4 or 6?; depth 80 cms.

45-*a*. Thick shallow plate with slightly flattened lip and an unmodified base; diameter 18.5 cms.; height 3 cms.; Smoked ware; Aromo variety.

45-*b*. Large open bowl with ring base and lip which is flattened obliquely on the interior; fired black; diameter 35 cms.; height 16 cms.; Smoked ware, Platanillo variety.

45-*c*. Large wide-mouthed jar with plain base; diameter of collar lip is 38 cms.; Red Daubed.

Comment. The large Red Daubed jar contained the plate within it and was covered by the inverted black bowl.

Find 48. Cache Unit located in Trench 6 or 4?; depth 75 cms.

48-*a*. Small collared jar with round base and lobed shoulders; diameter 8.5 cms.; height 7 cms.; thin wash of red purple dribbles around lobes; Red Line; Patterned and Modeled variety.

48-*b*. Wide-mouthed collared jar with round base; diameter 14 cms.; height 7.5 cms.; decorated with red-purple band around lip and three blobs of same color equidistantly placed about shoulder; Red Daubed.

48-*c*. Plate with round base and unmodified lip; diameter 8.5 cms.; height 1.8 cms.; red band on lip and three bands across plate; buff slip; Red Line type; Patterned and Modeled variety.

48-*d*. Shallow open bowl with ring base and modified gutter rim; diameter 19.5 cms.; height 6.5 cms.; Smoked ware type; Platanillo variety.

Find 49–Cache. Located in Trench 5; depth 40 cms.

49. A straight collared wide-mouthed jar with unmodified base; diameter 20.5 cms.; height 17 cms.; surface badly eroded, but evidence of red

slip; shape of collar and body very similar to Finds 7, 10, 20-*a*; classified as Pinilla Black-line-on-red on basis of shape.

Comment. This jar was accompanied by quartz crystals, Find 49-*a*.

Find   49–Grave Unit. Located in Trench 5; depth 3.85 m.

49-*b*. A three-legged metate with carved decoration.   This metate, along with a small sherd of polished buff ware, was found with 32 skeletons underneath a layer of boulders.

APPENDIX 4

HE-2 FINDS

Find 1. Trench 1.

1-*a*. Fragment of small open bowl, red slipped, with an "eared" rim and black parallel lines arranged radially between the "ears"; diameter about 11 cms.; height about 8 cms.; base is rounded; Girón type; Banded Lip variety.

1-*b*. Body and base fragments of a medium-sized (estimated diameter 15–20 cms.) brown-buff slipped jar; round base and strap handles; traces of red paint visible; probably Red Line, Red Daubed strap-handled collared jar.

Find 2. Trench 1.

2-*a*. Fragments of a closed-shape vessel with unmodified base; fire black-ened exterior; interior buff-slipped showing brush or cob markings; estimated diameter 25–30 cms.

2-*b*. Fragments of an open bowl with steeply slanted modified gutter rim and probably a rounded base; remnants of black paint on lip; diameter estimated at 36 cms.; Girón type; Banded Lip variety.

Find 3. Trench 1.

Red-slipped straight-collared jar with strap handles and a rounded base; diameter estimated at 18 cms.; height 16 cms.; orifice 10.5 cms.; found in inverted position; Red-slipped Miscellaneous.

Finds 4–6. Unit located in Trench 1.

4-*a*. Collared jar with rounded base and four loop handles on shoulder; buff with red line design; orifice diameter 8.5 cms.; Red Line type; Pito variety.

4-*b*. Large subglobular collared jar with rounded base; relatively straight flaring collar; lip flanged outward horizontally; orifice diameter 8 cms.; body diameter estimated at 34 cms.; collar interior and lip, body exterior covered with bright orange-red slip; collar exterior is buff; body interior is brushed; Red-slipped Miscellaneous.

4-*c*. Collared and spouted jar with ring base and highly polished orange-red slip; lip is horizontally flanged with a shallow groove and low ridge running around upper surface of the lip; spout is joined to lip by a short bridge; diameter 18 cms.; height 16.5 cms.; Coclé Red ware spouted jar.

4-*d*. Subglobular wide-mouthed collared jar with rounded base; collar interior and body exterior are red slipped; collar exterior is buff and brushed; diameter of body 25 cms., of orifice 15 cms.; height 19.5 cms.; Red slipped, squat jar.

4-*e*. Open ring-based dish or bowl with modified gutter rim; chocolate to dark brown slip interior and exterior; diameter 30 cms.; height 8 cms.; Smoked ware type, Platanillo variety.

5-*a*. Open bowl with rounded base and unmodified lip; decoration on interior only consisting of concentric black bands around interior below lip with pendent scroll elements; diameter 28 cms.; height 12 cms.; Girón type, Interior banded variety.

5-*b*. Shallow open bowl on a relatively short pedestal base, fluted shoulder, horizontally flanged and incised lip; diameter 17 cms.; total height 13 cms.; height of pedestal 6.5 cms.; all surfaces dark brown to black brown except for reddish areas on lip; Smoked ware, Venado Beach Incised.

5-c. Subglobular spouted jar with ring base and horizontally flanged lip with a broad shallow groove and low ridge running around its upper surface; spout is joined to lip by a short oval bridge; surface a gray-brown hue; body fluted; diameter 17.5 cms.; height 14.5 cms.; height of collar 5.5 cms.; Smoked ware spouted and fluted jar.

5-d. Subglobular collared jar with round base and a relatively straight high collar and rounded lip; lug appended to shoulder, place of attachment present for another on opposite side; collar exterior and lip are red slipped, remainder fired a buff-orange; diameter 10 cms.; height 8 cms.; height of collar 2.5 cms.; Red Line ware, Patterned and Modeled variety.

5-e. A high collared jar with rounded base and wide mouth; lip is unmodified; places of attachment for two missing loop handles on shoulder; body diameter 15 cms.; orifice diameter 8 cms.; total height 13 cms.; collar height 5 cms.; interior blackened by fire, exterior orange-buff slipped except for red band around lip and around collar base; Red Line type; Patterned and Modeled variety.

5-f. Wide-mouthed collared jar with rounded base and unmodified lip; place of attachment for two opposed loop handles; diameter 15 cms.; orifice diameter 11 cms.; height estimated at 12 cms.; decoration of red band on lip with red dribbles down collar exterior and over shoulder; originally buff-orange ground badly blackened by fire; Red Line type, Red Daubed variety.

5-g. Fragments of open bowl with unmodified lip and rounded base; diameter estimated at 46 cms.; height at 17 cms.; exterior fire clouded to dark brown and part of interior also, rest of interior a cream-buff slip; over this red bands have been applied in broad chevron pattern and a red band encircles the lip. Red Line type; Patterned and Modeled variety.

6. A three-legged stone metate; no carving; ovate-rectangular in shape; top 57×43 cms.; thickness 4 cms.; height 16 cms.

Comment. Human bone, badly decayed, was found with the Find 4 vessels, and powdered bone material as well as decayed human bone occurred with the Find 5 group. Find 5-g was found in fragments with one placed on top of the other. Finds 7 and 15 may also be related to this unit (see discussion of grave associations).

Find 7. Trench 1.

7-1. Collared and spouted jar with ring base, spout attached to rim by flat bridge; diameter 15.5 cms.; height 16 cms.; buff slip; Smoked ware spouted jar.

7-2. Chipped stone celt; length 12 cms.; spatulate shape.

Comment. Field notes suggest that Find 7 may have been part of Find Unit 5 grave as grave goods placed in the upper part of the shaft.

Find 8. Trench 2.

A red-slipped open bowl with ski-tip lip and round base; decoration is in a series of black bands running concentrically around interior wall just below lip; a black undulating band or snake bordered by two panels of black crosshachure covers the base interior; diameter 30 cms.; height 9.5 cms.; Girón Polychrome; Interior Banded variety.

Find 9. Trench 2.

Globular collared jar with round bottom and a widely flared rim over a constricted orifice; surface is smoothed and buff colored except for traces of a thin red paint or wash on the body and upper surface of the lip; diameter 14.5 cms.; orifice is 5.5 cms.; height is 15 cms.; unclassified.

Find 10. Trench 2.

10-1. A collared jar with a round base and two opposed straphandles on shoulder; ground color buff; lip is red banded and red stripes run vertically down collar, over shoulder and body to base; diameter estimated at 20 cms.; height estimated at 14–15 cms.; orifice at 16–18 cms.; Red Line type, Red Daubed variety.

10-2. An open bowl with a modified gutter rim and a ring base; color is brown except for black fire clouding on exterior; diameter 17 cms.; height 5 cms.; Smoked ware, Platanillo variety.

Comment. The jar was found in an upright position with the open bowl as a cover.

Find 11. Trench 2.

11-1. A spouted collared subglobular jar with ring base; spout is attached to lip by an oval bridge, and the lip is horizontally flanged with a broad shallow groove and low ridge running around its upper surface; diameter 20 cms.; orifice diameter 7 cms.; height 19 cms.; collar height 6 cms.; surface is smoothly polished and ranges from dark brown to black; Smoked ware spouted jar.

11-2. An open bowl with a ring base and "drooping lip"; entire interior and lip exterior are red slipped, remainder of exterior is orange-buff; red slip is soft and worn in many places; diameter 26 cms.; height 7.5 cms.; Coclé Red ware.

11-3. Red ware chalice; interior of collar and body are red slipped as is the body exterior; exterior of collar and pedestal are unslipped; diameter estimated at 12 cms.; height 17.5 cms. (height of collar is 6 cms., height of base is 4.5 cms.); Red ware chalice.

Comment. Powdered human bone was found in immediate association.

Find 12. Trench 2.

Globular collared jar with a round base and a high, straight, flared collar; interior is buff and brushed; collar interior is buff with evenly spaced red dribbles running down it; exterior collar and body red-slipped with a thin slip or wash; diameter estimated at 20–22 cms.; orifice 8 cms.; Red Slip miscellaneous.

Find 13. Trench 2.

A collared jar with a round base and out-curved rim and a lip which is almost horizontal; lip is incised with shell edged impressions arranged radially; inner and outer surfaces are soft (No. 2 rating on Mohs' scale), are orange-red in color, and may be slipped; lip edge is red painted; diameter estimated at 26 cms.; orifice at 7.5 cms; unclassified.

Find 14. Trench 2.

14-1. A relatively flat, thick, red plate with an unmodified base and a ski-tip lip; diameter estimated at 20 cms.; height at 3.5 cms.; upper surface and about 5 cms. of the lower surface next to the lip are covered with a fugitive red slip or wash; Red slipped miscellaneous.

14-2. Collared and spouted jar with the usual groove and median ridge on upper lip surface; spout joined to lip by bridge; ringed base; diameter 19 cms.; height 18 cms.; exterior is covered with a brownish-red slip; Smoked ware spouted jar.

Find 15. Trench 2.

A large collared jar with a round base and an unmodified lip; interior is smoothed and brushed; collar interior and body exterior are treated with a thin red slip or wash; collar exterior is a buff cream color; diameter estimated at 38 cms.; orifice at 24 cms.; Red slipped miscellaneous; squat jar.

Comment. Powdered human bone appeared just below this vessel.

Find 16. Trench 2.

Incensario with missing handle and two nubbin legs; diameter 23 cms.; height of dish 4 cms.; under surface shows brushing marks and is a reddish buff; upper surface shows traces of red daubing; Red Line type, Red Daubed variety.

Find 17. Trench 2.

A short pedestal 6 cms. high and 12 cms. in maximum diameter; surface is dark brown with reddish areas; may be the base of a Venado Beach Incised vessel, Smoked ware.

Find 18. Trench 4.

A miniature collared jar with a round base and outcurving rim; diameter 5.5 cms.; height 6 cms.; all surfaces are rough and unfinished; the interior is fired to a buff color, the exterior ranges from an orange-red to buff; Plain ware.

APPENDIX 5

SHELL IDENTIFICATIONS[24]

HE-4

Trench 1
    Level 3: *Pitar (Lamelliconcha) tortuosus* Broderip
            Natica unifasciata Lamarck
            Tivela argentina Sowerby
    3 and 4: *Solen rubis* C. B. Adams
    4: Unidentifiable coral fragment
    7: *Anadara (Larkinia) grandis* Broderip and Sowerby
       Natica unifasciata
       Pitar (Lamelliconcha) tortuosus
       Tivela argentina
       Dosina dunkeri Philippi
       Tellina (Eurytellina) hertleini Olsson

Mound III
       Pinctada mazatlanica Hanley
       Spondylus (species?)
       Solen rubis
       Cypraea (Macrocypraea) cervinetta Kiener
       Oliva (Oliva) splendidula Sowerby [worked on edge]
       Anadara (Anadara) tuberculosa Sowerby
       Cerithidea valida C. B. Adams

Trench 7
    Level 2: *Ostrea columbiensis* Hanley
        3: *Strombus peruvianus* Swainson

Trench 10
    Level 1: *Semele pacifica* Dall
            Ostrea columbiensis
            Anadara (Larkinia) grandis
        2: *Anadara (Larkinia) grandis*
        3: *Anadara (Larkina) grandis*

Surface
       Pitar (Lamelliconcha) tortuosus
       Dosinia dunkeri

HE-1

Surface

       Anadara (Larkinia) grandis
       Conus patricius Hinds
       Cypraea (Pseudozonaria) arabicula Lamarck

---

[24] Gratitude is herewith expressed for the generous help of the Department of Mollusks, Harvard University, in the identification of the shells from He-4 and He-1. Primary references were Keen (1958) and Olsson (1961). Shell identifications by Willey and Stoddard for Co-2 and He-8 were made before either reference was published.

CO-2

Pit 1

20–30 cm.
level: *Ostrea chilensis* Philippi [now *Ostrea corteziensis* Hertlein]
    Ostrea mexicana Sowerby [listed by Olsson as *Ostrea (Alextryonia?)*
      palmula Carpenter]
    Pitar (Lamelliconcha) tortuosus
    Scapharca tuberculosa Sowerby [probably *Anadara (Anadara)*
      tuberculosa]
    Natica unifasciata
    Thais haemostoma

60–70 cm.
level: *Anadara (Larkinia)grandis*
    Ostrea chilensis [see above]
    Scapharca tuberculosa [see above]
    Cardium ringens Swainson [not listed in either Keen or Olsson]
    Fasciolaria salmo Wood

130–140 cm.
level: *Anadara (Larkinia) grandis*
    Ostrea chilensis [see above]
    Scapharca tuberculosa [see above]

Pit 3

10–20 cm.
level: *Andara (Larkinia) grandis*
    Ostrea chilensis [see above]
    Ostrea mexicana [see above]
    Scapharca tuberculosa [see above]
    Natica unifasciata

HE-8

Pit 2

0–10 cm.
level: *Anadara (Larkina) grandis*
    Pitar (Lamelliconcha) tortuosus
    Ostrea chilensis [see above]
    Tivela gracilior Sowerby
    Dosinia dunkeri
    Polymedosa [genera only]
    Natica unifasciata

20–30 cm.
level: *Ostrea chilensis* [see above]
    Tivela gracilor
    Dosinia dunkeri
    Prothothaca grata Say
    Pitar (Lamelliconcha) tortuosus
    Polymesoda [genera only]

EXPLANATION OF PLATES 1–23

PLATE 1

He-4: Carved manatee bone of Find 10 and El Hatillo type effigy vessel. *a-c*, Find 10; *a*, length of longest fragment is 49 cms.; *b*, length of decorated area is 7 cms.; *c*, length of baton head is 5 cms.; *d*, El Hatillo type, El Hatillo variety, vessel P–13, height 17 cms.

PLATE 2

El Hatillo type ceramic remains.
- *a*, El Hatillo type, El Hatillo variety, vessel P–9, diameter 13 cm.
- *b*, El Hatillo type, El Hatillo variety, Find 30-2, length 19 cm.
- *c*, El Hatillo type, El Hatillo variety, Find 22-1, diameter 17.5 cm.
- *d*, El Hatillo type, Achote variety, Find 35-*a*, height 18 cm.

PLATE 3

El Hatillo and Parita types ceramic remains.
- *a*, El Hatillo type, Jobo variety, Find 10-2, diameter 15 cm.
- *b*, El Hatillo type, Jobo variety, Find 10-14, diameter 13 cm.
- *c*, Parita type, Anón variety, Find 124, diameter 19.5 cm.
- *d*, Parita type, Yampí variety, vessel P–24, diameter 23.5 cm.

PLATE 4

Parita type ceramic remains.
- *a*, Parita type, Níspero variety, vessel P–6, height 25 cm.
- *b*, Parita type, Níspero variety, vessel P–6.
- *c*, Parita type, Caimito variety, vessel P–3, diameter 17.5 cm.
- *d*, Parita type, Caimito variety, vessel P–3.

PLATE 5

Parita and Macaracas types ceramic remains.
- *a*, Parita type, Ortiga variety, vessel P–33, diameter 40 cm.
- *b*, Parita type, Ortiga variety, vessel P–33.
- *c*, Parita type, Ortiga variety, vessel P–39, estimated diameter 36 cm.
- *d*, Macaracas type, Pica-pica variety, Find 368-3, diameter 22 cm.

PLATE 6

Macaracas type ceramic remains.
- *a*, Macaracas type, Pica-pica variety, Find 368-4, diameter 11 cm.
- *b*, Macaracas type, Pica-pica variety, Find 368-4.
- *c*, Macaracas type, Pica-pica variety, Find 375-1, diameter 10 cm.
- *d*, Macaracas type, Pica-pica variety, Find 375-1.

PLATE 7

Macaracas type ceramic remains.
- *a*, Macaracas type, Higo variety, Find 368-1, diameter 27 cm.
- *b*, Macaracas type, Higo variety, Find 368-1.
- *c*, Macaracas type, Cuipo variety, Find 373-3, diameter 38 cm.
- *d*, Macaracas type, Cuipo variety, Find 373-3.

270

PLATE 8

Macaracas and Calabaza types ceramic remains.
  a, Macaracas type, Cuipo variety, Find 369-1, diameter 13 cm.
  b, Calabaza type, Calabaza variety, Vessel P-21, diameter 20.5 cm.
  c, Calabaza type, Calabaza variety, Find 45, diameter 17 cm.
  d, Calabaza type, Calabaza variety, Find 45.

PLATE 9

He-4 Ceritó variety and "cord marks" on Macaracas vessels.
  a, Calabaza type, Ceritó variety, vessel P-15, diameter 15.5 cm.
  b, Cord marking on underside of Pica-pica miniature pedestal plate, Find
     375-3, diameter 9.5 cm.
  c, The same on Find 375-4, diameter 10 cm.

PLATE 10

Girón and Red Line types ceramic remains.
  a, Girón type, Interior Banded variety, He-2, Find 5-a, diameter 28 cm.
  b, Girón type, Interior Banded variety, He-2, Find 8, diameter 30 cm.
  c, Red Line type, Red Daubed variety, He-1, Find 14-c, diameter 20 cm.
  d, Red Line type, Red Daubed variety, He-1, Find 21-f, estimated diameter
     42 cm.

PLATE 11

Red Line and Pinilla Black-line-on-red ceramic remains.
  a, Red Line type, Red Daubed variety, He-1, Find 18-c, diameter 16.5 cm.
  b, Red Line type, Pito variety, He-1, Find 22, diameter 14 cm.
  c, Pinilla Black-line-on-red variety, He-1, Find 10, diameter 16 cm.
  d, Pinilla Black-line-on-red variety, He-1, Find 20-a, estimated diameter
     22 cm.

PLATE 12

Miscellaneous vessels.
  a, He-1, Find 24-14, White-and-black-on-red ware, diameter 33.5 cm.
  b, He-1, Find 15, unclassified, diameter 13.5 cm.

PLATE 13

Girón Banded Lip variety ceramic remains.
  a, b, e, Radial Banded subvariety.
  c, Circumbanded subvariety.
  d, Scalloped subvariety.
  f, g, Crosshatched subvariety.

PLATE 14

Examples of plastic decoration on Co-2 ceramic remains.
  a, Slash punctation.
  b, Applique ridge notching.
  c, Punctation.
  d, Lip engraving.
  e, Fingernail punctation.

f, Fine line incising.
g, Reed punctation and lip grooving.
h, Shell edge stamping.
i, Semilunar punctation and scoring.
j, Broad line incision.
k, Applique ridging.
l, Linear punctation.
m, Reed punctation.
n, Pinching.
o, Fluting.
p, Lip grooving.

PLATE 15

Miscellaneous and unclassified sherds at He-4.
 a, Trench 5, 0–50 cm.; black and red on cream; 6–7 mm. thick.
 b, Trench 8, 25–50 cm.; black on red; 5–6 mm. thick.
 c, Trench 8, 75–100 cm.; black and red on cream; 7–8 mm. thick.
 d, Trench 8, 50–75 cm.; black and white on buff; 10 mm. thick.
 e, Mound III, eroded; black and red on cream; 7 mm. thick.
 f, Same vessel as (b).
 g, Trench 8, 25–50 cm.; red and purple on cream; 6–7 mm. thick.
 h, Trench 7, 300–490 cm.; modeled relief, eroded surface with black on cream, traces of orange slip; 4–7 mm. thick.
 i, Trench 8, 25–50 cm.; red crosshachure on cream; 6 mm. thick; similar to five sherds from the top two levels at Isla Muertos in the Bahia de Muertos near David in Chiriquí (Linares, personal communication).
 j, Mound III; black and red on cream; 8–9 mm. thick.
 k, Trench 1, 0–100 cm.; black on cream; 6 mm. thick.
 l, Mound III; smudged black on red; 6–7 mm. thick.
 m, Trench 7, 200–300 cm.; modeled relief, black and red and cream on buff; 8 mm. thick.
 n, Trench 8, 75–100 cm.; red and purple on cream; 6–7 mm. thick.
 o, Mound III; black and red and purple on cream; 5–8 mm. thick.
 p, Same vessel as (g).
 q, Trench 5, 0–50 cm.; black and red on cream; 8–12 mm. thick.
 r, Trench 7, 300–490 cm.; black and red on cream; 8–10 mm. thick.
 s, Trench 2, 0–40 cm.; incision through red wash or thin slip, buff paste; 5 mm. thick.
 t, Trench 8, 75–100 cm.; black and red on cream; 6–8 mm. thick.
 u, Trench 5, 0–50 cm.; black on cream; 5–6 mm. thick.
 v, Same vessel as (l).

PLATE 16

Miscellaneous and unclassified sherds at He-1.
 a, Pit 9; black and red on cream; 5 mm. thick.
 b, Probably same vessel as (a).
 c, Probably same vessel as (a).
 d, Pit 2, 0–25 cm.; black and red on cream; 6 mm. thick.
 e, Trench 2, 0–50 cm.; black and white on buff; 5–8 mm. thick.
 f, Pit 1, 75–150 cm.; black on white or cream, negative; 5 mm. thick; similar to the "Lost Color ware" of Chiriquí in design and technique.
 g, Pit 2, 0–25 cm.; black on white or cream, negative; 7–10 mm. thick; similar to the "Lost Color ware" of Chiriquí in design and technique.

h, Pit 2, 0–25 cm.; black and red on cream; 7 mm. thick.

i, Probably same vessel as (*h*).

j, Trench 1, 0–50 cm.; black and red on cream; 7–8 mm. thick.

k, Trench 1, 0–50 cm.; black and white on red; 7–10 mm. thick.

l, Pit 2, 0–25 cm.; black and white on red; 6 mm. thick.

m, Trench 1, 50–100 cm.; black on cream; 4–6 mm. thick.

n, Pit 2, 50–75 cm.; black on cream or white; 5 mm. thick.

o, Pit 2, 25–50 cm.; black and white on red; 7 mm. thick.

p, Trench 1, 50–100 cm.; black on red; 8 mm. thick.

q, Trench 1, 0–50 cm.; black and white on red; 4 mm. thick.

r, Pit 1, 25–50 cm.; black and white on red; 8–9 mm. thick.

s, Pit 4, 0–50 cm.; black and red on white or cream; 8 mm. thick.

t, Pit 1, 0–25 cm.; black and red on orange; 8–10 mm. thick.

u, Pit 1, 25–50 cm.; black on white; 5–7 mm. thick.

v, Probably same vessel as (*u*).

w, Pit 9; purple on buff; 7 mm. thick.

x, Trench 1, 50–100 cm.; smudged black on red; 5–7 mm. thick.

y, Trench 1, 150–240 cm.; red slip on red paste; 3–5 mm. thick.

z, Pit 1, 0–25 cm.; black and red on cream; 5–6 mm. thick.

a', Pit 2, 25–50 cm.; black on white; 9 mm. thick.

PLATE 17

Miscellaneous and unclassified sherds at He-1.

a, Pit 2, 0–25 cm.; El Tigre, cream-buff; 13–15 mm. thick.

b, Pit 2, 0–25 cm.; El Tigre, cream-buff (rim below); 13–15 mm. thick.

c, Trench 1, 0–50 cm.; El Tigre, buff-red; 10 mm. thick.

d, Pit 2, 0–25 cm.; El Tigre, buff-red; 8–11 mm. thick.

e, Pit 2, 0–25 cm.; El Tigre, cream-buff; 15 mm. thick.

f, Pit 2, 0–25 cm.; buff, eroded; 4 mm. thick.

g, Trench 1, 0–50 cm.; El Tigre, buff-red; 10–11 mm. thick.

h, Pit 2, 25–50 cm.; orange-red; 3–4 mm. thick.

i, Trench 1, 0–50 cm.; eroded buff with incision; 4 mm. thick.

j, Pit 1, 75–150 cm.; eroded buff with incision; 5 mm. thick.

k, Pit 2, 0–25 cm.; buff, polished; 4–6 mm. thick.

l, Trench 2, 50–100 cm.; smoked; 6 mm. thick.

m, Pit 2, 0–25 cm.; buff; 6 mm. thick.

n, Pit 1, 25–50 cm.; smoked; 5–6 mm. thick.

o, Pit 2, 50–75 cm.; red; 7–8 mm. thick.

p, Trench 1, 0–50 cm.; orange-buff; 6–7 mm. thick.

q, Trench 1, 50–100 cm.; smoked; 5 mm. thick.

r, Trench 2, 50–100 cm.; orange-buff; 4 mm. thick.

s, Pit 2, 0–25 cm.; buff; 5 mm. thick.

t, Pit 2, 0–25 cm.; buff; 6–9 mm. thick.

u, Trench 1, 0–50 cm.; smoked; 5 mm. thick.

v, Trench 1, 100–150 cm.; smoked; 6 mm. thick.

w, Pit 2, 0–25 cm.; red (underside scored); 5 mm. thick.

x, Pit 2, 0–25 cm.; red interior and rim band on cream; 5–6 mm. thick.

y, Pit 2, 25–50 cm.; eroded buff; 5 mm. thick.

z, Trench 1, 0–50 cm.; buff; 6–7 mm. thick.

a', Trench 1, 0–50 cm.; smoked; 6–8 mm. thick.

b', Trench 3, 0–100 cm.; smoked; 5–6 mm. thick.

c', Pit 2, 25–50 cm.; red; 8 mm. thick.

d', Pit 2, 50–75 cm.; cream; 8 mm. thick.

e', Pit 1, 25–50 cm.; buff, pottery stamp fragment; 10 mm. thick.

f', Pit 1, 25–50 cm.; buff, pottery stamp fragment; 7 mm. thick.

g', Pit 2, 0–25 cm.; red; 6 mm. thick.

h', Pit 2, 25–50 cm.; red; slip; 7–10 mm. thick.

PLATE 18

Stone artifacts from He-4.

a, Find 219; 25.5 cm. long.

b, Trench 10, 100–125 cm.; Level 5; 12.7 cm. long.

c, Find 372; 6.0 cm. long.

d, Mound III; 9.2 cm. long.

e, Find 370; 13.0 cm. long.

f, Mound III; 7.5 cm. long.

g, Trench 6, 0–50 cm.; Level 1; 6.8 cm. long.

h, Trench 7, 150–200 cm.; Level 2; 4.5 cm. long.

i, Trench 10, 150–175 cm.; Level 7; 5.2 cm. long.

j, Trench 10, 50–75 cm.; Level 3; 10.2 cm. long.

k, Trench 7, 200–300 cm.; Level 3; 9.0 cm. long.

l, Trench 1, 300 cm.; Level 4; 4.5 cm. long.

m, Trench 10, 100–125 cm.; Level 5; 7.5 cm. long.

n, Trench 10, 75–100 cm.; Level 4; 8.5 cm. long.

PLATE 19

Worked bone and shell at He-4, He-1, and Co-2.

a, He-1, Find 24; 8.5 cm. long.

b, Co-2, Pit 1, 140–150 cm.; bone tube; 7.2 cm. long.

c, Co-2, Pit 1, 140–150 cm.; bone tube; 5 cm. long.

d, He-4, Mound III; 10.4 cm. long.

e, He-4, Mound III; bone tube; 7.6 cm. long.

f, He-4, Mound III; bone tube; 9.7 cm. long.

g, He-4, Mound III; shell (*Anadara grandis*); maximum diameter 5.5 cm.

h, He-4, Mound III; 5.5 cm. long.

i, He-4, Mound III; 9.3 cm. long.

j, He-4, Mound III; fish vertebrae; maximum diameter 4.3 cm.

k, He-4, Mound III, fish vertebrae; maximum diameter 1.8 cm.

l, He-4, Mound III; fish vertebrae; maximum diameter 1.5 cm.

m, He-4, Find 10; bone tube; 13.5 cm. long.

n–v, He-4, Find 381; perforated shell (probably spondylus); lengths range from 3.3–4.5 cm.

PLATE 20

Worked stone at He-1.

a, Miscellaneous collection; 10 cm. long.

b, Pit 9; 10.2 cm. long.

c, Find 24; 10.3 cm. long.

d, Find 24; 9.5 cm. long.

e, Find 24; 4.3 cm. long.

f, Trench 1, 50–100 cm.; 5.5 cm. long.

g, Trench 1, 0–50 cm.; 5.5 cm. long.

h, Pit 2, 25–50 cm.; 5.5 cm. long.

i, Find 24; 8.5 cm. long.

j, Pit 1, 0–25 cm.; 5.5 cm. long.

k, Trench 1, 0–50 cm.; 2.5 cm. long.

l, Trench 2, 0–50 cm.; 3.3 cm. long.

m, Trench 1, 0–50 cm.; 4.3 cm. long.

n, Trench 1, 0–50 cm.; 3.5 cm. long.

o, Surface collection; 6.8 cm. long.

p, Trench 2, 0–50 cm.; 8.5 cm. long.

q, Trench 1, 0–50 cm.; 5.7 cm. long.

r, Trench 3, 0–100 cm.; 6.2 cm. long.

s, Trench 1, 0–50 cm.; 5.3 cm. long.

t, Find 27; 4 cm. long.

PLATE 21

Worked stone at Co-2.

a, Pit 2, 125–125 cm.; 21 cm. long.

b, Miscellaneous collection from riverbank; 11.8 cm. long.

c, Pit 2, 210–220 cm.; 9 cm. long.

d, Miscellaneous collection; approximate dimensions 5×5 cm.

e, Miscellaneous collection from riverbank; 9.6 cm. long.

f, Pit 1, 30–40 cm.; 7.3 cm. long.

g, Pit 1, 130–140 cm.; 4.7 cm. long.

PLATE 22

Metate from He-1.

a, b, Find 14; 52 cm. long.

PLATE 23

Metates from He-1.

a, Find 14; 52 cm. long.

b, Find 49; 46.5 cm. long.

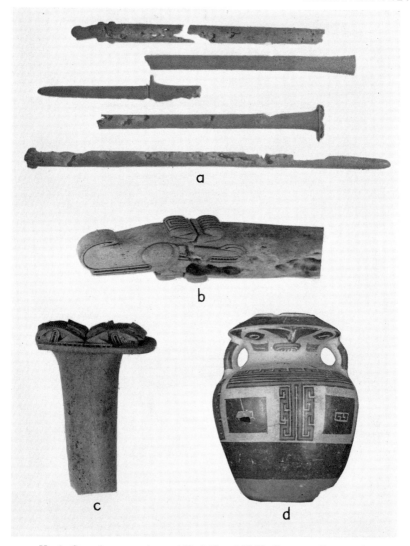

He–4: Carved manatee bone of Find 10 and El Hatillo type effigy vessel.
(For explanation, see p. 270.)

El Hatillo type ceramic remains.

(For explanation, see p. 270.)

El Hatillo and Parita type ceramic remains.
(For explanation, see p. 270.)

Parita type ceramic remains.

(For explanation, see p. 270.)

Parita and Macaracas types of ceramic remains.

(For explanation, see p. 270.)

Macaracas type ceramic remains.

(For explanation, see p. 270.)

Macaracas type ceramic remains.

(For explanation, see p. 271.)

Macaracas and Calabaza types ceramic remains.

(For explanation, see p. 271.)

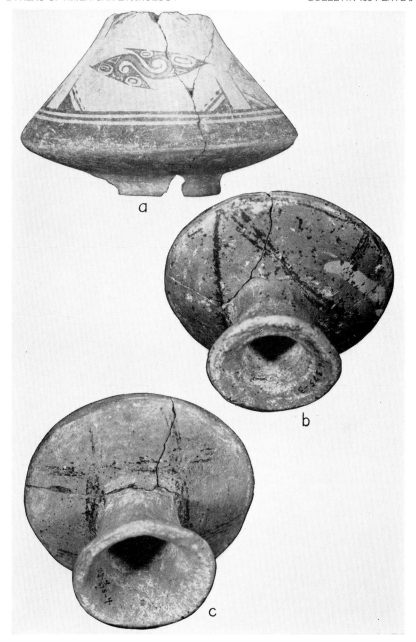

He–4 Ceritó variety and "cord marks" on Macaracas vessels.

(For explanation, see p. 271.)

Girón and Red Line types ceramic remains at He–2 and He–1.

(For explanation, see p. 271.)

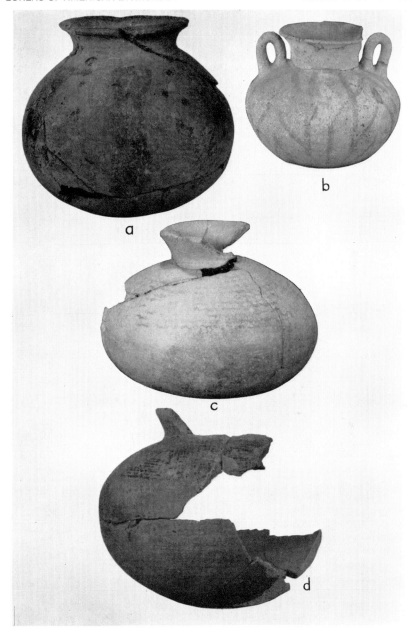

Red Line and Pinilla Black-line-on-red ceramic remains at He–1.

(For explanation, see p. 271.)

Miscellaneous vessels at He–1.

(For explanation, see p. 271.)

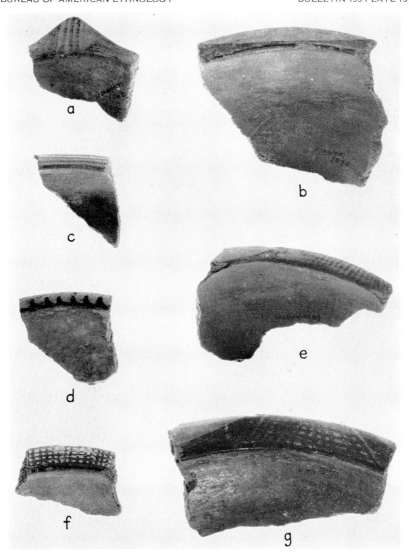

Girón Banded Lip variety ceramic remains.

(For explanation, see p. 272.)

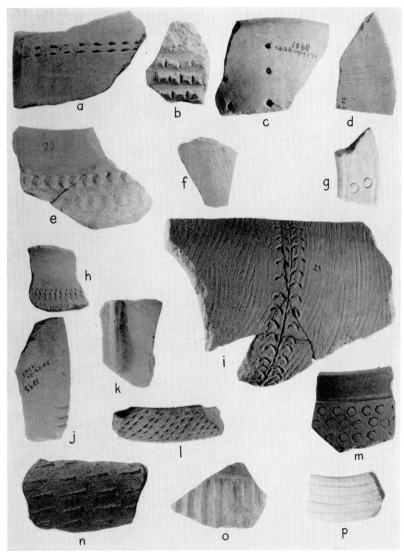

Examples of plastic decoration on Co–2 ceramic remains.

(For explanation, see p. 272.)

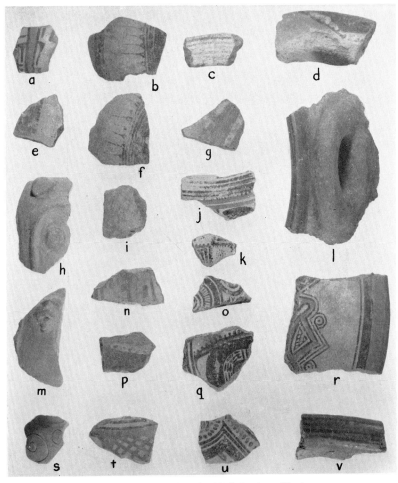

Miscellaneous and unclassified sherds at He–4.

(For explanation, see pp. 272–273.)

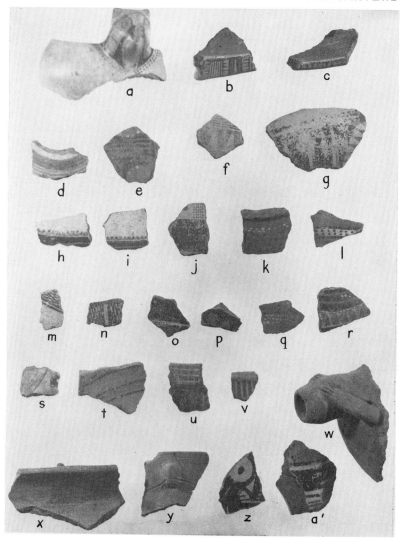

Miscellaneous and unclassified sherds at He-1.

(For explanation, see p. 273.)

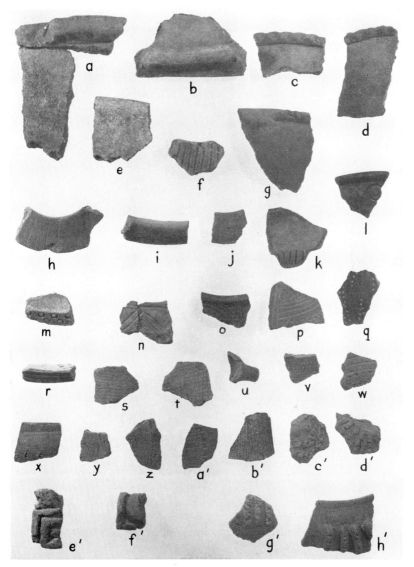

Miscellaneous and unclassified sherds at He–1.

(For explanation, see pp. 273–274.)

Stone artifacts from He-4.

(For explanation, see p. 274.)

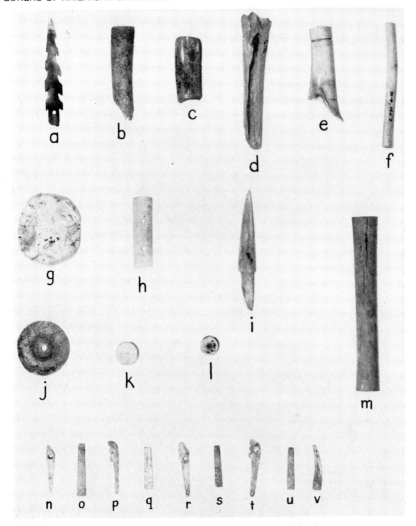

Worked bone and shell at He–4, He–1, and Co–2.

(For explanation, see p. 275.)

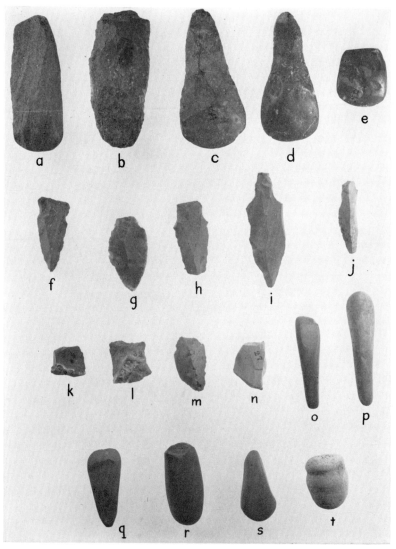

Worked stone at He-1.

(For explanation, see p. 275.)

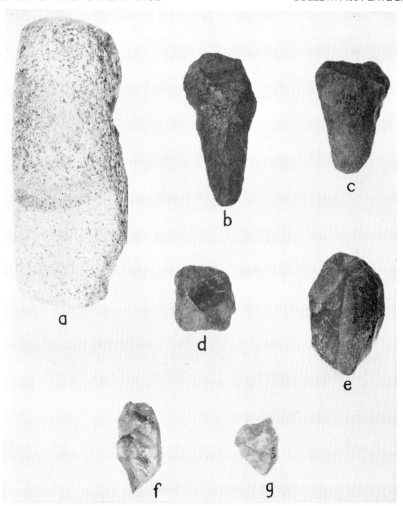

Worked stone at Co–2.

(For explanation, see pp. 275–276.)

Metate from He–1.

(For explanation, see p. 276.)

Metates from He-1.

(For explanation, see p. 276.)

Views of mounds at He–4.   (Photographs by Richard H. Stewart, courtesy National Geographic Society.)

Views of excavations at He–1.   (Photographs by Richard H. Stewart courtesy National
Geographic Society.)

INDEX

Achote variety, *see* Pottery.
Acker, John W., 97
Acker, Mitchell, xi
Adornos, modeled, 14, 53, 170, 215, 226
Agate, 222
Agriculture, 1, 3, 20, 151, 153, 155, 184, 209, 220, 221, 222, 227
Aguadulce, 2 (map)
Alligators, 3
American Philosophical Society, xi
Anadara (*Anadara*) *tuberculosa*, 268, 269
A. (*Larkinia*) *grandis*, 150, 268, 269
Andean areas, 226
Andean-Equatorial phylum, 3
Applique, *see* Design elements.
Archeological Society of Panama, xi, 12, 24
Aristide Girón site, *see* Girón site.
Armadillo, 1
Armor, cotton, 4
Arrowheads, triangular cross section, 14, 16
Artifacts, bone, 8, 20, 150–151, 183, 205
   copper, 210
   metal, 8
   shell, 8, 150–151, 183
   stone, 8, 147–149, 183, 187, 201–204, 205, 217–218, 229
Ashes, 224
Ash layers, 26(fig.), 27, 30, 35, 204, 205
Awl, bone, 150, 206, 227, 228, 245
Ax, bone, 150
   stone, 30, 207
Azuero Peninsula, 1, 6, 15, 166, 225, 233

Balboa, Vasco Nuñez de, 16, 234
Baldwin, Elizabeth, xii
Bananas, 3
Bark cloth, indications of, 222
Barlovento, Colombia, 227, 228–229
Barquisimeto region, 233
Barriles, in Chiriquí, 11, 12
Basalt, 147, 148, 183, 202
Batons, bone, 150, 153
   ceremonial, 150
Beads, jade or jadite, 149
   shell, 150, 152, 231
Beakers, pottery, 20, 226
Beans, 1, 3
Bells, bronze, 14
   copper, 231
Biese, Leo P., xii, 12, 18
Birds, 20, 48
   effigies of, 48, 53, 67, 82, 133, 140, 201, 215
   hunting of, 4
   See also Bone, bird.

Bivalves, small, 20
Blades, stone, 4
Bollaert, William, 10
Bone, animal, 28, 209
   artifacts of, 8, 20, 150–151, 183, 205
   bird, 28, 152, 210
   human, 14, 28, 30, 152, 153, 204, 205, 206, 207, 208, 210, 218, 219, 224
   manatee, 150, 224
   remains, 20
   worked, 204, 210, 226, 227, 228
Boquete cemetery, 10
Bottles, 8, 75, 134, 140, 147, 197
   angled, 128
   bird, 38, 48, 59, 125, 140
   Calabaza, 38
   carafe, 96 (fig.), 129
   cylindrical, 48
   effigy, 51
   El Hatillo type, 125
   globular, 40, 42, 47, 48, 51, 62
   gourd-shaped, 49, 120, 122, 125
   handled, 97
   pyramid-shaped, 40, 42, 47, 128, 140, 152
   ring-based, 120
   shoulder, 51, 76
   spouted, 28, 51, 53, 63, 107, 120, 129, 140
   subglobular, 51, 67
Bow and arrows, 4
Bowls, 226
   bird effigy, 28, 38, 48, 49, 51, 53, 57, 59, 67, 73, 88, 133
   black polished, 145
   casuela-shaped, 232
   collared, 53
   composite silhouette, 227
   deep, 8, 17, 21, 46, 97, 135, 136, 176
   divided, 228
   double rim, 15, 77
   drooping lip, 143, 206, 213, 214
   flaring, 206
   globular, 53, 57, 73, 75, 140, 172, 178, 179
   gutter rim, 42, 143, 145, 198, 201, 209
   incised, 219
   incurving rims, 42, 49, 53, 67, 75, 76, 86, 97, 106, 131, 135, 136, 142, 143, 175, 200, 207, 232
   insloping, 197, 227
   interior banded, 130
   modified-gutter rims, 143, 145, 198

277

Pottery—Continued
Girón Red variety, 19 (chart), 169
(fig.), 170, 171, 185, 187, 241
grave, 7, 35
gray-brown, 37, 50, 145, 147
grayish, 170
gray to gray-buff, 128, 129, 145
grooved lip, 160 (chart)
Guacamayan ware, 181, 182 (figs.)
Herrera Phase, 14, 151, 186, 223–
224, 225, 231, 232, 233
Higo variety, 6, 16, 29, 34, 40,
46, 50, 77, 82, 93, 95, 96 (fig.),
97, 101 (fig.), 103 (fig.), 106,
107, 109, 110 (fig.), 113, 114, 117,
119, 129, 140, 181, 241
Interior banded variety, 17, 151,
158, 159 (chart), 161, 162 (chart),
166, 167 (fig.), 168, 169 (fig.), 170,
188, 189 (chart), 190, 191 (chart),
192, 194, 204, 214, 218, 225, 241
Jobo variety, 27, 38, 61, 62–66, 150,
153, 232, 241
"killed," 224
La Arena, 19 (chart), 21, 22
La Arena Phase, 224–225
La Loma polychrome, 231
La Mula, 21, 22, 186
La Pitia, 232
La Villa, 17, 22
Lost-color ware, 14, 121
lugs, 170, 186, 200, 201, 215
Macaracas, 6, 14, 16, 17, 22, 27,
29, 34, 35, 37, 38, 42, 43, 46, 47,
48, 50, 51, 63, 66, 73, 75, 88, 95,
96 (fig.), 98 (fig.), 99 (fig.), 101
(fig.), 102 (fig.), 103 (fig.), 104
(fig.), 107, 109, 115, (fig.), 116
(fig.), 118 (fig.), 125, 134, 148,
149, 151, 158, 181, 185, 188, 190,
192, 193, 200, 205, 207, 210, 223,
224, 231, 232
Macaracas polychrome, 19 (chart),
27, 40, 53, 61, 77, 82, 93, 95–120,
128, 153, 181, 241
Miscellaneous, 242
modeled ware, 14, 17, 18
Momil polychrome wares, 231
Monagrillo, 19 (chart), 20, 21, 229
monochrome, 20, 29, 34, 37, 133–
134
Níspero variety, 5, 16, 38, 67, 68
(fig.), 70 (fig.), 71 (fig.), 72 (fig.),
75, 76, 79, 94, 95, 97, 121, 125,
133, 140, 241, 248
nodes, buttonlike, 170, 186, 197
notched, 17
Ocós Phase, 230
orange slipped, 119
Orange to brick red, dark red, or
brown, 50
Orange to dark brownish-red, 48,
49, 50, 67
orange wash, 15, 79

Pottery—Continued
Ortiga variety, 6, 14, 46, 47, 68, 69,
73, 75, 79, 82, 83 (fig.), 84 (fig.),
85 (fig.), 87 (fig.), 89 (fig.), 90
(fig.), 91 (fig.), 92 (fig.), 93
(fig.)–95, 106, 117, 121, 125, 128,
138, 142, 185, 190, 192, 193, 241
painted, 16, 17, 21, 233
Palmasola, 233
Paneled red ware, 21, 193, 205, 241
Parita, 6, 14, 17, 19 (chart), 21, 22,
27, 29, 34, 35, 37, 38, 40, 42, 43,
46, 47, 48, 53, 63, 66–95, 97, 109,
117, 120, 125, 134, 135, 151, 181,
185, 188, 190, 192, 193, 210, 223,
224, 241
Patterned and modeled variety,
206, 207, 208, 209, 215, 218, 222,
242
pear-shaped, 85, 86, 97
Pica-pica variety, 6, 16, 35, 37, 40,
42, 43, 46, 47, 82, 88, 90, 93, 94,
95, 96 (fig.), 98 (fig.), 99 (fig.),
101 (fig.), 102 (fig.), 103 (fig.),
104 (fig.), 105, 106, 107, 108, 109,
111, 112, 113, 114, 117, 119, 121,
136, 140, 141, 142, 147, 153, 181,
192, 241
Pinilla black-line-on-red variety,
199–200, 201, 206, 209, 218, 242
Pito variety, 196, 206, 207, 208,
215, 218, 222, 242
Plain ware, 6, 16, 22, 242
plastic decorated, 6, 19 (chart), 20,
160 (chart), 161
plastic treatment, 141–142
Platanillo variety, 145, 151, 182
(figs.), 198, 204, 206, 207, 208,
209, 214, 218, 219, 222, 242
Portacelli Period, 231
pot covers, 40, 42, 135, 140, 153
punctate, 17, 20
purple, 48, 50, 75, 204
purple line, 130
purple on red, 188
Radial banded, 158, 163, 164 (fig.),
165, 190
red, 14, 50, 88, 97, 106, 113, 129,
131, 133, 182, 185, 197, 209
red, bright or almost crimson to
dark carmen, 9
red, dull to dark brown, 15, 63
red and black on white, 233
Red and cream ware, 233
Red and white ware, 130–132 (fig.),
142, 242
Red bordered by black, 233
Red-buff, 7, 20, 26, 29, 34, 35, 37,
38, 40, 42, 43, 46, 47, 73, 100,
113, 128, 131, 132 (fig.), 133,
134–137, 139 (fig.), 140, 141, 142,
145, 152, 153, 185, 186, 195, 197,
233, 242

Pottery—Continued
Red daubed, 35, 38, 130, 134, 146
  (fig.), 157 (chart), 158, 161, 162
  (chart), 180, 181–182, 184, 188,
  189 (chart), 190, 191 (chart), 192,
  193 (chart), 194–197, 198, 204,
  205, 206, 207, 208, 209, 215, 217,
  218, 219, 221, 222
Reddish-orange to brown-red, 97
Red line ware, 19 (chart), 20, 21,
  38, 130, 131, 134, 184, 188, 189
  (chart), 190, 191 (chart), 192,
  194–197, 204, 206, 207, 208, 215–
  216, 218, 221, 222, 223, 231, 242
red-on-buff, 43, 130, 195
red on plain, 233
red on white, 228, 231, 232
red painted, 204, 226, 229
red to buff, 168
red slipped, 12, 14, 22, 66, 69, 73,
  75, 79, 86, 88, 98, 105, 111, 127,
  129, 131, 136, 138, 142, 163,
  166, 171, 172, 174, 176, 186, 197,
  198, 199, 201, 204, 206, 209, 214,
  216, 217, 218, 227, 228
red unslipped, 170, 197, 216
rings, hollow, 15
rough scored, 158, 160 (chart)
Sandy-buff ware, 147
Sangre variety, 35, 42, 145, 151,
  182 (figs.), 198, 204, 208, 209,
  223, 242
Santa Maria Phase, 16, 18, 151,
  161, 192, 210, 221, 222, 224, 230,
  231
Santa Maria polychrome, 161, 163
Sarigua, 19 (chart)
Scalloped, 158, 164 (figs.), 166
scarified, 12, 13 (chart), 14, 230
shapes, 49, 50, 51, 52 (fig.), 53, 59,
  61, 62, 67, 68 (fig.), 69, 75, 76,
  79, 83, 97, 109, 113, 120
Smoked buff ware, 147
Smoked ware, 18, 19 (chart), 21,
  35, 37, 42, 43, 128, 130, 133, 134,
  135, 144, 145, 146 (fig.), 151,
  198–199, 204, 207, 208, 209, 213,
  214–215, 218, 219, 223, 231, 242
striated, 20, 227
supports, 142
temper, crushed rock, 8, 67, 97, 113,
  120, 127, 131, 134, 145, 147, 163,
  171, 176, 177, 185
temper, sand, 8, 165, 186
temper, shell, 165
temper, sherd, 8
Tocuyano, 232
unclassified, 200–201
unpainted, 17, 18
Venado Beach incised variety, 17,
  18, 182, 199, 206, 207, 242
Venezuelan, 232–233
Veraguas plain, 16
White and black on red ware, 200,
  207, 242
white slip, 185

Pottery—Continued
Yampí variety, 14, 46, 66, 69, 79,
  80, 81 (fig.)–82, 95, 100, 102,
  105, 111, 117, 181, 185, 190, 192,
  193, 241
yellow ware, 20
See also Bottles; Bowls; Ceramic
  remains; Chalices; Design elements; Handles; Incensarios;
  Jars; Plates; Urns.
Pottery bases, 8, 53, 135
annular, 40
flat, 117
pedestal, 8, 53, 75, 97, 100, 105,
  109, 113, 114, 117, 130, 134, 135,
  142, 143 (fig.), 170, 171, 172,
  181, 186, 197, 233
plain, 42, 135, 145, 147, 201
rattle, 113
ring, 8, 17, 37, 40, 42, 46, 53, 94,
  106, 120, 134, 135, 142, 143, 152,
  170, 186, 197, 199, 204
rounded, 195, 196, 198, 200
Pottery legs, 15, 16, 129, 142, 232
Pottery lips, 97, 109, 111, 113, 130, 136,
  176, 195
drooping, 129, 134, 177, 219
flanged, 176
flattened, 197, 199
grooved, 215
gutter, 144
horizontally flattened, 35, 37
incised, 198, 215
unmodified, 197, 199
Pottery rims, 53, 79, 86, 97, 105, 111,
  130, 131, 133, 134, 136, 145, 171,
  172, 226
drooping lip, 181
flanged, 79, 81, 82
gutter, 134, 142, 143
modeled, 227
pedestal, 198
ski-tip, 194
squared-off, 17
Pottery spouts, 120, 125, 171, 186
Preceramic stone complex, 19
Projectile points, 4, 12, 18, 152
bone, 4, 222, 247
fine chipped, 18
flint, 206
fluted, 13, 18, 226
lanceolate-shaped, 226
microlithic, 228
shouldered, 202
stone, 4, 147, 149, 202, 222
Protothaca grata, 269
Pueblo Nuevo, 12
Punctation, see Design elements.

Quartz, 127, 171, 202
Quebrada Honda, 76

Rancheria region, Colombia, 231, 233
Rancho Sancho de la Isla, Coclé
  Province, 12